郑州文艺人才
宣传推介工程

北京大学特展

李仁清传拓艺术

李仁清 李 正 编

中州古籍出版社
·郑州·

图书在版编目（CIP）数据

李仁清传拓艺术 / 李仁清，李正编 . — 郑州：中州古籍出版社，2019.5

ISBN 978-7-5348-8680-5

Ⅰ.①李… Ⅱ.①李…②李… Ⅲ.①传拓技术—河南 Ⅳ.①G263

中国版本图书馆 CIP 数据核字（2019）第 097530 号

《"郑州文艺人才宣传推介工程"系列丛书》编委会

主　任： 黄　卿

副主任： 徐西平　裴保顺　王丽艳　石大东　王书广　徐大庆
　　　　　宋建国　李　芳　任　伟

主　编： 王丽艳

副主编： 沈良斌　马建领　刘冰洁

编　委： 李汝洋　李　黎　靳艳妍　林学东　郭　森　李海涛
　　　　　马齐苒　曹　玲

封面题字： 宿白先生
主　编： 李仁清　李　正
拓　印： 李仁清　李泽民　李　正
修　复： 王琴琴　徐　雪　彭　清
策划编辑： 王小方　宗增芳
责任编辑： 吕兵伟
责任校对： 杨守民
出版发行： 中州古籍出版社出版发行
　　　　　　地址：郑州市郑东新区祥盛街 27 号 6 层
　　　　　　邮编：450016
印　刷： 郑州新海岸电脑彩色制印有限公司
开　本： 787 毫米 ×1092 毫米　　1/8
印　张： 34.5
印　数： 1—2500 册
版　次： 2019 年 5 月第 1 版
印　次： 2019 年 8 月第 1 次印刷
书　号： ISBN 978-7-5348-8680-5
定　价： 580.00 元

本书如有印装质量问题，由承印厂负责调换。

作者简介

李仁清,男,1963年生,河南商城县人。文博界著名传拓技师,从事传拓工作30余年,现为河南省省级非物质文化遗产(传拓技艺)传承人。

1982年入河南省古建筑研究所工作,为河南省碑刻、石窟的"四有建档"做了大量传拓工作,曾参与河南省中小型石窟、古桥和小浪底等项目调查与测绘。传拓足迹遍布河南、上海、南京、山东、陕西、山西等省市。工作中对传拓技法进行了深入探索和研究,开创了独特的高浮雕拓法,传拓技艺日臻成熟。2008年以个人的传拓成果出版了《中国北朝石刻拓片精品集》。近年,对河南省中小型石窟造像(文物拓印建档项目)、北宋皇陵圆雕和桂林高浮雕摩崖造像进行了传拓。在河南登封"天地之中"、"丝绸之路"申遗项目中,高浮雕拓片被列为精品档案。2014年9月,由河南省和郑州市文物局批准成立郑州仁清金石传拓艺术博物馆。2016年5月18日"国家级古籍修复技艺传习中心李仁清传习所"在该馆揭牌。应国家古籍保护中心之邀,2013—2016年,为第一、第二、第三期全国传拓技术高级培训班授课。

举办展览及媒体报导李仁清传拓情况如下:
2010年河南卫视为高浮雕传拓技艺,制作《拓片人生》专题片。
2012年参加文化部主办的"中国拓片联合申报国家级非物质文化遗产技艺展"。
2012年《中国文化报》对高浮雕传拓技艺进行了整版报导。
2013年应邀在台湾佛光山举行高浮雕拓片展。
2013年《中华遗产》杂志对高浮雕传拓技艺进行了长篇报导。
2016年6月18—26日《大国工匠》剧组拍摄高浮雕传拓技艺专题片。10月5日至今,《大国工匠》第五集"大工传世",在CCTV-1台、CCTV-4台、CCTV-13台和英语、俄语、法语等多频道面向世界播出。
2016年12月26日《了望》周刊对高浮雕传拓进行了专题报导。
2017年6月1—7日应北京大学图书馆邀请举办李仁清传拓艺术专题展。

About the Author

Li Renqing, male, born in 1963 in Shangcheng County, Henan, is a renowned rubbing specialist among Chinese heritage circles, who has worked in rubbing for more than thirty years and is now a holder of provincial-level intangible cultural heritage (rubbing techniques) in Henan.

In 1982, Li began working for the Henan Provincial Ancient Architecture Research Institute, where he made a lot of rubbings for the documentation of steles and grottoes across Henan and took part in surveying and mapping small to medium-sized grottoes, ancient bridges, and Xiaolangdi among other projects in the province. He traveled across Henan, Shanghai, Nanjing, Shandong, Shaanxi, and Shanxi among other Chinese provinces and cities making rubbings. While working, he conducted extensive research into rubbing techniques, and pioneered a rubbing technique for high reliefs, which added to his mastery of rubbing skills. In 2008, he published his rubbings under the title of *Selected Rubbings of Stone Inscriptions from the Chinese Northern Dynasty*. Rubbings he made in recent years including those of small and medium-sized grotto statues (for cultural heritage documentation) and the sculptures in the round in the Northern-Song imperial mausoleum complex in Henan, as well as of the high-relief cliff sculptures in Guiling. High-relief rubbings were contained as a quintessential element in the application for the World Heritage Site inscription of "The Center of Heaven and Earth" in Dengfeng, Henan, and of the "Silk Roads". In September 2014, the Zhengzhou Renqing Epigraphical Rubbing Art Museum was established under the auspices of the cultural heritage agencies of Henan and Zhengzhou. On May 18, 2016, the "Li Renqing Apprenticeship Institute, National-level Ancient Texts Restoration Training Center" was unveiled at the aforesaid museum. Li was engaged by the National Ancient Books Conservation Center to lecture for the first three National Rubbing Technique Advanced Training Sessions in 2013-2016.

Exhibitions and Media Coverage of Li:

In 2010, Henan TV produced the television documentary on rubbings of sculptures in high relief, *Tapian Rensheng* (Life of a Rubbing Artist).

In 2012, participated in the "China Rubbing Exhibition in Application for Inscription into National Intangible Cultural Heritage" sponsored by the Ministry of Culture.

In 2012, the *China Culture Daily* reported in a full page on the technique of rubbing for sculptures in high relief.

In 2013, exhibited high-relief rubbings at Fo Guang Shan, Taiwan.

In 2013, the *Chinese Heritage Magazine* reported on the technique of rubbing for sculptures in high relief at length.

During June 18-26, 2016, the *Daguo Gongjiang* (Great Artisans of the Nation) crew shot on the technique of rubbing for sculptures in high relief. Since October 5, 2016, *Daguo Gongjiang* Episode 5: Preservation of the Rubbing Craft has been broadcast on CCTV-1, CCTV-4 and CCTV-13 in multiple languages including English, Russian, and French.

On December 26, 2016, the *Outlook Magazine* reported on high-relief rubbings.

During June 1-7, 2017, held the Li Renqing Rubbing Art Exhibition at the invitation of the Peking University Library.

　　李正，男，1992年7月出生，祖籍河南省商城县，因从小受父亲李仁清先生影响，对传拓产生了浓厚的兴趣。2011年9月至2015年7月就读于广东工业大学物流管理专业，并获得管理学学士学位；2016年9月至2019年7月就读于郑州大学历史学院文物与博物馆专业，师从韩国河教授，主要研究方向为秦汉考古。

实践经历：

2012年至2014年，参与河南省济源市济渎庙等千余种石刻造像拓印及后期的拓片修复工作；

2013年至2015年，参与桂林地域摩崖造像后期拓片的整理修复工作；

2016年5—9月，参加郑州大学荥阳官庄遗址的发掘工作；

2016年，在国家图书馆学习拓片的编目和整理；

2016年，参与央视纪录片《大国工匠》的拍摄；

2017年7—9月，在古荥郑州大学历史学院文化遗产保护研究基地进行文物的修复和整理工作；

2017年6月，参与北京大学图书馆邀请举办的李仁清传拓艺术专题展，

2017年9月—2018年6月，在北京考古工地进行踏勘、勘探、考古发掘等工作；

2018年7月，参加国家古籍保护中心主办的"第四期全国传拓技术高级培训班"，并获得毕业证书；

2013—2018年，参与河南中小型石窟的拓印及后期拓片修复工作，

2015—2018年，参与郑州市周边拓印建档项目，并参与后期的拓片修复工作。

Li Zheng, male, born in July 1992 in Shangcheng County, Henan, is the son of Li Renqing. He has developed a strong interest since childhood in rubbing due to his father's influence. He studied logistics management from September 2011 to July 2015 at Guangdong University of Technology, from which he graduated with a bachelor's degree in management. From September 2016 to July 2019, he attended the School of History, Zhengzhou University, where he studied Heritage and Museums under the tutelage of Prof. Han Guohe and was focused in research on archeology concerning the Qin and Han dynasties.

Work experience:

From 2012 to 2014, participated in making and repairing rubbings of well over 1,000 stone statues at the Jidu Temple among other heritage sites in Jiyuan, Henan.

From 2013 to 2015, participated in the sorting and repairing of rubbings made of cliff statues in Guilin.

May through September 2016, participated in Zhengzhou University's excavation of the Guanzhuang site in Xingyang.

In 2016, studied rubbings cataloguing and sorting at the National Library of China.

In 2016, participated in the shooting of the CCTV documentary film Daguo Gongjiang (Great Artisans of the Nation).

From July to September 2017, repaired and sorted out cultural objects the Zhengzhou University School of History's Cultural Heritage Conservation Research Base in Guxing.

In June 2017, participated in the Li Renqing Rubbing Art Exhibition held at the Peking University Library.

From September 2017 to June 2018, made field surveys and excavations at an archaeological site in Beijing.

In July 2018, attended and graduated with a certificate from the "Fourth National Rubbing Advanced Training Session" provided by the National Ancient Books Conservation Center.

From 2013 to 2018, participated in making and repairing rubbings of statues in small and medium-sized grottoes in Henan.

From 2015 to 2018, participated in making and repairing rubbings of statues in the areas around Zhengzhou.

在北京大学李仁清传拓艺术展上的致词

（代序 I）

北京大学常务副校长 吴志攀

尊敬的李仁清先生，尊敬的我们兄弟单位的领导专家、老师、同学，大家上午好！

我代表学校向李仁清先生能到我们学校举办这次精美的展览表示感谢，向所有支持这个展览布展的各位老师各位专家们表示感谢。我去过巩义很多次，因为是实习基地的原因。但是我还没去过本次展览拓片涉及的这个洞窟，自己还是挺孤陋寡闻的。今天看到李先生在巩义打来的拓片，我才知道巩义的石窟里还有这么精美的石像。而且李先生拓片技术非常好，让我们看到石像生动的细节。我们这看到的同学、老师，有一点精神是特别值得学习和赞叹的，就是这些完全是用手工一点点用鬃刷敲打出来的，他的这种耐心，这种细致，以及拓片效果这样完美，是我们今天做科研，今天写作业，今天做习题，以及今天做社会调查等工作都需要的一种精神，就是大国工匠的精神。我们的祖先就是以这样心态工作的。我们现在有很多机器，有很多代替手工操作的方式，效率提高了，但有时我们也没那个耐心了，手也笨拙了，解决问题的办法也变少了。但是李仁清先生这个展览给我们上了非常生动的一课，对于每个人来说都非常的受教育。他的这种精神，他的这种手工艺的传承能保持到今天是我们所有在校生所有在校老师都要学习的，我再一次代表学校向他表示感谢。

谢谢您，李老师！

Speech at the Li Renqing Rubbing Art Exhibition, Peking University

(Preface I)

Wu Zhipan, Executive Vice President at Peking University

Dear Mr. Li Renqing, experts, teachers, and students from fellow universities, good morning!

On behalf of Peking University, I would like to thank Mr. Li Renqing for his beautiful exhibition at Peking University, and the teachers and experts for their support in the run-up to this exhibition. I have been to Gongyi many times, because it is where our training base is located. But I never went to the grotto where the rubbings for this exhibition were made. Quite ill-informed I was. Not until I saw the rubbings Mr. Li made in Gongyi did I become aware that there are so beautiful stone statues in Gongyi grottoes. These rubbings, so skillfully made by Mr. Li, allow us to view the vivid details of the statues. As our teachers and students may have noticed, there is one thing that is particularly worth learning and admiration, and it is that all this is tapped out, bit by bit, with a bristle brush. His patience, his painstaking attention to detail, and as a result so perfect rubbing effects, represent a spirit that we all need in our research today, in our homework today, in our social surveys today, and it is the spirit of the craftsman. Our forefathers just worked with such a spirit. We have many machines now, many means to replace manual work, and we have higher efficiency, but at times we are not that patient, our hands are clumsy, and so we have fewer ways to solve problems. But Mr. Li's exhibition teaches us a lesson that is valuable to everyone. Mr. Li's spirit, his effort to keep the craft alive, is something that all our teachers and students today should learn. Again, I would like to express thanks to him on behalf of the university.

Thank you, Mr. Li.

李仁清传拓艺术展序言

（代序Ⅱ）

胡海帆

2017年6月1日至7日"国家级古籍修复技艺传习中心李仁清传习所·李仁清传拓艺术展"在北京大学图书馆举办。这是一次高水平传拓技艺的展示。

传拓技术是中国古人一项了不起的发明。传拓让甲骨、彝器、碑刻、砖瓦陶等历代金石器物的铭文图像，以纸质墨本形式原大复制，赖纸寿千年而永久保存。千余年来，拓本与古籍一道，构成了记载、保存和传播中华文明的纸文献主体。

传拓术历史悠久，文献记载最早见于《隋书·经籍志》，提到汉魏石经自洛迁邺毁没于北齐神武执政期间，隋秘府留存其拓本——"其相承传拓之本，犹在秘府"，当拓于石没之前，可见传拓最迟在南北朝时期已经产生。现已知最早、有确切纪年的存世拓本，是1900年发现于敦煌莫高窟第十七窟的唐拓本《温泉铭》，拓本裱纸尾书有永徽四年八月墨跋，现藏法国巴黎国家图书馆。唐人书籍、诗歌中传拓的记载，说明唐代传拓已经普及。宋代不仅传拓极为流行，还启发了四大发明之一印刷术的产生。迄今，存世尚有上百种的宋拓本，被公认是博物馆、图书馆拓本类藏品中的皇冠。

历史上，拓工创造了许多拓法，使捶拓技艺不断创新，除了传统的平面拓，清中期又发明了全形拓，将青铜器立体地呈现于纸上，这已是一种艺术创作了。因此拓本不仅承载了金石的文献和艺术内容，还因为自身的技艺发展，成为一种新的艺术形式。

今天奉现给观众的是李仁清先生制作的、以汉至宋刻高浮雕拓为主的部分代表作。李仁清从事传拓三十余年，拓技精湛，现为河南省省级非物质文化遗产（传拓技艺）传承人。

其传拓作品有几个特点：

一、注意资料的完整性。能将碑石的阳、阴、侧、额、座一应拓全，已是不易，完整再现整个洞窟、整座石阙乃至高达十米的巨碑全形更令人拍案称奇。一些石刻旧拓人们很熟悉，但见其各面俱全，浮雕纹饰毕现之新拓时，仍让人有耳目一新需重新认识的感觉，如本展北齐刘碑造像。传世旧拓对碑刻正文以外的部位，往往缺漏。这主要囿于古人只重视文字的传统，以及考虑制作成本和难度，以致形成长期以来拓不全的现象。然而，随着现代学科对古代社会研究的细化和深入，所有可以反映古代社会信息的材料都进入研究者的视野，完整本的价值更为人们所重视，也成为鉴伪的有效手段。

二、注意提高拓片的艺术观赏性。李拓尽力表现出图像层次感，不同部位以不同墨色处理，乌金蝉翼，浓淡相宜，十分精美和生动。如本展北魏释迦牟尼像、安阳灵泉寺隋刻神王像、巩义宋陵将军等，形神兼备、栩栩如生，拓技之妙让人赞叹。

三、作者在拓技创新方面的探索"高浮雕拓法"尤其值得称道。众所周知，限于纸的拉伸限度，拓片宜表现起伏不大的平面，不善于表现高浮雕，这使得以往高浮雕拓片几无踪迹。而作者长期研究实践，开创了一套拓制高浮雕、圆雕的技法，拓艺也日臻成熟。此法虽极其耗时费力，但却将以往难于表现的、凹凸相差悬殊的立体塑像展现出来，本展北魏巩义石窟寺全窟拓（仅展局部）可谓代表，不仅大大提高了拓片的资料价值，为石刻保护修复提供了形象的、原样大小的"样式雷",也为后世留下了艺术价值与欣赏价值更高的收藏品,为传播弘扬民族传统文化做出了自己特有的贡献。

在数字化时代的今天,古老的传拓技术,仍是文博领域复制保存金石文字的最佳方法,非但没被淘汰,还因其独特、无可替代的艺术性和表现力,伴随着拓艺新发展,仍焕发着青春的活力。我们希望,通过展览观众可领略古代石刻艺术和传拓艺术的魅力,感受中华传统文化的博大。也希望作者数十年精益求精、追求完美和创新,为社会创造经典的"大国工匠"精神,得到弘扬。这是社会提倡和亟需的精神。

Preface for the Exhibition of Li Renqing's Rubbing Artworks

(Preface II)

Hu Haifan

From June 1 to June 7, 2017, the "Exhibition of Li Renqing's Rubbing Artworks by Li Renqing Apprenticeship Institute of National Ancient Books Conservation Center" was held at the Peking University Library. The exhibition showcased superb rubbing techniques.

Rubbing techniques are a proud innovation of ancient Chinese. It is through this particular technique that we are able to permanently preserve texts and images engraved on ancient metal and stone wares, such as oracles, bronze wares, steles, bricks and roof tiles, in paper format, which is significantly more durable than stone carvings. Over the past thousand years in China, rubbings and ancient books have been the two primary vehicles for record retention, information preservation and civilization development.

Rubbing techniques have a long history. The earliest record of rubbing techniques is in the *Book of Sui: Classics*, in which the author wrote that the classics engraved on stones in the Han and Wei Dynasties were all destroyed in the Shenwu Era of the Northern Qi Dynasty after the capital city was relocated from Luo to Ye. The rubbings of the original were preserved in the Palace Library of the Sui government. A quote from the book is as follows. "The corresponding rubbings still remains at the Palace Library". The aforementioned rubbings must have been created before the mass destruction, which indicates that the rubbing technique had, at least, appeared by the Southern and Northern Dynasties. The earliest pre-existing rubbing, whose year of creation has been confirmed and verified, is the rubbing of the *Inscription of Hot Spring*, created in the Tang Dynasty, discovered in 1900 at the 17th cave of the Mogao Caves. The rubbing was dated in August in the fourth year of the Yonghui Era at the end. It is now collected at the National Library of France in Paris. The records of rubbing techniques in books and poems published in the Tang Dynasty demonstrate that rubbings had proliferated by then. In the Song Dynasty, the prevailing rubbing techniques gave rise to the invention of woodblock printing. Up to this date, there are hundreds of rubbings dating back to the Song Dynasty. It is publicly acknowledged that these rubbing works are the most magnificent rubbings among all the collections in museums and libraries.

Over the years, rubbing art kept advancing as rubbing artists continuously created a number of rubbing techniques. Apart from the traditional 2-D rubbing technique, in the mid Qing Dynasty, 3-D rubbing, which presented 3-D bronze wares on paper, was invented. This could be considered as a type of art creation. Therefore, rubbings are not only media of communication that serve to preserve contents of art and texts, but also artworks, a new form of art.

Today, we are presenting to our audience Mr. Li Renqing's rubbing works, most of which are high relief rubbings of artworks from the Han Dynasty to the Song Dynasty. Having over 30 years of experience in rubbing, Li Renqing possesses superb rubbing skills. He is currently the inheritor of Provincial Intangible Cultural Heritage of Henan Province (rubbing technique). His works have the following characteristics:

1. Completeness. It is not easy to reproduce an entire tablet, including its front, back, sides, top and bottom, not to mention reconstructing a whole cave, a stone statue or a giant stone tablet that stands 10 meters high. Although some old rubbings may be familiar to many people, Li's new rubbings still impress and refresh the audience with their stupendous completeness and intricate

designs of patterns, inviting viewers to reexamine the work. One of the examples is the reproduction of the Tablet of Liu Bei Temple originally established in the Northern Qi Dynasty displayed on this exhibition. Due to the fact that ancient Chinese typically had a preference for texts over designs, and also in consideration of the technical difficulty in and the high financial cost of reproducing the entire tablet, the existing old rubbing of this tablet only contains the body part of the text. However, as more extensive and thorough research has been conducted on the ancient Chinese society, current researchers are interested in everything that reflects the world in the past. People, therefore, begin to place a high value on the completeness of rubbings. Completeness, as a result, also becomes an effective way to distinguish a counterfeit from a real one.

2. Artistic appeal. Li's work is famous for its vividness and faithfulness. He is good at applying the right shade of color to the right area to maintain a delicate balance between heavy and light, strength and tenderness, static and dynamic. For example, the portrait of the Gautama Buddha in the Northern Wei Dynasty, the portrait of the God of the Lingquan Temple in Anyang, carved in the Sui Dynasty, and the portrait of the general buried in Northern Song Mausoleum, Gongyi, are all real to life. It is such a marvel of hand that Li's skills take the audience by surprise.

3. Exploration and Innovation. "High-relief rubbing" is rather impressive. As we all know, due to the flexural rigidity of paper, rubbings are normally 2-dimentional rather than 3-dimentional. As a consequence, there are very few "high-relief rubbings" preserved in the world. Nevertheless, after years of research and exploration, Li developed a set of skills specifically tailored to the creation of high-relief and 3-dimensional rubbings. Progressively, his skills improved. Although to employ this technique is extremely time-consuming, it successfully transfers 3-dimensional statues onto 2-dimensional paper, which was something hard to achieve in the past. The rubbing of the entire Shiku Temple in Gongyi, built in the Northern Wei Dynasty, displayed on this exhibition (only partially), provides a perfect example. This technique not only duplicates the original stone carving and increases the material value of the rubbing, but also provides the later generations with splendid artworks that possess high artistic and aesthetic values while making a contribution to promoting the traditional Chinese culture.

Even in this digitalized world, the ancient rubbing technique is still the most effective method to restore and preserve stone carvings in the cultural heritage conservation field. The technique is not at all obsolete. Instead, because of its irreplaceable artistic and aesthetic values and its recent new development, the rubbing technique has been further revitalized. We hope that our audience could have a glimpse of the charm of the stone carving and rubbing art in ancient times and learn about the great traditional Chinese culture through this exhibition. We also hope that we could, like the artist, be meticulous, persistent and diligent in the pursuit of perfection and innovation. This is the spirit of "Chinese craftsmen", a spirit that we shall all advocate and our society urgently needs.

为文艺塑名家　为城市添魅力
——"郑州文艺人才宣传推介工程"系列丛书序言
（代序Ⅲ）

文化是一个民族的精神和血脉，文化是一座城市的特质和灵魂。造诣精深、德艺双馨的文艺名家，则是一座城市文化品位的生动体现。

为充分发挥文化在国家中心城市建设中的引领和支撑作用，培养造就一批文化名家、艺术大师，郑州市2018年开始实施"郑州文艺人才宣传推介工程"，遴选文化艺术界取得突出成就、在全国具有一定影响力、德艺双馨的郑州文艺领军人才进行宣传推广，通过举办一场展览（演）、出版一本个人专著、召开一次专家座谈会等形式，向国内外展示其艺术形象、艺术成果和明德风尚，进一步提升其社会影响力，并在全市营造出尊重人才的浓厚氛围，引领全市文化艺术人才队伍健康成长。

本套丛书作为"郑州文艺人才宣传推介工程"的重要组成部分，这一本本专著是我市文艺工作者坚持"深入生活、扎根人民"、坚持与时代同步伐、坚持以人民为中心、坚持以精品奉献人民、坚持用明德引领风尚的丰硕成果，代表了他们在不同领域所达到的新高度，从不同角度展现了郑州的内在气质和文化情怀，对郑州文化大发展大繁荣具有特殊的感召作用和标志意义。同时，这些文艺人才还有很长的路要走，希望他们坚定文化自信，更上一层楼，用健康向上的文艺作品和做人处事陶冶情操、启迪心智、引领风尚，也期待不断涌现出更多的优秀文艺人才，讲好郑州故事、传播好郑州声音，不断提升郑州城市文化软实力，切实承担起举旗帜、聚民心、育新人、兴文化、展形象的使命任务。

《"郑州文艺人才宣传推介工程"系列丛书》编委会

2019年6月

To Distinguish Literary and Artistic Figures and Add Charm to the City

Preface to the Series of Books for the Publicity and Promotion Program of Zhengzhou Literary and Artistic Talents

(Preface Ⅲ)

Culture is in the ethos and blood of a nation, and in the temperament and soul of a city. The highly accomplished literary and artistic figures of virtue and competence embody the cultural taste of their city.

To give full play to the culture's role in leading and supporting the construction of central cities of the nation and foster a group of cultural celebrities and masters of art, Zhengzhou began to implement the Publicity and Promotion Program of Zhengzhou Literary and Artistic Talents as of 2018. The program conducts publicity and promotion centering on the leading literary and artistic figures of virtue and competence from Zhengzhou who have nationwide influence for their outstanding achievements through such forms as staging an exhibition (a performance), publishing a monograph and convening a seminar to display their images and achievements in artistic creation as well as their virtues, with a view of enhancing their social impact, building an intense atmosphere of respecting talents, and contributing to the healthy growth of the municipal team of literary and artistic talents.

This series of books, as an important component of the Publicity and Promotion Program of Zhengzhou Literary and Artistic Talents, represents rich work results of this city's literary and artistic workers who always go deep into the common people's life, keep abreast of the times, take a people-centered approach, persist in turning out excellent works for the people and set examples of virtue. These books reflect the authors have reached new heights in their respective fields, manifest the temperament and cultural passion of Zhengzhou from different perspectives, inspire all in concern to contribute to the development and prosperity of local culture, and on this account hold signature significance. Still these literary and artistic talents have a long way to go. It is hoped that they will firm up their cultural confidence and seek further progress to edify, inspire and guide people with their works full of positive energy and their way of conducting themselves. It is also hoped that even more excellent literary and artistic talents will emerge; that they will do a good job in telling Zhengzhou stories and spreading the voice of Zhengzhou and will continuously help enhance the cultural soft power of Zhengzhou; and that they will earnestly undertake missions and tasks to hold high the banner, win popular support, forge new talents, and invigorate culture and project good images of Zhengzhou.

Editorial Board of the Series of Books on the Publicity and Promotion Project for Zhengzhou Literary and Artistic Talents

June 2019

目 录

高浮雕传拓技艺	001
嵩山 / 东汉三阙	001
北魏 / 巩义石窟寺	099
北朝 / 石刻造像	165
北魏 / 释迦牟尼佛	166
东魏 / 嵩阳寺造像碑	172
北齐 / 刘碑寺造像碑	186
隋唐 / 灵泉寺洞窟	211
北齐 / 林州洪谷寺塔龛	234
北宋 / 巩义宋陵石像	238
掠影 / 艺术展	245
跋	248

高浮雕传拓技艺

李 正

一、传拓的起源和发展

（一）传拓技法产生的时间

"拓"，也可称为传拓、墨拓、锤拓、打拓，是将宣纸用水浸润之后，使用扫刷、砸刷等工具，将其贴附于石刻或器物上，然后使用墨汁（朱砂等颜料）将铸刻于器物上的文字或图案捶印下来，凹陷处的纹饰和阴文因不着墨色而呈白色，凸起之处的阳文和图案则呈现墨色。用这种技法制作出的成品称为拓片或拓本，是中国特有的保存金石文献的方式，也是中国古代重要发明之一。

传拓的起源现已难以考证，《隋书·经籍志》中著录了《秦皇东巡会稽刻石》一卷，汉《熹平石经》三十四卷，三国魏《正始石经》十七卷。其后魏徵注曰："后汉镌刻七经，著于石碑，皆蔡邕书。魏正始中又立三体石经，相承以为七经正字。后魏之末，齐神武执政，自洛阳徙邺都（《北齐书》卷二《神武》下载：'……乃议迁邺……诏下三日，车驾便发，户四十万狼狈就道'），行至河阳，值岸崩，遂没于水。其得至邺者，不盈太半。至隋开皇六年，又自邺京载入长安，置于秘书内省，议欲补缉，立于国学。寻属隋乱，事遂寝废，营造之司因用为柱础。贞观初，秘书监臣魏徵始收聚之，十不存一。其相承传拓之本，犹在秘府。"这里的"相承传拓之本"显然说的都是拓本。由此证明，传拓术最晚在齐神武执政后自洛阳迁都前（即东魏天平年，公元534年以前）就发明了，可惜没有留下这个时期的拓本。现在存世最早且有确切纪年的拓本是唐太宗李世民撰文并书写的《温泉铭》，此铭原石在陕西温泉，久佚。拓本1900年于敦煌莫高窟第十七窟发现，今在法国巴黎图书馆，末尾有墨书"永徽四年八月□日围谷府果毅儿"一行，据此可以断定，此本当是唐永徽四年，即公元653年以前

所拓。唐代传拓虽已普及，但唐拓本如今留存却极少，除《温泉铭》外，还有欧阳询《化度寺邕禅师舍利塔铭》、柳公权《金刚经》《神策军碑》较为可信。宋代不仅传拓极为流行，还启发了四大发明之一印刷术的产生。迄今，存世尚有上百种的宋拓本，被公认是博物馆、图书馆拓本类藏品中的桂冠。

（二）传拓技法产生的条件

1. 墨的发明和使用

中国是发明墨最早的国家，古代人类出于书写的必要，很早就开始使用有颜色的颜料。早在仰韶时期，彩陶纹饰、甲骨文、竹简木牍等都留有先人使用墨料的痕迹。由此可见，中国使用墨的时间可以追溯到新石器时代。但是人类最早使用的墨，多为天然墨，其质地较差，难以书写，从而促使了人造墨的产生。目前所发现最早的人工制墨，是1975年湖北云梦睡虎地四号古墓中出土的战国中期墨块，同墓中出土的石砚和研墨的石头上还留有研磨过的痕迹。由此可见，在战国时期，古人已经开始研磨书写了。

2. 石刻的大量出现

商、周用来刻字的主要是甲骨和青铜器，多用以占卜、祭祀，或记载重大事件。战国秦汉以后金器衰落，石器逐渐成为铭文的重要载体。我国正式的石刻当从战国时代的《石鼓文》开始，之后石刻快速发展，秦至汉间已有数百种之多。正是大量石刻的出现，为传拓技术的发明提供了重要的条件。

3. 纸的发明及使用

在上古时代，祖先主要依靠结绳记事，殷商时期开始将文字镌刻于龟甲和兽骨之上，春秋时期又利用竹片和木片以及缣帛作为纸张发明之前书写典籍、文书等文字载体的主要材料。但由于这些材质都有自身的局限性，如缣帛过于昂贵，竹片略显笨重，

限制了文化的传播与发展，于是就促使了纸的发明。1957年陕西省博物馆在西安东郊灞桥附近的一座西汉墓中发掘出了一批"灞桥纸"实物，其制作年代不晚于西汉武帝时期，之后在新疆的罗布淖尔和甘肃的居延等地都发掘出了汉代纸的残片。由此可见，纸作为中国的四大发明之一，西汉初期已经出现。但是这个时期的纸极为粗糙，且造价高昂，难以广泛普及。公元105年，造纸术经过东汉宦官蔡伦改进之后，降低了成本，提高了质量及产量，从而得以广泛流传。至隋唐时期，宣纸诞生，为传拓技法的产生提供了重要的物质基础。

二、传拓的工具

（一）上纸工具

1. 扫刷（棕刷）：扫刷是上纸的第一道工序，其材质是棕椰树生长的棕丝和剑麻纤维，用途是在上纸时将宣纸刷平，并将气泡扫出，使之与碑刻贴合。使用之时，扫刷要与碑刻垂直，以防将纸张划破。新买的扫刷用前需用针锥将里面棕毛挑直并剪平，之后在粗砂纸或石质较粗的砂石上来回打磨半小时左右，感觉棕丝光滑柔软不刮手方可使用。

2. 砸刷（打刷）：早期所用砸刷为木锤，将毡子垫在宣纸上对碑刻进行敲打，但其对濒危石刻会有损伤，不建议采用此种方法。20世纪中后期将木锤改进为由猪鬃毛制作而成的打刷，并于拓印高浮雕时在打刷外套上一层薄袜，其大小可依据碑刻或浮雕的大小而定。主要用来将宣纸均匀的打入碑刻及浮雕的凹陷处，使宣纸紧密贴合在拓件上面。其效果是为了在纸干之后不易绷起，便于上墨，同时能够将字口及细节表现的更加清晰。

3. 毡子（薄厚适中）：用羊毛加工粘合而成，柔软富有弹性。

4. 湿毛巾：在野外工作时，难免会遇到大风及碑刻倾斜角度过大，上纸难度过高等问题。上纸时，用湿毛巾将宣纸紧按在碑刻或浮雕上，用湿度保持纸和碑刻的粘合性，再用砸刷将其砸实。

（二）上墨工具

1. 扑子：又称"拓包"，是上墨的主要工具，一般根据所拓器物的大小和字迹情况自己制作。制作扑子的材料：棉花、棉布或绸布、线绳、毡子、海棉、薄塑料布等。方法：①把毛毡剪成圆形，每层小1—2毫米，形成锥形，大小以自己适用为宜，然后用薄塑料把毡片扎紧，注意要使扑面紧绷无皱褶，但此种方法多适用于平面石刻。②高浮雕、圆雕是立体雕像，表面多凸凹不平，所以传拓高浮雕、圆雕就不能采用第一种方法制作而成的大拓包上墨，而是将其用于着墨。用于上墨的拓包需用海绵剪出大小不同的金字塔形，大的如鸡蛋，小的宛若黄豆（扑子大小需跟据我们所拓器物的纹饰来定），然后再用棉布包扎紧即可。拓包的制作不同地区有着不同的方法，以上墨均匀、个人习惯为准。因墨汁易干，毛毡很快会变硬，下次拓印时易造成上墨不均匀的情况，所以每次使用完毕后，需将拓包用塑料袋或密封袋包裹，保持湿度及毛毡的弹性。

2. 拓板：也称为"墨板"，是上墨的辅助工具，形似乒乓球拍，略大。主要是将墨汁直接倒在上面，或用毛笔蘸于其上，辅助扑子上墨之用。墨板多用于拓印大碑，而南方则很少使用，仅以两个大拓包对拍上黑即可。

3. 毛笔、排笔：材料以羊毫为宜，作上墨和上水之用。使用前需用清水浸泡，洗净表面胶质。

（三）后期修复工具

1. 浆糊：是按传统书画装裱和古书揭裱所用浆糊的制艺制成，主要用来将破损的拓片粘接起来，以作修复保护之用。早期是用面粉作为材料，先将其倒入清水洗净，把面筋取出（以防虫蛀），然后把洗出的淀粉放入桶内沉淀，再把沉淀后的淀粉用开水充熟即可。近年来则改用小麦淀粉，用开水充熟直至透明即可使用。

2. 拓片粘接纸条：纸条采用较薄的宣纸，以拓片纸张厚度或略薄于纸张为宜，将其剪为0.5—1.5厘米宽（可视拓片破碎情况来定），并根据拓片破损长度在拓片背面涂抹浆糊，再将纸条粘接其上。

3. 毛笔：可以将浆糊均匀地涂抹在宣纸条上。

4. 喷壶：后期修复粘接之前需要用喷壶将拓片打湿，并将拓片破损之处拼接起来，再使用宣纸条粘接。这样不仅便于粘接，还可防止粘接之后拓片起皱、错位等情况出现。

三、传拓的对象及步骤程序

（一）传拓的对象

传统的传拓对象：青铜器、刻石、碑碣、墓志、塔铭、经幢、造像记、石阙、摩崖、石经、画像、建筑物附属题刻等。而高浮雕传拓技艺的创新则大大拓展了这一范畴，不仅可以传拓高大的高浮雕及圆雕，还可以对木雕、历史建筑、大自然山体、古村庄、原始森林和现代雕刻等进行传拓，使传拓技法的运用更为广泛。

（二）叠纸、闷纸、裁剪

拓印平面石刻：如若工作量较小，建议根据碑刻大小选择合适尺寸的宣纸，若尺寸不合适，可对宣纸进行裁剪。纸张四边可依需要留出空白，3厘米左右为宜。首先将纸多次折叠为方形或长方形，每一折时需将纸错开2毫米左右，以便揭开。然后将折叠好的宣纸用湿毛巾包住，放入自封袋内，待其湿透还原后使用。若拓印石窟或大体量的雕像时，需提前闷纸，取大量清水把宣纸放入水中湿透取出，放于干净平板上，然后用塑料板放置在宣纸上，双手按压或者人立其上将纸内的水挤压出来，过程需缓慢轻柔，力度过大极易损坏纸张。之后将宣纸用洁净的毛巾包裹好，放入塑料袋或密封袋内保存，防止水分流失。

（三）清洁碑刻

许多碑刻常年放在野外，字口及纹饰处多有灰尘及泥垢，需用柔软刷子或棉布毛巾对表面进行清洁，保持字体纹饰的清晰度。若遇难以扫除的脏污，可用竹签或棉棒小心剔除，不可用力，以防损坏碑刻。所有碑刻都需清洁干净再进行传拓，尤其是风化严重之处，字体及纹饰模糊不清，用柔软毛刷把浮在表面的灰尘扫净即可。早期，有些人会采用火烧的办法清洁碑刻，但是经过高温火烧后的碑刻容易变酥，多次捶打就会碎裂，不利于保护文物，现已不再使用。

（四）平面石刻与高浮雕、圆雕上纸、捶纸方法

平面石刻上纸主要采用干、湿两种方法。干纸上法：一般用于条件或时间有限，需快速拓印时，但其多用于平面石刻，高浮雕则难以实施。首先用喷壶或毛巾将水均匀地喷洒在宣纸上，然后用毛巾把宣纸摁在石刻本体上。如有褶皱，则把喷湿的宣纸揭起，用扫刷扫平后再用打刷把宣纸打入纸口。湿纸上法：是将提前闷好的湿宣纸轻轻揭开，覆盖在碑刻之上，再行捶打。因闷好的宣纸干湿均匀，所以传拓多采用湿纸上法。

高浮雕上纸、锤纸方法：平面拓片从上纸到成品多为整纸，不易破碎，取回之后即可直接登记入库，步骤简单。而高浮雕由于凸凹不平，用干纸会导致干湿不均，用湿毛巾摁纸时也会上下左右移动，加宽造像本体尺寸，所以不宜采用干纸上法。需提前闷纸，把宣纸剪开，按1∶1比例摁压在实物本体，然后用毛巾逐步一层一层把宣纸按入雕像的凹陷处。由于高浮雕的立体效果，导致其无法像平面碑刻一样使纸张和碑刻完全贴合，难以增大纸张和高浮雕的粘合度，这已使上纸不易，若遇天干风大时，上纸难度还会倍增。上纸时，先将宣纸揭开，然后将纸张按压在浮雕上方的空白处，并用毛巾将四角固定。之后采用正投影方法，一一裁剪浮雕凸起之处，如有褶皱，则把皱褶处理在空白之处。上纸完毕后，用大小不同的打刷，根据雕像纹饰角度的差异轻轻把宣纸打入实体与之结合。但要注意因高浮雕起伏不平，受力面积很小，不宜用力过度。同时用打刷之前，需将薄袜子套在打刷之外，对石刻及宣纸的纤维都是一种很好的保护。如遇大风天气，可先将宣纸完全揭开，然后从下方将纸张卷起，再将纸张一点一点展开，用湿毛巾按压在浮雕的两边及凸起之处，最后用砸刷将四边砸实，可以有效避免风力将纸张吹起。传拓高浮雕时难免会遇到碑刻过大，纸张不够，需要接纸，尤其注意两张相连的纸要重叠2厘米左右宽，并用砸刷反复捶打接口处，以防揭纸时分开。这期间的每一步都繁琐复杂、费时费力，所以需要有极大的耐心和细心才可完成。

（五）上墨

上墨：待宣纸干到90%以上时便可开始上墨。对于平面上墨，运用大扑子（适合自己手握的扑子），上下左右一遍一遍地均匀扑墨即可，但要注意碑刻的纹路和线刻清晰度，尤其要表现出历代碑刻的基理和沧桑感。

高浮雕上墨方法：拓印前需对石刻对象的数据进行测量，同时还要对浮雕石刻的年代和风格进行探究，以便后期进行粘接修复。高浮雕上墨所用扑子与平面碑刻不同，因高浮雕凹凸不平，我们通常所用的拓印平面碑拓的拓包无法直接上墨，无论造像大小都需小扑子来完成。上墨时需把扑子当作绘画毛笔一样运用，

时中时侧，不同造像的雕刻技法，运用不同角度的手法。同时要心静如水，戒急戒躁，似水墨画般墨分五色，近浓远浅。上墨之后，需在不同的角度、位置来观看透视效果，不足之处再加以补墨。

（六）拓片的揭取

高浮雕拓片不同于平面拓片，平面碑刻揭取后，是一幅完整的成品。而高浮雕拓片揭取时，需从左向右或从下往上，根据雕像的纹路按造像的顺序卷轴式揭取。在揭取过程当中，应提前准备好一自封袋，把所有揭取的碎片装入袋中，哪怕指甲般大小的碎片也不可遗失，保证后期修复的完整性。

（七）拓片的粘接修复

高浮雕拓片的粘接、修复是高浮雕传拓中非常重要的一环，直接影响成品的整体效果。揭取之后的拓片破碎成成百上千片，需要通过打湿、拼接、粘接、裁剪等一系列工序才可修复，所费时间为拓印的几倍有余。修复前，首先将拓片取出，背面朝上平铺于桌面，用喷壶将水均匀撒在纸面上，湿度保持在将宣纸拉平不起褶皱为宜。然后利用拼图的原理将破碎的纸片一片片拼接在破损处，并用水打湿，将缝隙对齐，由此补全整张拓片。尤其注意，整张拓片必须完全展平，破损处的碎片四边也需对齐不留缝隙和褶皱，否则粘接完成后图像会因此而走形，失去原图的韵味。拼接完成后，取出补纸，用毛笔蘸上浆糊涂抹其上，根据对接缝隙的长短粗细用宣纸条进行粘接，并用手掌按压，将补纸粘牢。但要注意涂抹浆糊时不宜过多，否则按压时易导致浆糊溢出，不利于折叠保存。待粘接完成后将拓片正面翻转上来，对照原物照片进行比对，若有走形和褶皱之处需将该处补纸揭开重新粘接，直至与原物一致。之后将拓片放置晾干，再将四边裁剪整齐，方可折叠，入袋保存。

四、高浮雕传拓的价值

我国的碑刻传拓技术已经有一千多年的历史，但传拓作品多围绕着平面碑刻，遇有石窟或造像碑中的高浮雕类，多是空缺留白，或是仅拓出佛像的背光图案。而高浮雕传拓的创新，能够对高大的陵墓石刻及石窟中的巨龛佛像等高浮雕及圆雕进行传拓，并将其层次感、艺术感展现出来，既可保持造像石刻的原真性，又提高了石刻作品内容的可读性。

高浮雕传拓技艺是在结合传统平面碑刻和青铜器全形拓技艺基础之上，采取正面投影原理，运用青铜器全形、平面、乌金、蝉翼和镶拓相综合的技法，通过上纸、砸纸、上墨、揭取、粘接、修复等一系列传拓工艺流程将大体量的高浮雕及圆雕石刻作品从立体形象转换到平面粉本的一项新技艺。它通过时代风格、艺术特色，决定拓印手法，再根据实际情况调制墨色、选择扑子用法，加上揭取粘接等一系列程序才可完成。每一步都需要平静和耐心，任何一点浮躁的情绪都会造成功亏一篑。因为拓印者面对的是凹凸不平的石雕面，纸张随需而剪，拓成揭取下来的是无数张碎片，后期的拼接作业是一项在细心中求真实，在碎片中求完美的工作。所以人们在事后看到的每一张美丽、动人的画卷，都要经过传拓者在高架上、在石窟中弓背曲身的拓印、细心分块的揭取和耐心细微的拼合等层层难关之后才能完成。所以比起平面传拓，熟练运用高浮雕拓印技艺的难度非常高，只有通过长时间的实践才可掌握。

高浮雕传拓技艺，不仅可以1∶1保留文物作品原大尺度与艺术风格，而且能在石刻本体的基础上，通过精湛的墨拓技巧拓印出精美的纸上画卷。虽然说现今的3D打印等高科技技术快速发展，但这一古老技艺仍能传承至今并被延续，除了它自身具有的顽强生命力之外，最值得关注的是它所特有、无可替代的艺术性和表现力。从保存文物资料的角度看，它比文字的记述、摄影资料、测绘图纸等更加真实和精细，也更有助于学术研究。并且它不仅能较为完整、精确地呈现高浮雕石刻的纹理、衣饰和工匠的雕凿印迹，甚至在石刻上出现的裂隙或剥蚀等情况，也可记录下来，为进行保护、观察提供准确信息。总之，这一传拓技术的成功，对现在或将来的石刻保护与开展学术研究、建立科学档案、开展文物工作交流、宏扬传统文化艺术等，都有着重要的意义。

The Technique of High-Relief Rubbing

Li Zheng

I. Origin and Development of Rubbing

1. When the Technique Originated

Rubbing, known as *ta*, or *chuan-ta* (lit. "impression rubbing"), or *mo-ta* ("ink rubbing"), or *da-ta* ("tap-rubbing") in Chinese, is the process of rubbing characters or designs on implements onto water-saturated Xuan paper attached to their surfaces with ink (or paint like cinnabar) by using brushing or hammering tools. The depressed parts of designs and characters in intaglio, when rubbed, look white because they cannot be impressed onto paper, whereas the rest parts are rubbed in ink. The final product(s) made with this technique is (are) known as *ta-pian* (rubbing) or *ta-ben* (book of rubbings). It is a unique way of preserving stone and bronze inscriptions in China, as well as one of the major inventions in ancient China.

The origin of rubbing is hardly verifiable. *The Records of Classics and Books* in *the History of Sui* mentions *Carvings in Stone During the First Emperor of Qin's Eastward Inspection Tour to Kuaiji* in one volume, *Stone Inscriptions of the Years of Xiping of the Han Dynasty* in 34 volumes and *Stone Inscriptions of the Years of Zhengshi* of Wei in the Three Kingdoms period in 17 volumes. Wei Zheng, a well-known Tang scholar, says in an annotation, "Later in the Han Dynasty, the Seven Classics, calligraphed by Cai Yong [famous Han calligrapher] are inscribed on stone steles. In the years of Zhengshi, the Kingdom of Wei created the Three-Script Inscription (*San-ti Shi-jing*), which has been passed down as the right version of the Seven Classics. In late Wei Dynasty, when the Shenwu Emperor of Qi was in reign, the capital was moved from Luoyang to Yedu (Shenwu, vol. 2, The Book of Northern Qi , writes, '...so [they] decided to move to Ye.....Three days after the imperial edict was issued, the carriage procession set out and 400 thousand households were hard-pressed to follow'). When they arrived to the south of the Yellow River, it happened that the bank was breached and the inscribed steles were flooded. Less than half of them reached Ye. In the 6th year of Kaihuang reign in the Sui Dynasty, the rulers moved the steles from Ye to Chang'an, where they were placed inside the Inner Department of the Secretariat *(Mi-shu Nei Sheng)*. A motion was thus set forth to complement the steles and erect them in the State Academy. Soon the Sui Dynasty was in chaos, so the matter was dropped. The steles were used as column bases. In the early years of Zhenguan, I, Wei Zheng, director of the Secretariat, started collecting them. One out of ten of them remain. The book of their rubbings has been preserved in the office of the Secretariat." Here, "the book of their rubbings" is obviously what we are talking about. It can thus be proven that the technique of rubbing had been invented during the reign of the Shenwu Emperor of Qi before he moved the capital from Luoyang (i.e. in the years of Tianping of Eastern Wei, prior to 534 CE) at the latest. Unfortunately, no rubbings of inscriptions from that period have been passed down. The oldest book of rubbings preserved and specifically dated is the *Hot Springs Inscription* written and calligraphed by Li Shimin, the Taizong Emperor of Tang. The original inscribed stone was placed in Wenquan, Shaanxi and is long gone. The book of rubbings, discovered in 1900 in Grotto 17 of the Mogao Grottoes in Dunhuang is now collected by the Library of Paris, France. Toward the end of the book, a line is written in ink, which says, "Guoyier, Weigu Prefecture, on the □th day of the 8th month in the fourth year of Yonghui". From this it can be determined that the rubbings were made before 653, or the 4th year of Yonghui of Tang. Though rubbings were rather common in the Tang Dynasty, very few Tang books of rubbings have been preserved. Besides the *Hot Springs Inscription,* there are also verifiable Tang books of rubbings like the *Inscription for the Pagoda of Buddhist Master Yong's Relic at Huadu Temple* calligraphed by Ouyang Xun, *Diamond Sutra and Stele to Shence Army* by Liu Gongquan. In the Song Dynasty, rubbings were extremely popular and they inspired the invention of printing, one of the Four Great Inventions. By now, over 100 Song books of rubbings have been preserved. They are universally seen as treasures under the category of rubbings in the collections of museums and libraries.

2. Prerequisites for Emergence of the Technique

1) Invention and Use of Ink

China is the first country in the world to have invented ink. To meet their need of writing, ancient Chinese started using colored paints since a very long time ago. Traces of ink have been found on patterned colored pottery, inscribed shells and oracle bones, bamboo and wooden slips dating back to the period of the Yangshao Culture, which means that the use of ink in China can be traced back to the Neolithic era. However, the earliest ink used by mankind was mostly natural ink, which is inferior in quality and hard to use. This had prodded the invention of artificial ink. The earliest artificial ink discovered so far is ink bars of the mid-Warring States period unearthed at Tomb 4 of Shuihudi Ancient Tombs in Yunmeng, Hubei in 1975. On the inkstone unearthed in the same tomb, there are traces of ink grinding. It can thus be seen that ancient Chinese started grinding ink for writing in the Warring States period.

2) Mass creation of stone inscriptions

Inscriptions of the Shang and Zhou dynasties are mainly found on oracle bones and bronze ware, mostly for divination, sacrifice or recording major events. In the Warring States period and Qin and Han dynasties, metal ware declined, and stone ware gradually became an important medium for inscription. The history of stone inscription officially starts with the Shi-gu-wen or "Stone Drum Inscription" dating to the Warring States period. Later, stone inscription developed rapidly. There were already hundreds of stone inscriptions in the Qin and Han dynasties. The mass creation of stone inscriptions constituted an important prerequisite for the invention of the technique of rubbing.

3) Invention and Use of Paper

Prior to recorded history, our ancestors mainly kept records by tying knots. In the Shang Dynasty, people started to inscribe characters on tortoise shells and oracle bones. In the Spring and Autumn period, bamboo slips and wooden pieces and silk cloth were used as the main media for writings such as books and documents. However, these materials have inherent limitations. For instance, silk cloth was too expensive, and bamboo slips were slightly awkward, which constrained the dissemination and development of culture. Thus, paper was invented. In 1957, Shaanxi Museum discovered some Baqiao paper in a Western Han tomb near Baqiao in the eastern suburb of Xi'an. The time of its production was no later than the reign of the Wudi Emperor of Western Han. Later, some scraps of Han paper were also unearthed in Lop Nor, Xinjiang and Juyan, Gansu. It can be seen that as one of the Four Great Inventions of China, paper had appeared in the early Western Han Dynasty. However, paper then was extremely coarse and expensive to make, and thus hard to be put to wide use. In 105 CE, the technique of papermaking was improved by Cai Lun, an Eastern Han eunuch, who reduced its cost and improved its quality and output. Thanks to him, paper can be widely used. In the Sui and Tang dynasties, Xuan paper was developed, providing an important physical condition for the emergence of the rubbing technique.

II. Tools for Rubbing

1. Tools for Pasting Paper

1) Sweeping brush (mane brush) The sweeping brush is used for the first step, i.e. pasting paper. It is made of coir or sisal fiber and used to brush the Xuan paper to squeeze the air from in between when the paper is attached to the inscription. When used, the brush should be perpendicular to the surface so as to void damaging the paper. The hair of a newly bought sweeping brush should be "combed" tidy with an awl and then cut to the same length. Later they should be polished or grinded with sandpaper or coarse gravel for half an hour so as to make the coir feel soft and smooth before the brush can be used.

2) Hammer-brushing (Tap-brushing) Initially a wooden hammer was used to beat a matt placed on the Xuan paper attached to a tablet inscription. Such a method is not advisable and disused because it causes damage to endangered stone inscriptions. In the late 20th century, the wooden hammer was replaced with a bristle brush. When a high-relief was rubbed, the bristle brush was placed into a thin sock and its size could be determined by that of the tablet inscription or relief. The tapping brush is mainly used to tap Xuan paper evenly into the recessed parts of tablet inscriptions and reliefs so that the paper is closely attached to carvings to be rubbed. The desired effect is that when the paper goes dry, it is not too tense for applying ink and the edges and details of characters can be imprinted more clearly.

3) Felt (of moderate thickness) The felt, made by sticking wool together, is soft and elastic.

4) Wet towel When one works in open air, wind is always likely and the stele may tilt so much that it become very difficult to attach paper. When paper is attached, a wet towel can be used to press Xuan paper onto the inscribed tablet or relief. The wetness can ensure the close attachment of paper to the tablet. Then the tapping brush is used to make the attachment firmer.

2. Ink-Applying Tools

1) Puff The puff, known as *pu-zi* or *ta-bao*, is the main tool for applying ink. Generally, it is made according to the size and inscription of the item to be rubbed. Materials used include: cotton, cotton or silk cloth, thread, felt, sponge, thin plastic, etc. Method: ①The felt is cut into round shapes, which taper 1-2 millimeters each layer upward and are stacked together to form a cone of a size suitable for the user. Then the thin plastic is used to bind the felt pieces together. It should be noted that surface of the puff should be tight and free of wrinkles. However, this method is usually suitable for stone carvings on a flat surface. ②High reliefs and circular engravings, as cubic sculptures, feature uneven surfaces. Therefore, the type of puff made with the first method cannot be used for applying ink if a high relief or circular engraving is rubbed... Puffs used to apply ink are made by binding sponge pieces cut into pyramidal shapes that can be as big as eggs or as small as beans. Their sizes should be determined by the patterns on items that need to rubbed. Techniques employed to make puffs may vary in different regions, though they should be handy for the actual user and can apply ink evenly. Because ink dries up easily and felt stiffens very quickly, when used next time, they are prone to leave ink application uneven. Therefore, puffs should be wrapped up in a plastic or air-tight bag so as to maintain their wetness and the elasticity of felt.

2) Ink board: Known as *ta-ban* or *mo-ban* in Chinese, the ink board is an auxiliary tool for applying ink. It is shaped like a table tennis bat, but slightly larger. Ink is poured directly onto the board, or put thereon with a writing brush to facilitate ink application with the puff. The ink board is mainly used to rub large inscribed tablets, but seldom used in the south of China, where two large puffs are patted against each other to apply ink.

3) Writing brush, flat writing brush (*pai-bi*): The writing brush or flat writing brush, made of wool, is used to apply ink and water. Before it is used, it should be steeped in water to wash colloids off its surface.

3. Repairing tools

1) Paste: Made by following the procedure of making paste for traditional calligraphy and painting mounting and remounting of ancient books. It is mainly used to stick a damaged rubbing together for restoration and protection. Earlier its raw material has been wheat flour, which is put into water and washed clean before gluten is removed (to avoid attracting vermin). Then the remaining starch is put into a bucket for precipitation. After that hot water is poured into the starchy sediments to make paste. In recent years, wheat starch is used instead. Hot water is poured into the starch until it goes translucent and ready for use.

2) Paper slips for joining pieces of rubbings: Paper slips, typically of thin Xuan paper as thick as or slightly thinner than the paper used for rubbing, are cut 0.5-1.5 centimeters wide (depending on the actual damage condition of the rubbing) and pasted onto the back of the rubbing where paste has been applied according to the dimensions of the damaged part.

3) Writing brush: The writing brush can be used to spread paste evenly onto Xuan paper slips.

4) Sprinkling can: Before a rubbing is mended, it needs to be wetted with a sprinkling can and the damaged parts should be pieced together before they are joined and reinforced with Xuan paper slips. Wetting the rubbing not only makes joining and pasting easier, but can prevent such things as wrinkling and displacement of the rubbing.

III. What and How to Rub

1. What to Rub

Traditional objects of rubbings include: bronze ware, carved stone, inscribed tablets, epitaphs, pagoda inscriptions, sutra pillars, statue-building inscriptions, stone *que* inscriptions, cliff carvings, carved bricks and stones, building inscriptions, etc. The innovation of high relief rubbing has greatly expanded the category. Now we can rub lofty high reliefs and circular engravings, as well as wood carvings, historic buildings, mountains in Mother Nature, ancient villages, primitive forests and modern sculpture. The use of the rubbing technique has become more extensive.

2. Folding, Processing and Cutting Paper

Rubbing planar stone carvings: If light work is desired, it is advisable that Xuan paper of an appropriate size be chosen. If the size does not fit, Xuan paper can be cut. Blank space, ideally around 3 centimeters, should be left on the four sides. Xuan paper should first be folded multiple times into a square or rectangular shape. Every fold should leave the two halves stagger by around 2 millimeters to make it easier to separate them. Then the folded Xuan paper is wrapped with a wet towel and placed into a ziplock bag and will be used until the soaked paper goes dry again. When a grotto or large-sized statue is rubbed, the *men-zhi* or paper-processing procedure needs to be carried out in advance. Xuan paper is first put into a large amount of water and then taken out and placed on a clean flat board after it is soaked. After that a plastic board is placed onto the Xuan paper and pressed with two hands or with the weight of the body to squeeze the water out of the paper. This step should be conducted gently. Two much force is especially prone to damage the paper. After that, the Xuan paper is wrapped with clean towels and kept in a plastic or sealed bag to prevent water loss.

3. Cleaning the Tablet Inscription

Because many tablet inscriptions are often put in the open air for years, there are often dirt and dust on character edges and designs. A soft brush or cotton towel is needed to clean their surfaces and keep the characters and designs clear. If there is dirt that cannot be easily removed, bamboo picks or cotton swabs may be used. But we should not exert too much force in case the inscriptions would be damaged. All tablet inscriptions should be cleaned before they are rubbed, particularly at places where serious weathering has blurred characters and designs; a soft-hair brush should be used to sweep dust off the surface. In the past, some people used fire to clean tablet inscriptions. However, tablet inscriptions heated by fire become crisp easily and may break up after being beaten many times. Such a method is not good to the protection of cultural relics. Now it is no longer in use.

4. The Method of Applying and Tapping Paper for Planar Stone Carvings, High Reliefs and Circular Engravings

There are two methods of attaching paper to planar stone carvings: the Dry Method and the Wet Method. The Dry Method: The Dry Method is generally used in case of limited conditions or time constraints when the rubbing should be done quickly. However, it is mostly used for planar stone carving. It is very hard to apply this method to high reliefs. First, sprinkle water evenly onto Xuan paper with a sprinkling can or towel. Then press it onto the stone inscription with a towel. If there are wrinkles, peel the wet Xuan paper, remove the wrinkles with the sweeping brush and attach the paper with the tapping brush. The Wet Method: West Xuan paper processed in advance is gently peeled to cover the tablet inscription before it is tapped. Because processed Xuan paper is evenly wet, the Wet Method has been preferred.

The method of applying and tapping paper for high reliefs and circular engravings: In most cases, rubbings of planar inscriptions can remain intact from paper application to the completion of the rubbing. They are not prone to be damaged. After being recovered, they are registered and stored directly with a simple procedure. In the case of high reliefs, due to their uneven surfaces, the Dry Method may result in uneven paper wetting; when a wet towel is pressed onto the paper, it may budge, to getting a rubbing larger than the actual size of the original high relief. Paper needs to be processed in advance and Xuan paper to be cut by a 1:1 ratio and pressed onto the inscription to be rubbed. Then towels are used to press the Xuan paper into the recessed parts gradually layer by layer. Because of the cubic effect of high reliefs, it is unlikely to make paper perfectly aligned as in the case of planar tablet inscriptions. It is hard to increase the adhesion between paper and high relief, which already makes it hard to apply paper; when it is windy, it will be far harder. When paper is applied, a piece of Xuan paper is separated, pressed onto the blank space above the relief and then fixed at the four corners with a towel. Afterwards, the method of orthographic projection is adopted to tailor the paper for the convex places one by one. If there are wrinkles, they should be at blank spaces. After paper is attached, tapping brushes of different sizes are used to gently tap Xuan paper so that it is aligned with the actual relief according to the different angles of statue designs. However, because high reliefs have uneven surfaces which result in very small stress areas, force should not be exerted in excess. Meanwhile, before tap-brushes are used, they should be sleeved in thin socks which give good protection to stone inscriptions and Xuan paper. If it is windy, first separate Xuan paper completely, then roll it up, and unroll it bit by bit from bottom upward. Use wet towels to press the two sides and convex parts of high reliefs. Lastly, use tapping brushes to ensure solid attachment and effectively prevent wind from detaching the paper. When high reliefs are rubbed, they are at times so large that pieces of paper need to be joined. It should be noted that two pieces of paper should overlap by 2 centimeters and be hammered repeatedly to ensure they will not come apart. Every step in the process is complex and time- and energy-consuming. Therefore, great patience and care is needed to execute them.

5. Applying Ink

Applying ink: When Xuan paper is 90% dry or drier, ink can be applied. For a planar inscription, use a large puff (suitable for the size of the hand) to apply ink evenly all over the paper. Make sure that the lines and carvings are rubbed clearly, with the texture and weathering highlighted.

The method of applying ink for high reliefs: Before being rubbed, the target stone inscription should be measured and the date and style of the relief be explored so as to facilitate later joining and mending. Puffs used to apply ink for high reliefs are different from those for planar tablet inscriptions. Because of their uneven surfaces, puffs generally used to rub planar tablet inscriptions cannot be applied to them. The rubbing of high reliefs, whatever their sizes, should be completed with small puffs. When ink is applied, the puff should be used in the same way as the writing brush by using the tip of the middle at some times and the sides at others. Corresponding to different carving techniques of statues, techniques involving different angles are employed. Meanwhile, the mind should be calm and free of anxiety and impatience. The techniques are similar to those of ink and wash painting, with nearer places in thicker color than father ones. After ink is applied, the perspective effect should be examined from different angles and different positions. Ink should be added where the effect is not perfect.

6. Detaching the Rubbing

Rubbings of high reliefs are different from planar inscription rubbings. After a planar inscription rubbing is detached, it is already a complete work. When a high-relief rubbing is detached, the detachment should be conducted from left to right or from bottom to top, according to the texture of the statue and the order of statue building. In the course of detachment, a zip-lock bag should be prepared to contain all rubbing pieces, including those as small as a fingernail, so as to ensure the completeness of the rubbing.

7. Joining and Mending of Rubbings

The joining and mending of high-relief rubbings is an important step which has direct impact upon the final product. After being detached, a rubbing may be in the form of hundreds or even thousands of pieces, which can be pieced together through a series of procedures including wetting, joining and cutting. The time needed may several times than that spent on rubbing. Before mending, first take out the pieces and place them front down on a desk. Sprinkle water on them evenly with a can and keep them stretched and wet to the extent that there are no wrinkles on the pieces. Then put the pieces together on by one at the missing parts, wet them, and align the edges to complete the entire rubbing. It should be noted that the entire rubbing must be fully spread and that there should not be any gaps or wrinkles at the edges of the pieces. Otherwise the design on the rubbing will be distorted and lose its original charm. After the joining, take out some patch paper and spread paste on it with a writing brush. Use Xuan paper slips for joining according to the dimensions of the gaps and press the joined places with the palms so that the patch paper is firmly attached. Care should be taken not to use too much paste in case it is squeezed out when pressed, which makes folding and storage less easy. After the joining is completed, turn the rubbing over and compare it to a photo of the original inscription. In the event that there is any distortion or wrinkle, the patch paper at the place should be detached and then rejoined until the design on the rubbing is consistent with the original. Later, air-dry the rubbing and trim its four sides before it is folded and placed into a bag for storage.

IV. Value of High-Relief Rubbing

China's inscription rubbing technique has a history of over 1,000 years. However, the works rubbed have mostly been planar tablet inscriptions. High reliefs in caves or on statue tablets have in most cases been left unrubbed, or only their backdrop design is rubbed. The innovation of high-relief rubbing has made it possible to rub lofty stone tomb carvings and huge grotto statues and represent their layering and artistic effect. It can not only preserve the authenticity of statues and inscriptions, but also improve the legibility of the contents of the stone carvings.

The technique of high-relief rubbing is an innovated new technique of rendering the three-dimensional designs of large-sized works of high relief and circular engraving onto planar paper, on the basis of traditional full rubbing techniques of tablet inscriptions and bronze ware, combining the techniques of full bronze rubbing, planar rubbing, *wu-jin* (black bronze) rubbing, "*chan-yi*" (cicada wings), and embedded rubbing, through a series of rubbing procedures including paper applying, paper tapping, ink applying, rubbing detaching, and mending. The actual rubbing technique is determined according to the style and artistic features of the times, and then the "color" of ink and the use of puffs are adjusted according to the actual conditions. Then the rubbing is detached and joined and mended to complete the entire process. Every step calls for calmness and patience. A bit of impatience may result in a total failure. Because the operator faces an uneven surface of stone sculpture, paper should be tailored as needed. When the rubbing is done, it is in the form of numerous pieces. The joining following the detachment is a task of seeking truth with carefulness and pursuing perfection in putting together the pieces. Therefore, every beautiful scroll people see afterwards is completed by a rubbers standing on a high stand, rubbing the inscription with the back bent, detaching the rubbing with care and piecing it together with patience and meticulosity. Therefore, compared to planar inscription rubbing, it is very hard to master the technique of high-relief rubbing, which can only be mastered through long-term practice.

The technique of high-relief rubbing cannot only retain the original size and artistic style of the cultural relic, but can produce exquisite designs with superb skills on the basis of the original design of the stone carving. Though high technologies like 3D printing have achieved rapid advancements, the ancient technique has been passed down and continued, which not only testifies to its vitality, but, more notably, proves its unique, irreplaceable artistic effect and expressiveness. From the perspective of cultural heritage preservation, such rubbings are more authentic and more elaborate than written records, photographic materials and drawings, and are more helpful to academic research. They can represent the texture, clothing and accessories of high-relief subjects and traces left by artisans, and record crevices or wear on the inscriptions, providing accurate information for protection and observation. In brief, the successful innovation of this rubbing technique is of great significance to present and future protection and research and archiving of stone carvings, to the exchange of cultural heritage, and to carrying forth traditional culture and art.

嵩山东汉三阙

Three Ques in the Eastern Han Dynasty at Mount Song

"嵩山三阙"是东汉太室石阙、少室石阙、启母阙三阙的合称。三阙位于河南省登封市，是我国现存最古老的庙阙，为第一批全国重点文物保护单位，现已申报世界文化遗产。三阙形制相仿，每阙均为对称的东西双阙，皆刻有阙铭和画像。画像内容颇为丰富，包括人物、车马出行、宴饮、百戏、蹴鞠、斗鸡、猎兔、驯象、杂技表演、双龙穿壁、四灵、辟邪柏、夏禹化熊、动植物等，图文宽博朴厚、气象恢宏。三阙为研究汉代中原地区庙阙制度、建筑形制、汉代画像及书法提供了珍贵的实物资料。

太室石阙位于登封中岳庙南约一里处。东汉元初五年（118）四月建，吕常等造。阙身雕刻画像。西阙正面（南面）刻阙铭，隶书28行，行9字。两铭间有额，阳文篆书，3行，行3字，额题"中岳泰室阳城嵩高口"，额下刻有东汉延光四年三月颍川太守杨君题名。画面用减地平雕手法，由于画像久露荒野，风雨剥蚀，已漫漶不清，保存下来的有60余幅。其中有斗鸡图、车骑出行、杂技表演、虎食鬼及蛟龙、鸥、鹿、朱雀、虎等图像，形象生动古朴，对研究建筑史、书法和美术史有重要价值。

少室石阙在登封县城西六公里少室山下邢家铺村西，东汉延光二年（123）三月建。阙身刻画像。西阙正面（南面）刻阙铭，篆书，约36行，行4至8字。西阙北面上部有额，双勾阴文篆书3行，行2字，额题：少室神道之阙。东阙北面刻有"江孟李阳等题名"，隶书，4行，无年月。左右两阙分别雕刻蹴鞠图、辅首衔环、羊头、狐逐兔、头鸡、赛马、马戏、兽斗、玄鸟生商、四灵、羽人、车马出行、双兽争食、双龙穿壁、辟邪柏以及山水等图案约七十余幅。

开母庙石阙位于登封城东北三公里开母庙遗址前。堂溪协撰，东汉延光二年（123）建。阙文颂扬夏禹治水及夏后（涂山氏）启母的事迹。开母庙本名启母庙，为避汉景帝（刘启）讳，改作开母庙。阙身刻画像。阙铭刻于西阙北面（背面）及东侧，篆书36行，前11行，行7字，后25行，行12字。无额题。铭文下方刻东汉熹平四年（175）中郎将堂溪典"嵩高山请雨铭"，隶书，19行，行5字，字多剥蚀，现存11行。据请雨铭知开母庙石阙铭撰者为堂溪协。在铭文之间和其他块石中雕刻人物画像、启母化石、孔甲畜龙、鹳叼鱼、虎扑鹿、口中吐火、日御羲和、夏禹化熊、蹴鞠、果下马、犬逐兔、蛟龙穿环、郭巨埋儿、幻术、骑马出行、斗鸡、驯象、进谒、倒立、饮宴等七十余幅画像。

The "Three Ques of Mount Song" refers to the Taishi Que, Shaoshi Que and Qimu Que built in the Eastern Han Dynasty. The three ques are located at Dengfeng, Henan. They are the oldest existing gate towers in China and were included in the first batch of Major Historical and Cultural Sites Protected at the National Level. Currently, they are also nominated for the World Heritage List. The three ques are similar in appearance, each of which is flanked by two symmetrical towers on the east and west sides, both engraved with inscriptions and images. The subjects of the pictures engraved upon them vary, including human figures, carriages, revelries, folk dance, cuju games, cockfight, rabbit hunting, elephant crushing, juggling, soaring double dragons, the Four Holy Beasts, the cypress that blocks evil spirits, the transformation of Yu into a bear, and other plants and animals. The designs are magnificent and elegant. The three ques provide valuable physical materials for the research on the structure and architectural characteristics of ques in the Han Dynasty in the Central Plain, as well as on the paintings and calligraph of the Han Dynasty.

The Taishi Que is situated around 1 mile away from the Zhongyue Temple at Dengfeng. It was constructed in April in the fifth year of the Yuanchu Era (118 A.D.) by Lu Chang and others. The que is heavy with engraved images, with an inscription on the front side (southern side) of the western tower. The inscription was written in the clerical script, consisting of 28 lines, 9 words in each line . Between the two inscriptions lays a heading comprising 3 lines, 3 words in each line. The heading reads, "Yangcheng, Taishi, Zhongyue of Mount Song", beneath which is the signature of Mr. Yang, the governor of Yingchuan Prefecture, dated March in the fourth year of the Yanguang Era in the Eastern Han Dynasty. The pictures were sculpted in relief. Due to years of exposure to rushes of wind and torrents of rain, most of them are effaced. Only 60 of them survived the harsh weather. There are pictures of cockfight, running carriages, juggling, tigers that eat ghosts, dragons, owls, deer, phoenixes, and tigers. All these vivid sculptures are invaluable to the research on the history of architecture, calligraphy and art.

The Shaoshi Que is located to the west of the Xingjiapu village at the foot of Shaoshi Mountain four to six kilometers away from Dengfeng. It was built in March in the second year of the Yanguang Era in the Eastern Han Dynasty (123 A.D.). The que is also engraved with pictures. The inscription on the front side (southern side) of the western tower was written in the seal script, consisting of around 36 lines, 4 to 8 words in each line. At the top of the northern side of the western tower lays the heading, which was engraved in the seal script in a hollow font in intaglio. The heading, which has three lines, 2 words in each line, reads as follows, "The Que of Shaoshi Sacred Pathway". On the northern side of the eastern tower is the "signature of Jiangmeng, Liyang, and others" written in the clerical script, comprising 4 lines without a date. Both the towers are engraved with over 70 pictures that feature cuju games, adorned door knockers, sheep heads, rabbit-chasing foxes, roosters, horse racing, circus, fighting beasts, the bird giving birth to Shang, the Four Holy Beasts, immortals, running carriages, beasts fighting for food, double dragons, the cypress that blocks evil spirits, and other natural landscapes.

The Kaimu Que is three kilometers away to the northeast of the Dengfeng city, in front of the Kaimu Temple. It was built in the second year of the Yanguang Era in the Eastern Han Dynasty (123 A.D.). The inscription, written by Tang Xixie, tells the story of Emperor Yu who tamed the flood, as well as Emperor Yu's queen, the mother of Qi (Ms. Tushan). The Kaimu Que was originally called the Qimu Que. To show due respect to Emperor Jing of Han (whose name was Liu Qi), the temple was renamed Kaimu. The que is engraved with pictures. The inscription is engraved upon the northern side (back side) and eastern side of the western tower in the seal script. There are 36 lines, the first 11 lines with 7 words each, the remaining 25 with 12. There is no heading. Below the inscription is a line, which reads, "Inscription of the petition for rain at Mount Song". The inscription was written in the clerical script, comprising 19 lines, 5 words in each line, by the General of the Palace Gentleman, Tang Xixie, in the fourth year of Xiping Era in the Eastern Han Dynasty (175 A.D.). Most of it has worn off, with only 11 lines left. There are over 70 pictures engraved between the inscriptions and other stones, which feature human figures, the mother of Qi who transformed into a stone, Kong Jia who petted a dragon, cranes and fish, tigers pursuing deer, fire breathing, Xi He who governed the sun, Yu who transformed into a bear, cuju games, ponies, rabbit-chasing dogs, dragons going through hoops, Guo Ju who buried his son, magic, horse-riding, cockfight, elephant crushing, the meeting with the emperor, handstands, and scenes of banquets.

太室阙东阙南壁：东汉元初五年（118）建，拓片高305厘米，宽210厘米，2008年天地之中历史建筑群申报世界文化遗产建档时拓印。此壁内刻双龙穿壁、貘、朱雀、羊首和马等图案。形象古朴生动。

South wall of the east part of the Taishi Que: Completed in 118, the fifthfifth year of the Yuanchu era of the Eastern Han dynasty. The rubbing, 305 cm tall and 210 cm wide, was made in 2008 during the application for the World Heritage Site inscription of "The Centre of Heaven and Earth" historic monuments. On the south surface are engraved figures of two dragons winding through a circular motif, a tapir, a Vermilion Bird, a goat head, a horse, etc., which look simple yet vivid.

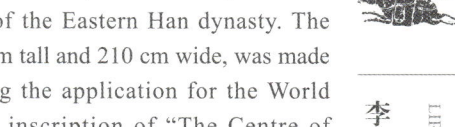

太室阙东阙北壁：东汉元初五年（118）建，拓片高305厘米，宽210厘米，2008年天地之中历史建筑群，申报世界文化遗产建档时拓印。此壁刻虎、二龙交尾、玄武、兔、蛟龙、斗鸡等图案。保存较完整，形态夸张，富有浪漫气息画面。

North surface of the east part of the Taishi Que: Completed in 118, the fifth year of the Yuanchu era of the Eastern Han dynasty. The rubbing, 305 cm tall and 210 cm wide, was made in 2008 during the application for the World Heritage Site inscription of the "The Centre of Heaven and Earth" historic monuments. On the north surface are well preserved engraved figures of a tiger, two dragons whose tails are intertwined, a Black Turtle, a rabbit, a scaled dragon, fighting cocks, etc., which appear romantically exaggerated in form.

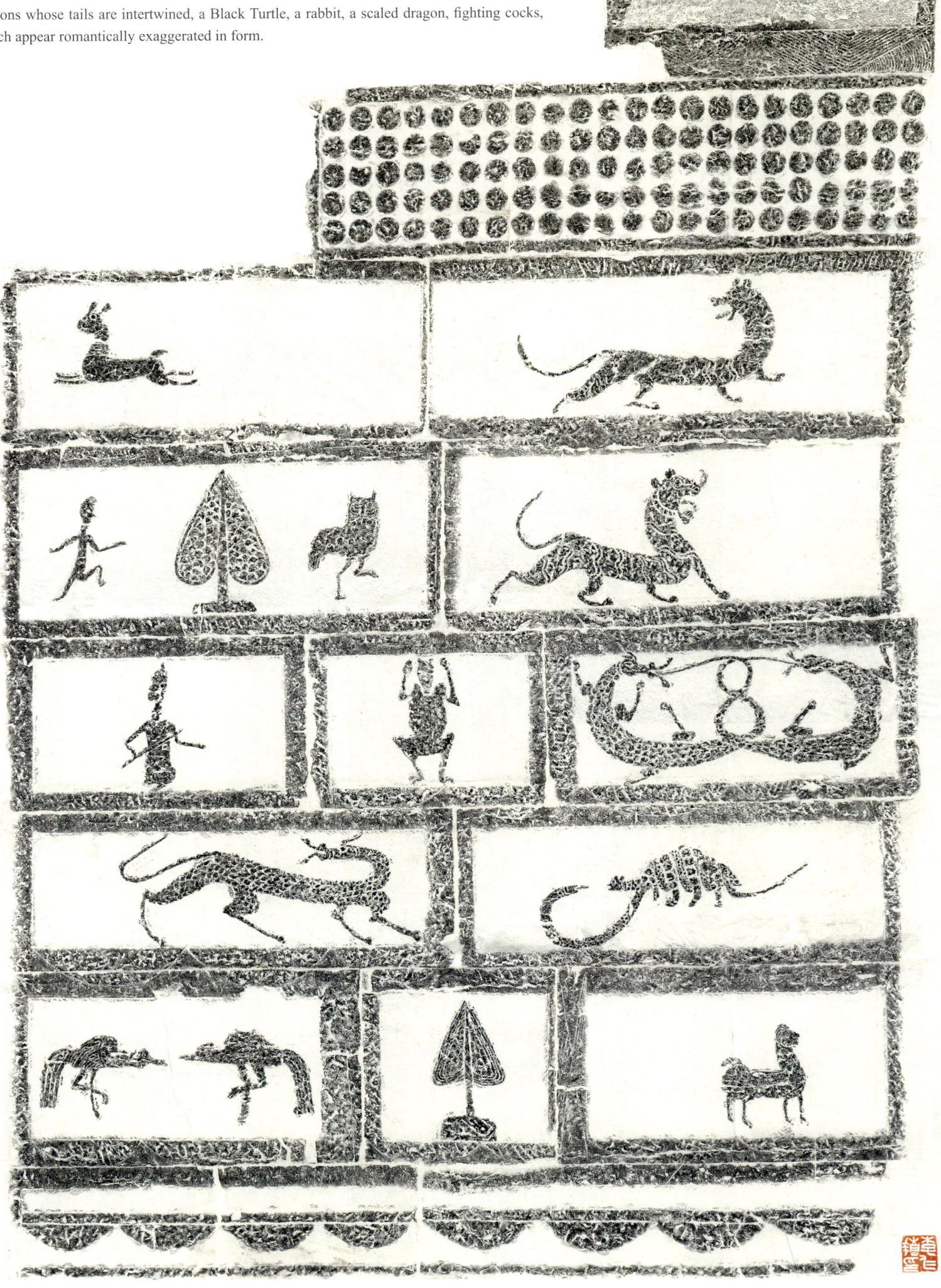

貘／太室阙东阙南面

李仁清传拓艺术

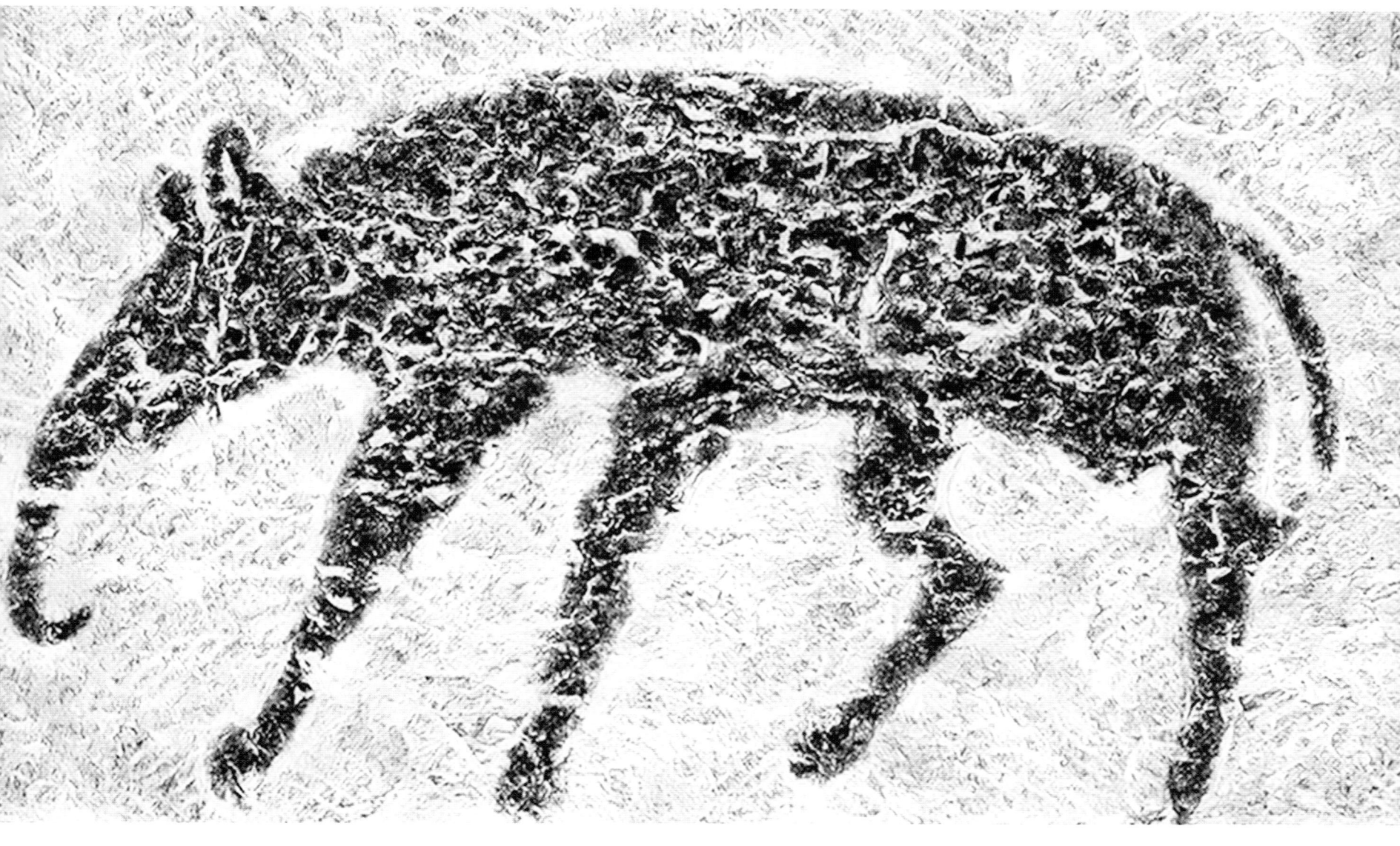

嵩山／东汉三阙／

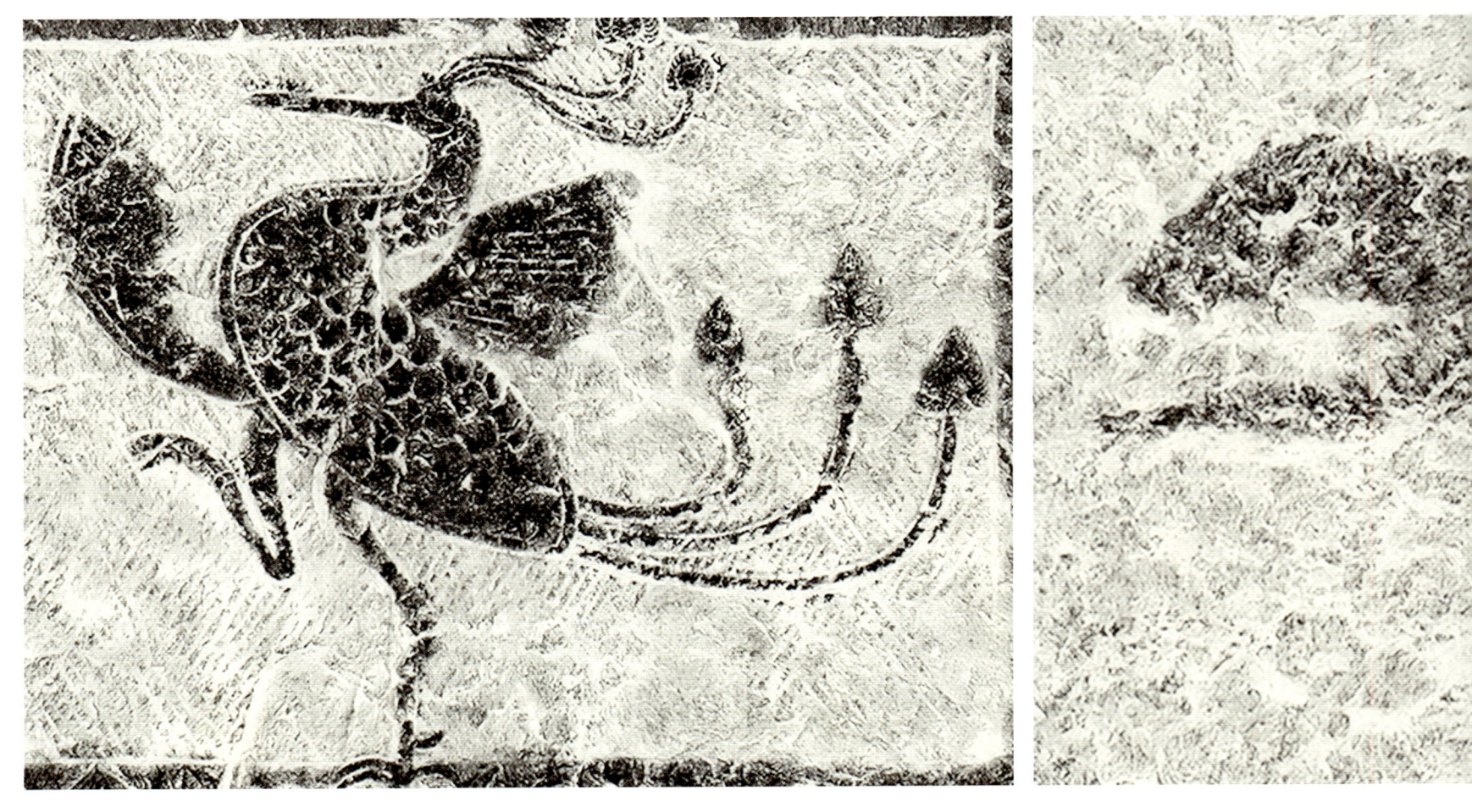

虎／太室阙东阙北面

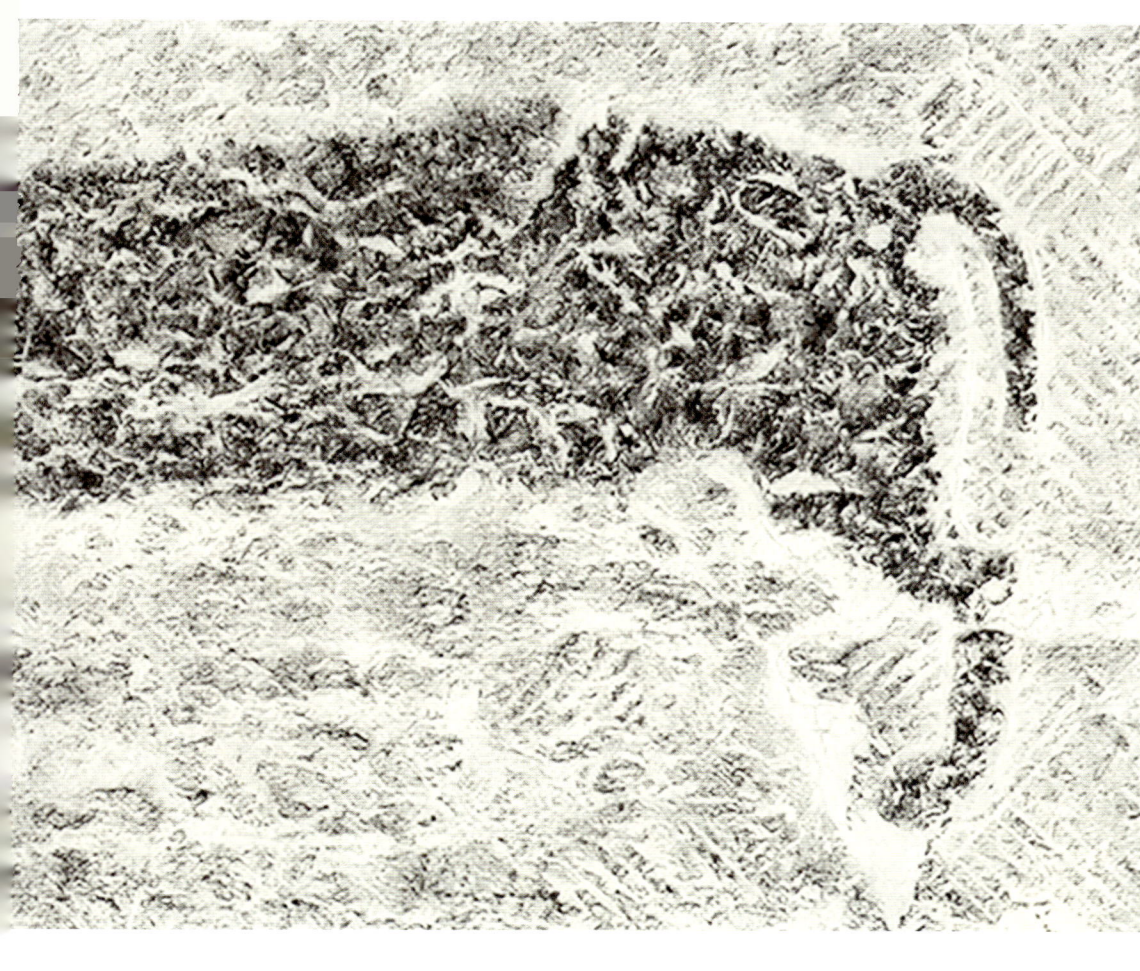

朱雀／太室阙东阙南面

马／太室阙东阙南面

嵩山／东汉三阙

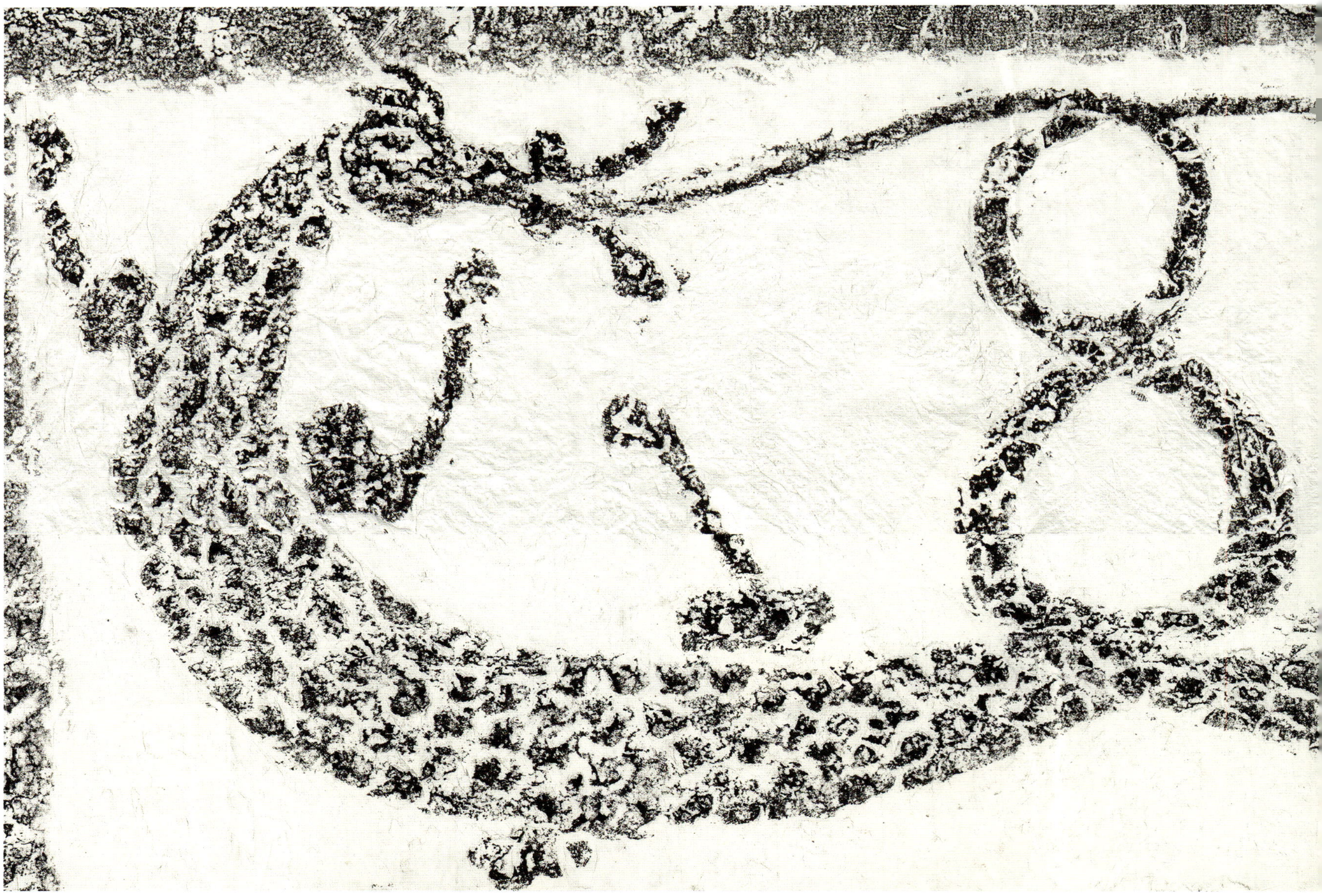

玄武／太室阙东阙北面

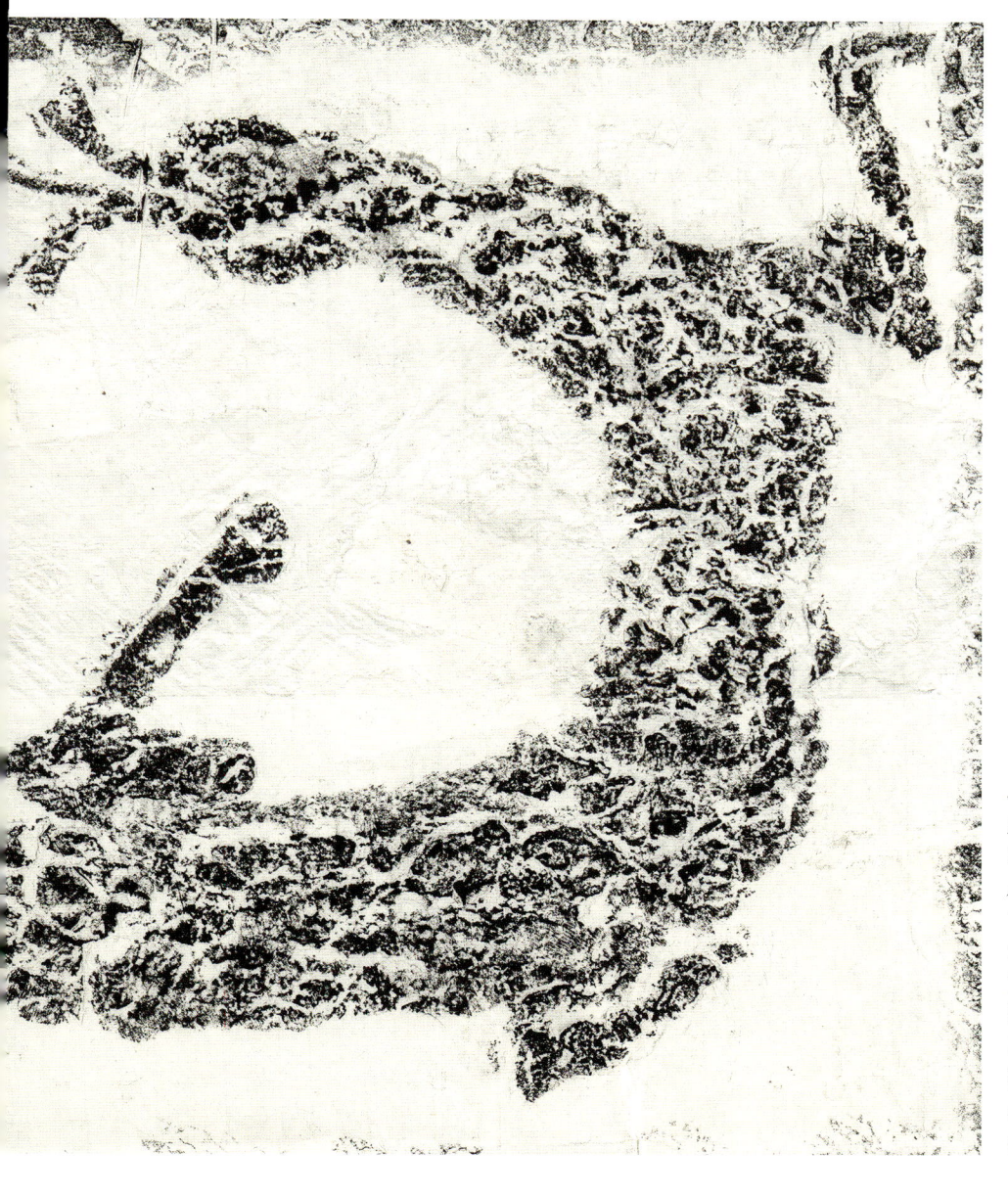

二龙交尾／太室阙东阙北面

嵩山／东汉三阙／

太室阙东阙东面：东汉元初五年（118）建，拓片高225厘米，宽62厘米，2008年天地之中历史建筑群申报世界文化遗产建档时拓印。上下两格残缺不全，第二方格刻两只水鸟、下刻鹿和猎犬捕兔画面。

East surface of the east part of the Taishi Que: Completed in 118, the fifth year of the Yuanchu era of the Eastern Han dynasty. The rubbing, 225 cm tall and 62 cm wide, was made in 2008 during the application for the World Heritage Site inscription of the "The Centre of Heaven and Earth" historic monuments. The top and bottom parts are incomplete; on the second part is an engraved figure of a pair of waterfowl, beneath which are a deer, and a hunting dog chasing a rabbit.

太室阙东阙西面：东汉元初五年（118）建，拓片高294厘米，宽80厘米，2008年天地之中历史建筑群申报世界文化遗产建档时拓印。此面刻双阙，比翼鸟和铺首衔环图案。

West surface of the east part of the Taishi Que: Completed in 118, the fifth year of the Yuanchu era of the Eastern Han dynasty. The rubbing, 294 cm tall and 80 cm wide, was made in 2008 during the application for the World Heritage Site inscription of the "The Centre of Heaven and Earth" historic monuments. There are engraved two que towers, a pair of lovebirds, and a door knocker.

水鸟／太室阙东阙东侧

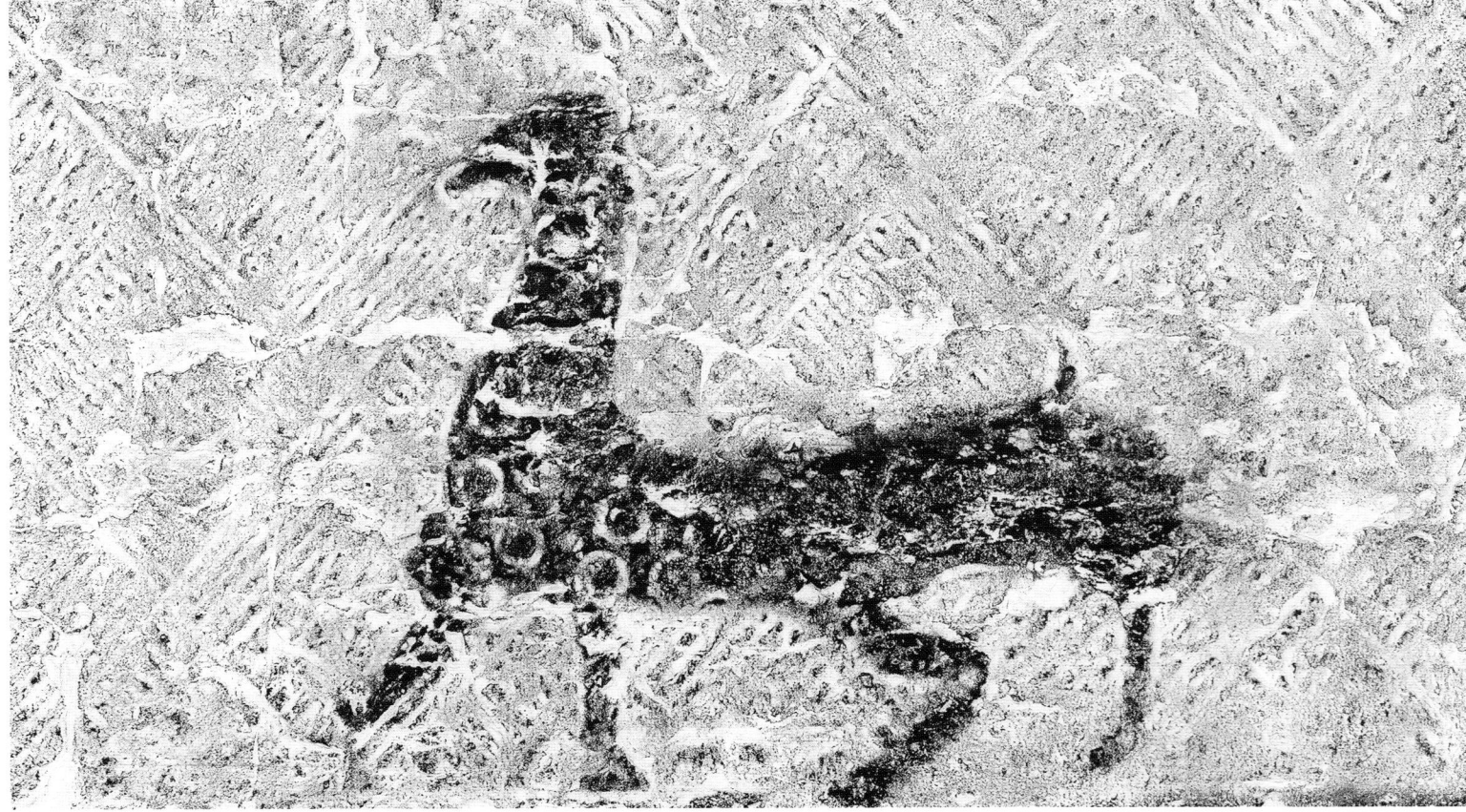

鹿／太室阙东阙东侧

铺首衔环／太室阙东阙西侧

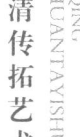
李仁清传拓艺术

嵩山／东汉三阙／

015

太室阙西阙南面：东汉元初五年（118）建，拓片高300厘米，宽200厘米，2008年天地之中历史建筑群申报世界文化遗产建档时拓印。此面下半部残缺不全，上层中部有阳刻篆书一"中岳泰室阳城□□□"9字题额，于其右侧刻一巨鳖，应是夏禹父亲神像，也是夏族的图腾之一。题额下面刻篆、隶各半的铭记和杂技马术、轺车出行等画面。

South surface of the west part of the Taishi Que: Completed in 118, the fifth year of the Yuanchu era of the Eastern Han dynasty. The rubbing, 300 cm tall and 200 cm wide, was made in 2008 during the application for the World Heritage Site inscription of the "The Centre of Heaven and Earth" historic monuments. The lower section of the surface is damaged and incomplete. On the middle part of the upper section is a nine-character inscription engraved in relief, "Zhongyue Taishi Yangcheng [three characters missing here]", to its right a sizable figure of turtle - presumably the divine image of the father of Yu the Great, and also one of the totems of the Xia dynasty. Below the inscription is a text engraved half in seal script and half in clerical script, as well as acrobatic, horse-riding, carriage trip and other images.

太室阙西阙北面：东汉元初五年（118）建，拓片高300厘米，宽200厘米，2008年天地之中历史建筑群申报世界文化遗产建档时拓印。上方右侧阴刻隶书阙铭，赞颂中岳神君的灵应和吕常等人建阙的缘由，为汉代石刻书体所罕见。铭记左侧刻骑行、鸱和虎食女鬼、朱雀、鹤叼鱼和龙等画面。

North surface of the west part of the Taishi Que: Completed in 118, the fifth year of the Yuanchu era of the Eastern Han dynasty. The rubbing, 300 cm tall and 200 cm wide, was made in 2008 during the application for the World Heritage Site inscription of the "The Centre of Heaven and Earth" historic monuments. On the right of the upper part is an inscription to the que towers, carved in clerical script, which praises the prophecy of the God of the Central Mountain and a gives an account of why Lü Chang among others built the que towers - a style of writing rarely seen for stone sculptures of the Han dynasty. To the left of the inscription are carved scenes of horse ride, an owl, a tiger eating a female ghost, a Vermilion Bird, a crane holding a fish in the mouth, a dragon, etc.

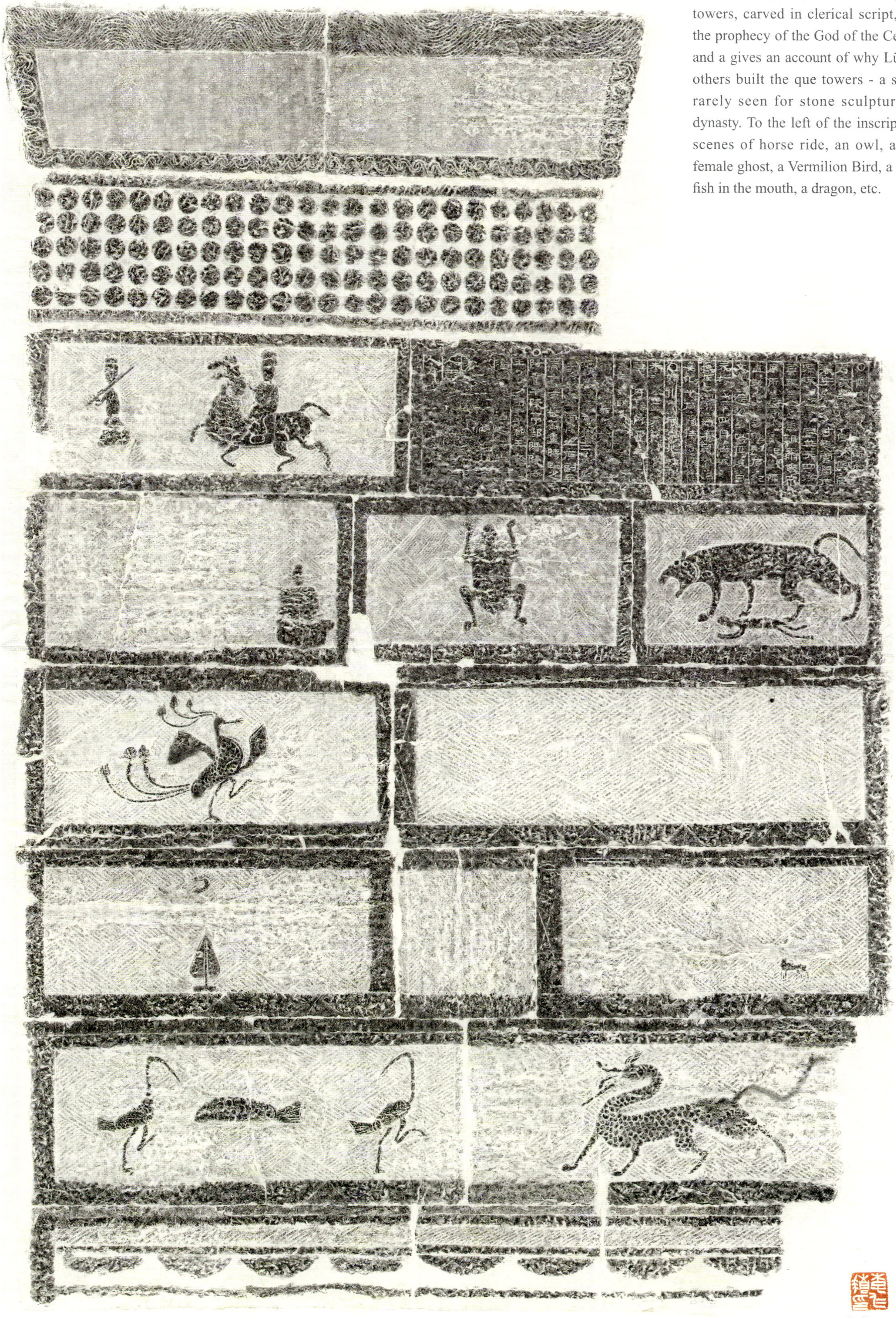

太室闕銘

嵩山/东汉三阙/

太室阙铭额

杂技马术／太室阙西阙南面

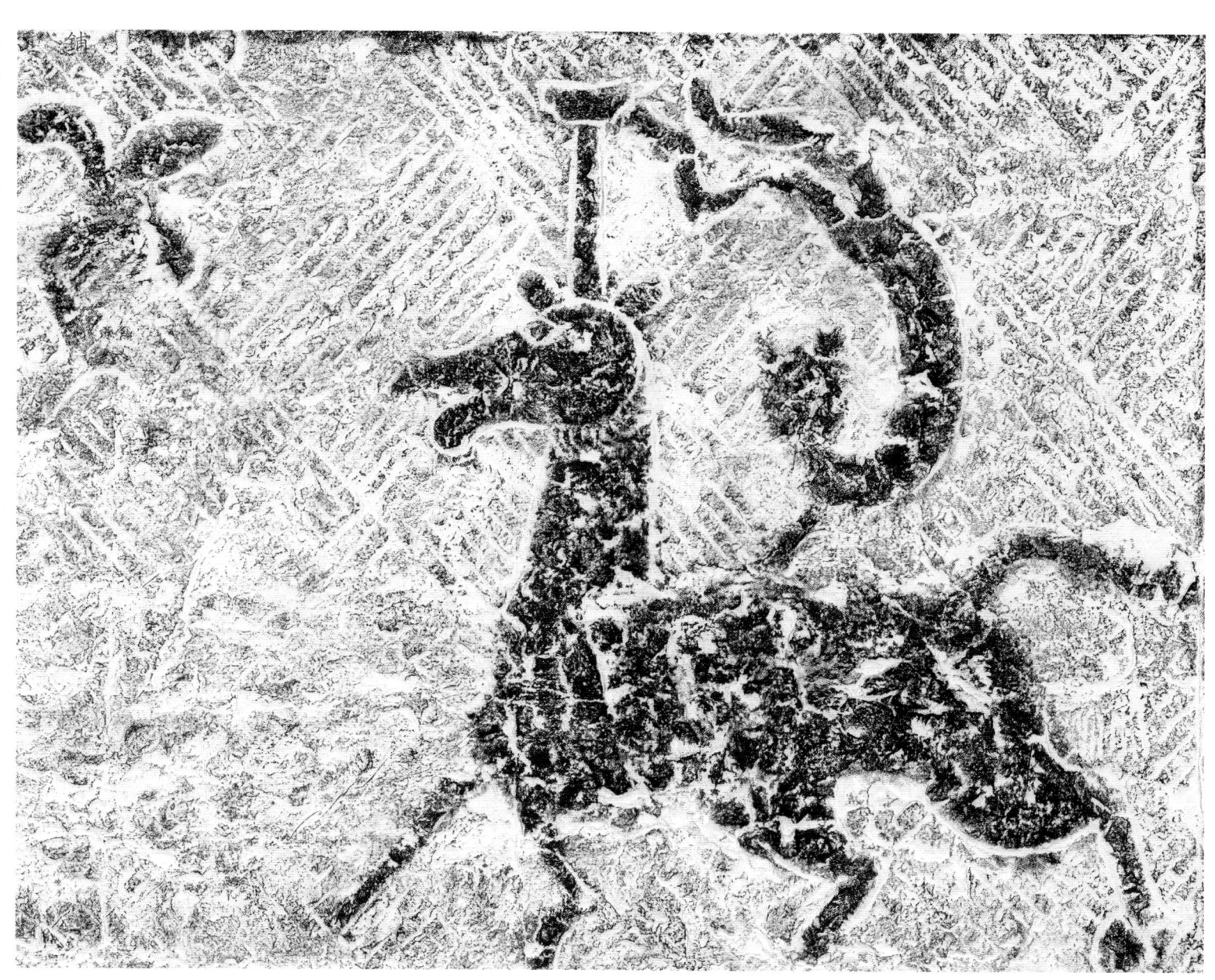

嵩山／东汉三阙／

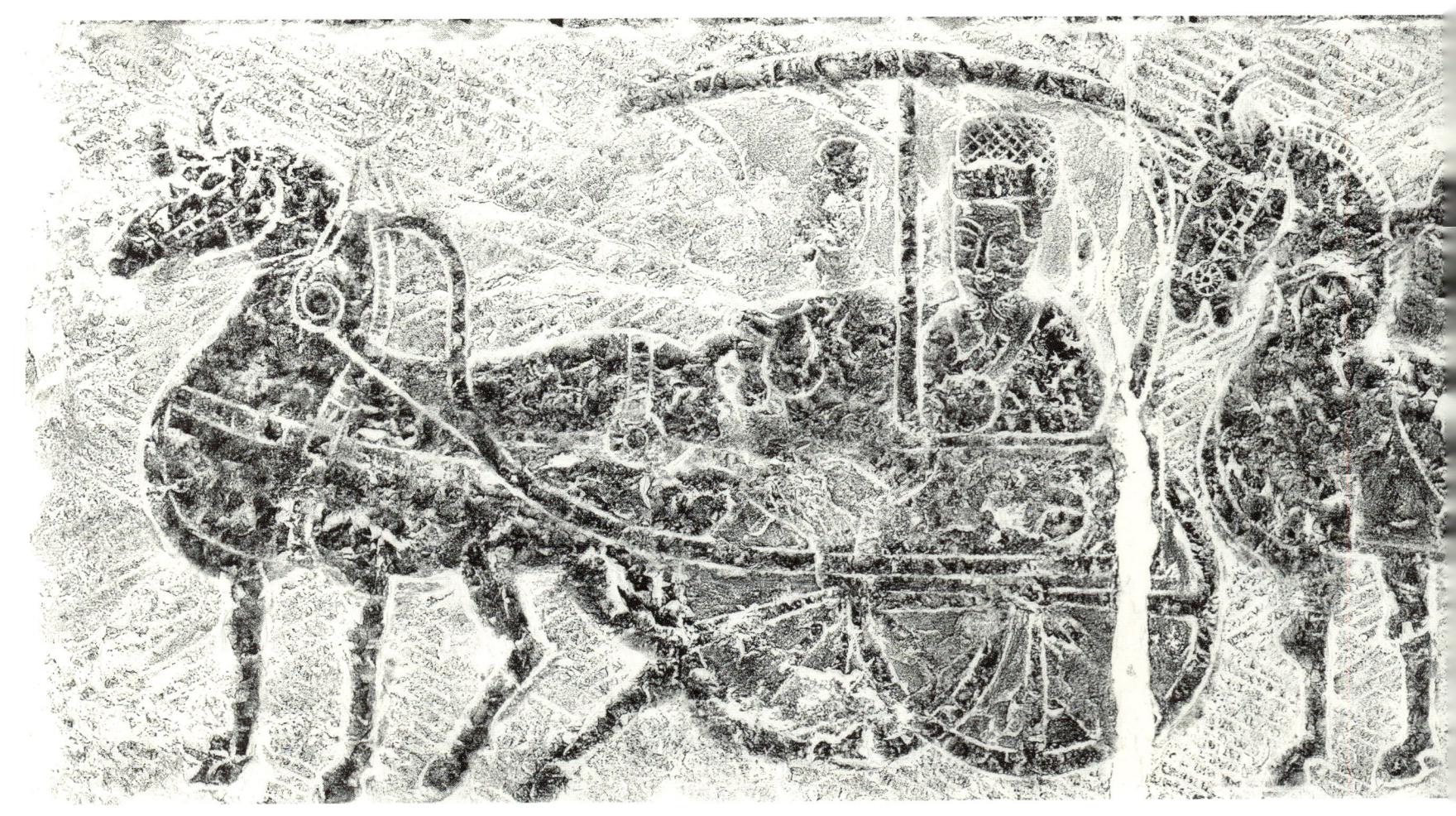

骑行／太室阙西阙北面局部

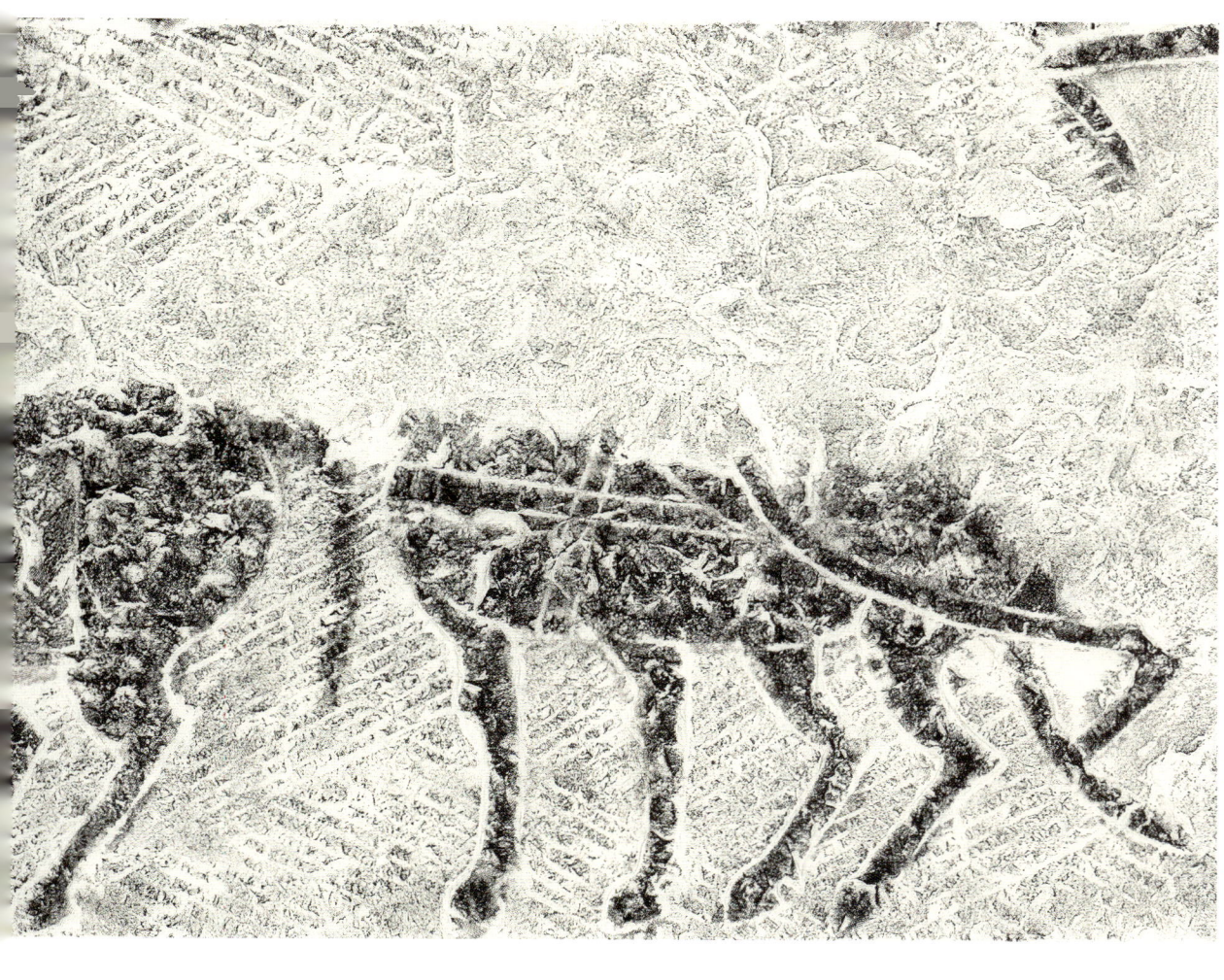

辎车出行／太室阙西阙南面

嵩山／东汉三阙／

李仁清传拓艺术

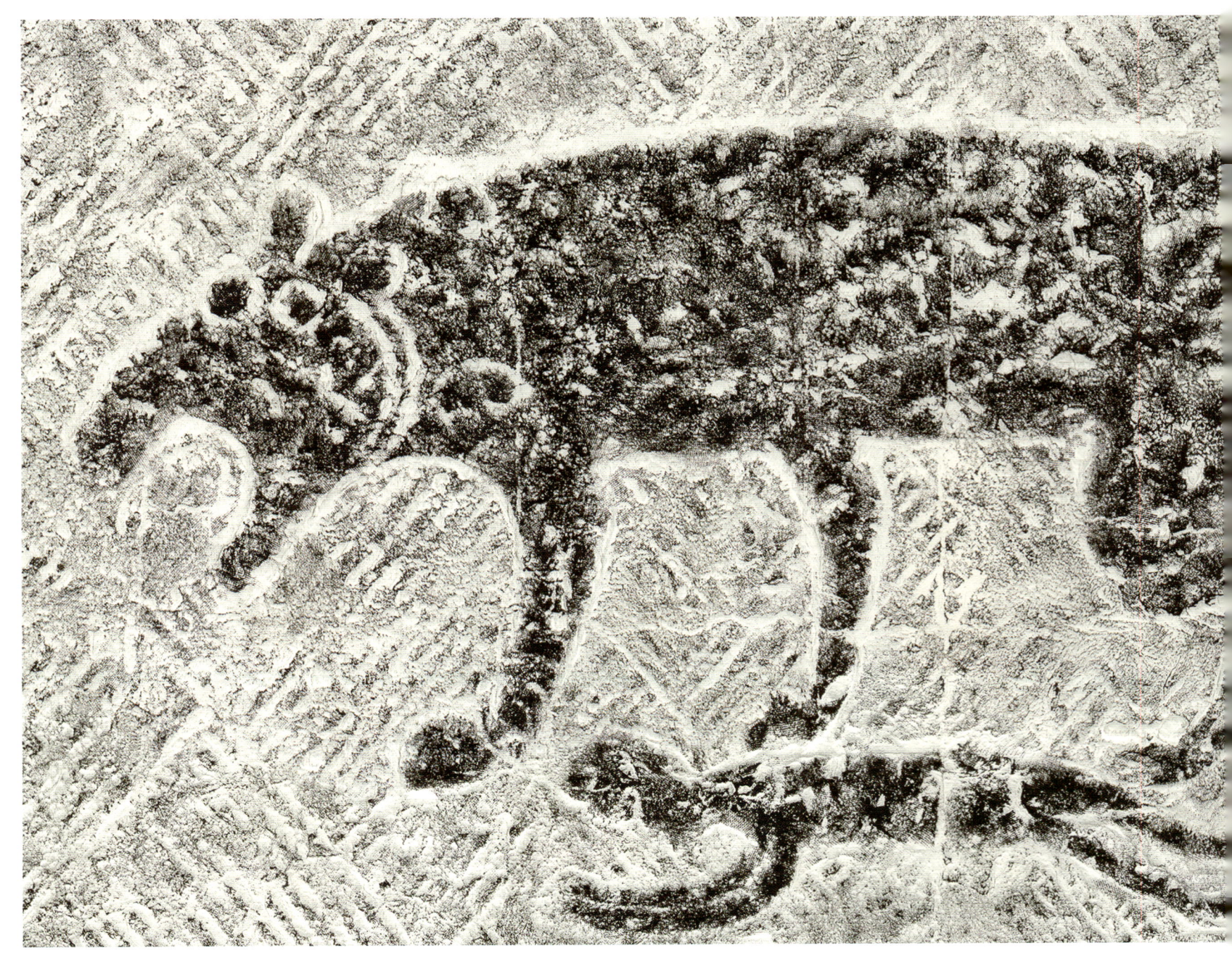

鹳叼鱼／太室阙西阙北面局部

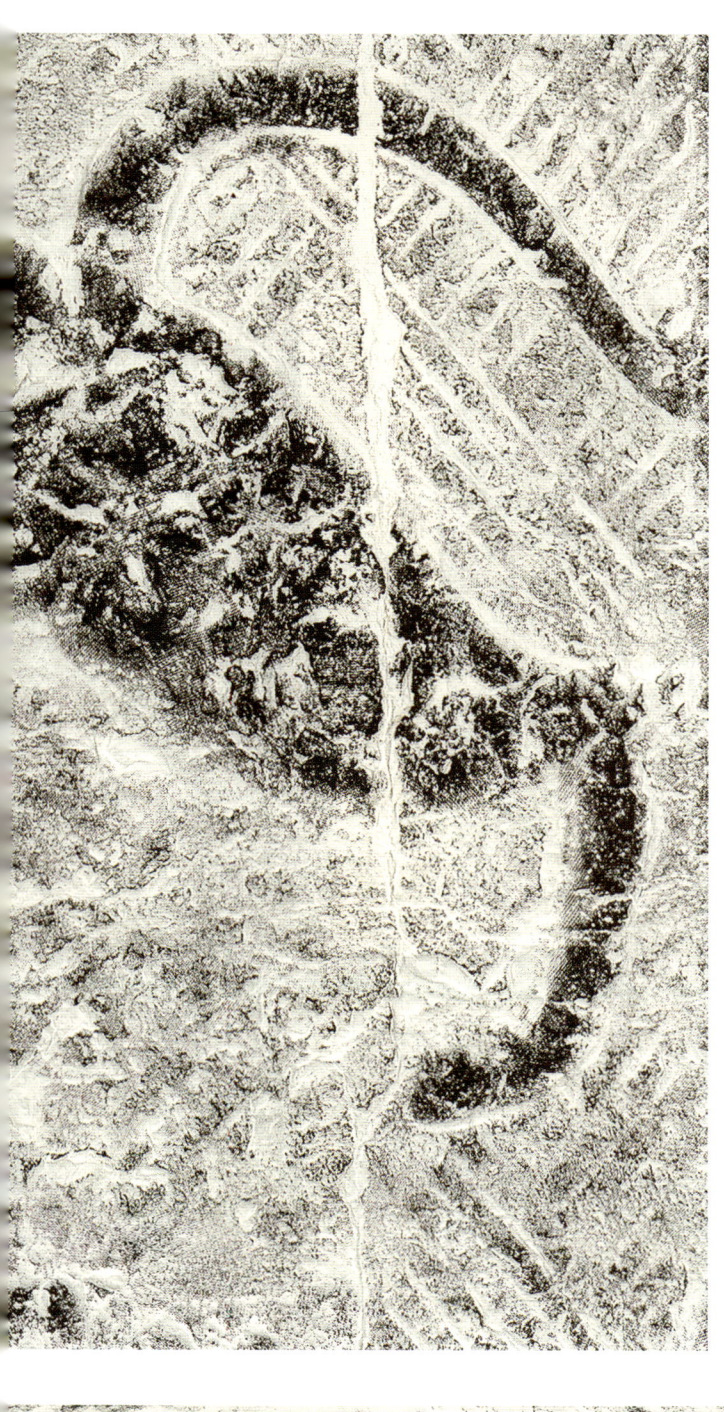

虎食女魃／太室阙西阙北面局部

嵩山／东汉三阙／

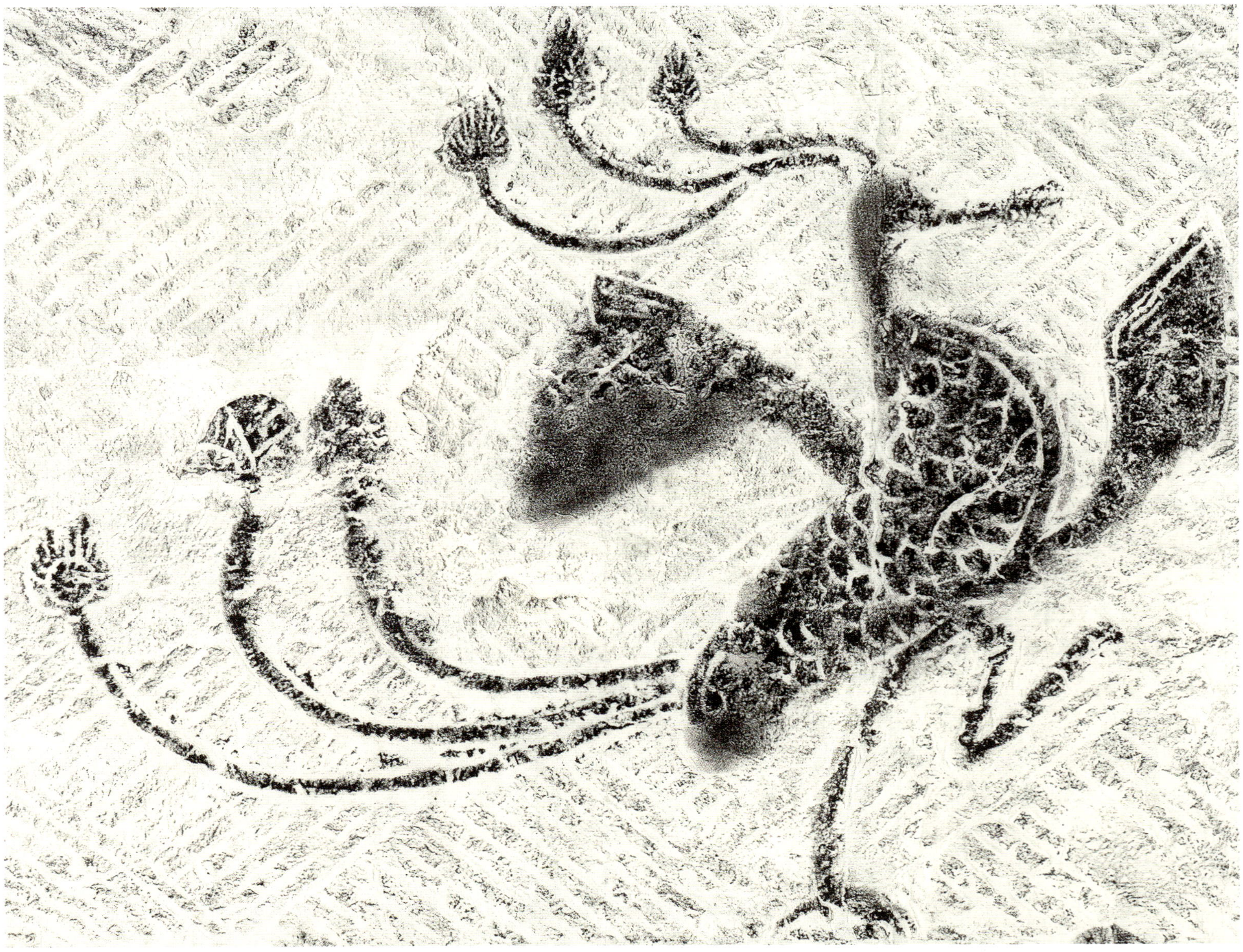

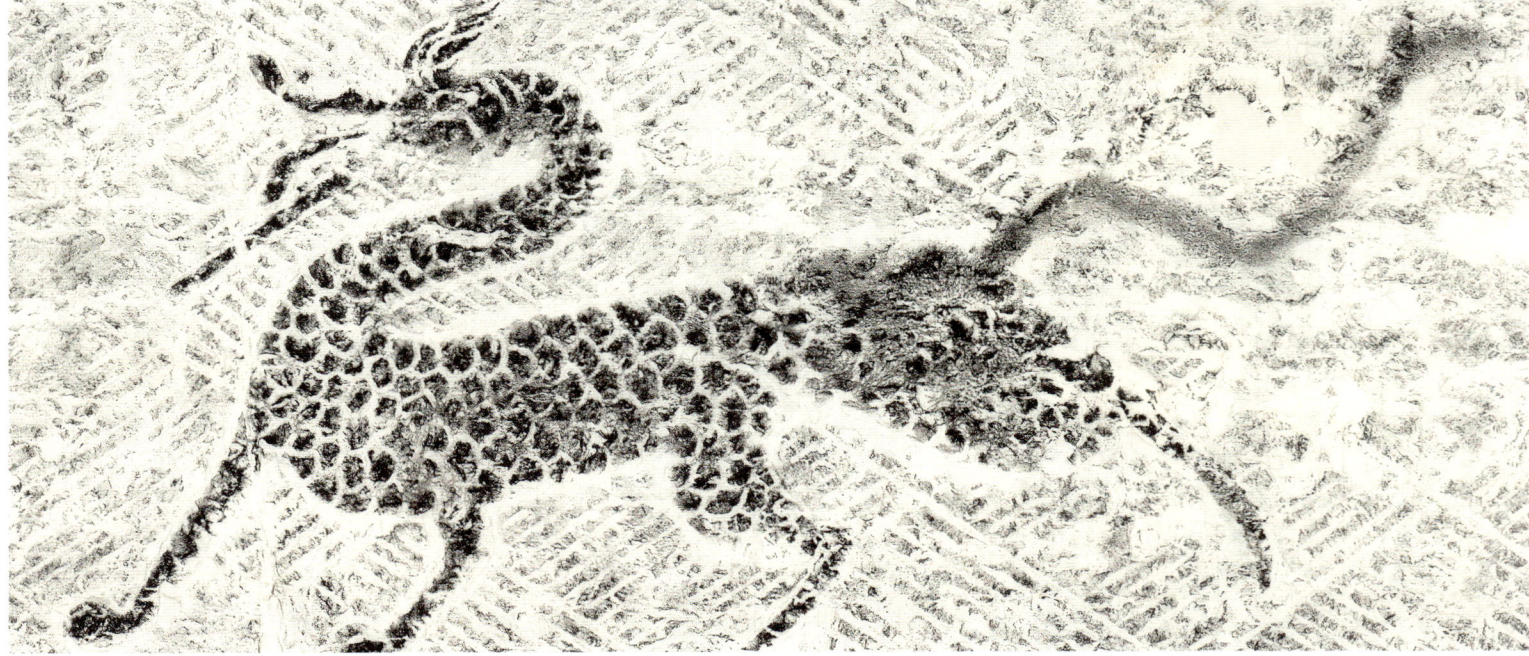

朱雀／太室阙西阙北面局部

龙／太室阙西阙北面局部

太室阙西阙东面：东汉元初五年（118）建，拓片高295厘米，宽80厘米，2008年天地之中历史建筑群申报世界文化遗产建档时拓印。画面残损严重，仅存下方铺首衔环图案。

East surface of the west part of the Taishi Que: Completed in 118, the fifth year of the Yuanchu era of the Eastern Han dynasty. The rubbing, 295 cm tall and 80 cm wide, was made in 2008 during the application for the World Heritage Site inscription of the "The Centre of Heaven and Earth" historic monuments. The carvings on the surface are heavily damaged except for an image of a door knocker that is well preserved.

太室阙西阙西面：东汉元初五年（118）建，拓片高225厘米，宽63厘米，2008年天地之中历史建筑群申报世界文化遗产建档时拓印。此面保存较完整，从上到下刻汉阙门、倒立、水鸟、三鱼共头和羽人画面。

West surface of the west part of the Taishi Que: Completed in 118, the fifth year of the Yuanchu era of the Eastern Han dynasty. The rubbing, 225 cm tall and 63 cm wide, was made in 2008 during the application for the World Heritage Site inscription of the "The Centre of Heaven and Earth" historic monuments. This surface is well preserved, and from top to bottom are carved images of a Han-dynasty *que* tower gate, headstand, waterfowl, three fish with a shared head, and a feathered human figure.

三鱼共头／太室阙西阙西面局部

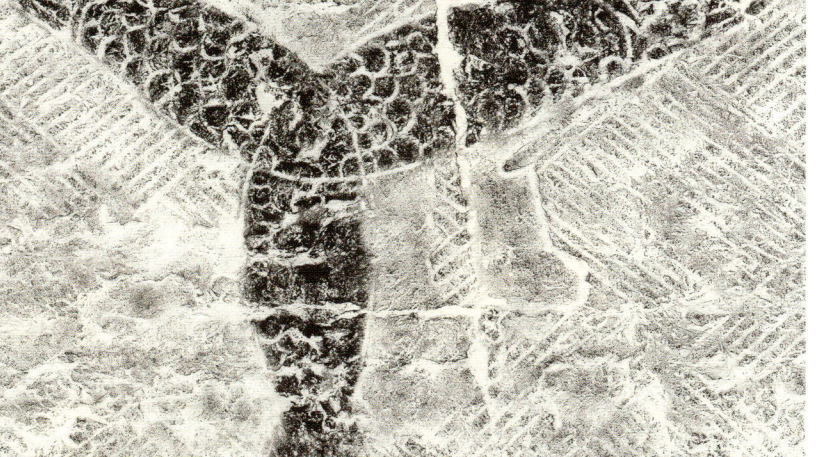

羽人／太室阙西阙西面局部

倒立／太室阙西阙西面局部

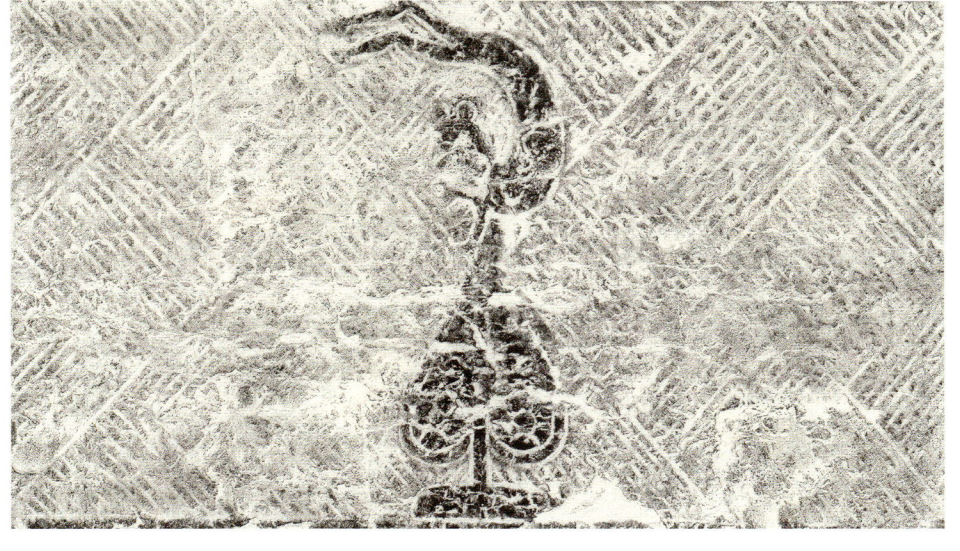

水鸟／太室阙西阙西面局部

嵩山／东汉三阙

少室阙东阙南面：东汉元初五年（118）至延光二年（123）建，拓片高305厘米，宽210厘米，2008年天地之中历史建筑群申报世界文化遗产建档时拓印。南面保存较完整，上刻减地浮雕，在辅首衔环两侧刻水鸟啄鱼、羽人、拜谒图、蹴鞠、四灵、马戏和双龙穿壁等图案。

South surface of the east part of the Shaoshi Que: Built between 118, the fifth year of the Yuanchu era of the Eastern Han dynasty, and 123, the second year of the Yanguang era of the dynasty. The rubbing, 305 cm tall and 210 cm wide, was made in 2008 during the application for the World Heritage Site inscription of the "The Centre of Heaven and Earth" historic monuments. The surface is well preserved. There is a carved door knocker, on both sides of which are images of waterfowl pecking at fish, feathered human figures, homage paying, ball games, the Four Symbols, circus, twine dragons winding through rings, etc.

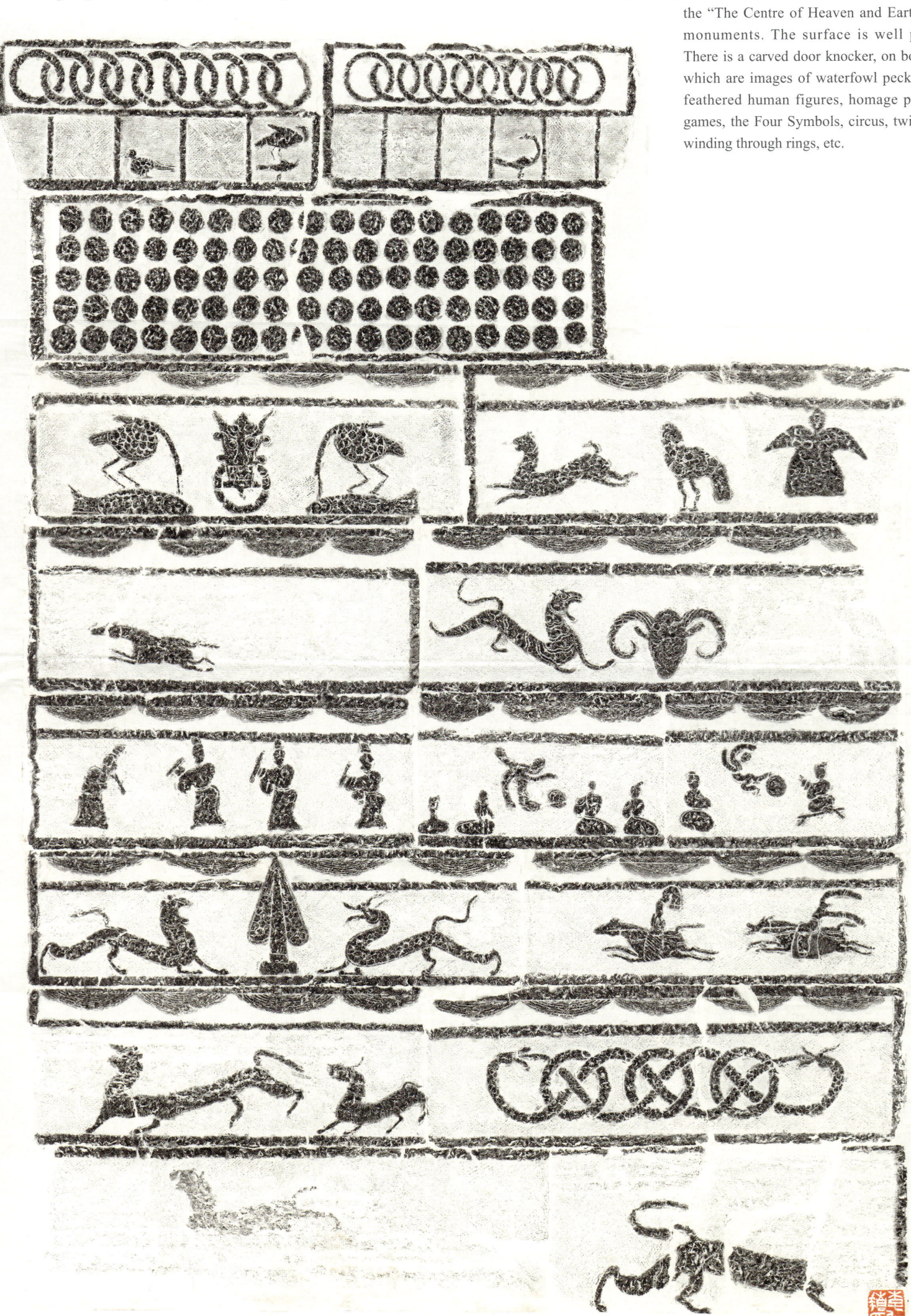

少室阙东阙南面：东汉元初五年（118）至延光二年（123）建，拓片高305厘米，宽210厘米，2008年天地之中历史建筑群申报世界文化遗产建档时拓印。北面刻一方铭记、狩猎图、驯象、车骑出行、宴饮、人物、斗鸡、骑行、玄鸟生商和双兽争食等画面。

South surface of the east part of the Shaoshi Que: Built between 118, the fifth year of the Yuanchu era of the Eastern Han dynasty, and 123, the second year of the Yanguang era of the dynasty. The rubbing, 305 cm tall and 210 cm wide, was made in 2008 during the application for the World Heritage Site inscription of the "The Centre of Heaven and Earth" historic monuments. On the surface are carved an inscription and scenes of hunting, elephant training, carriages and horses, feasting, human figures, cockfight, horse riding, the swallow descending and giving birth to the Shang, two beasts fighting for prey, etc.

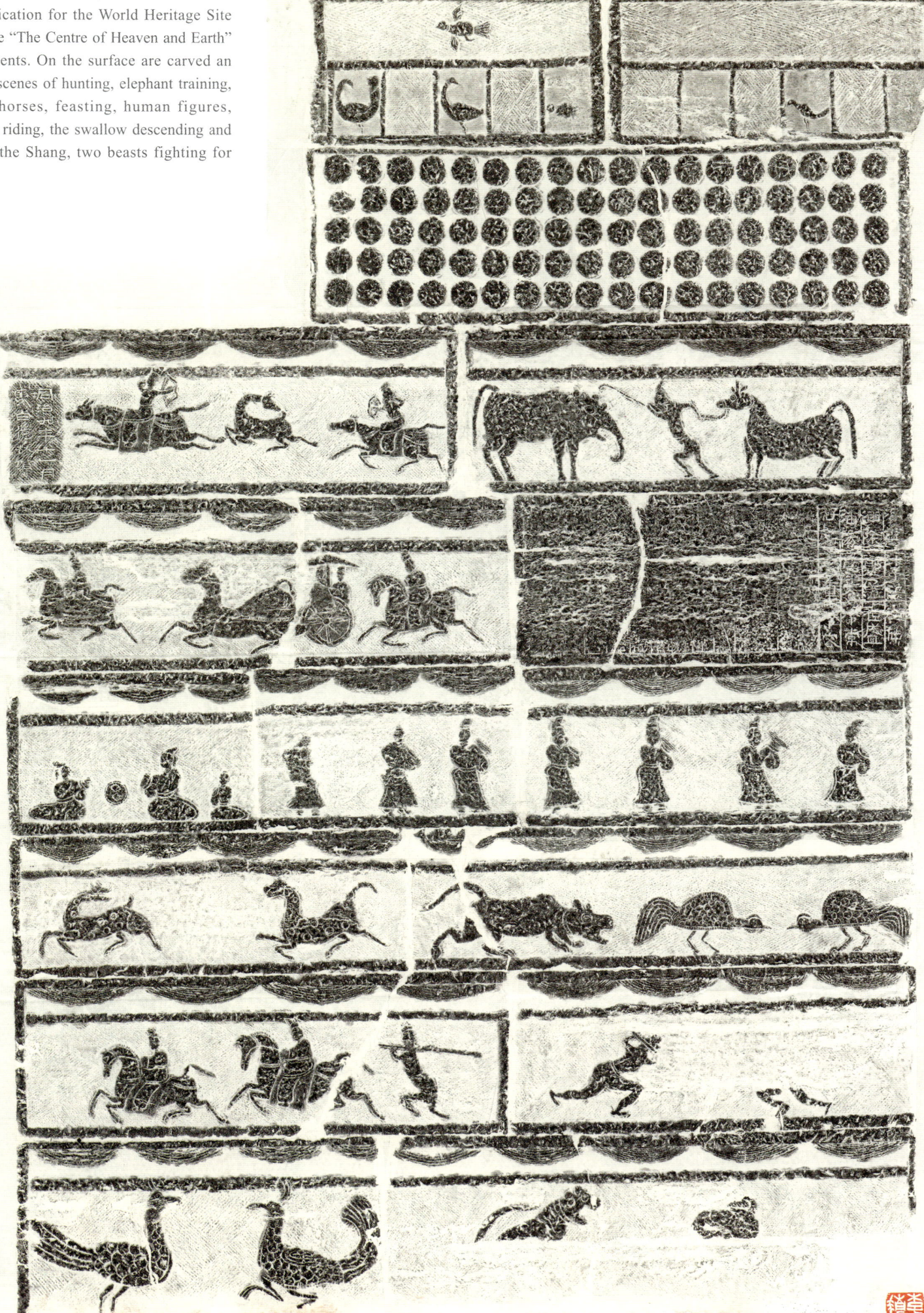

少室阙铭文

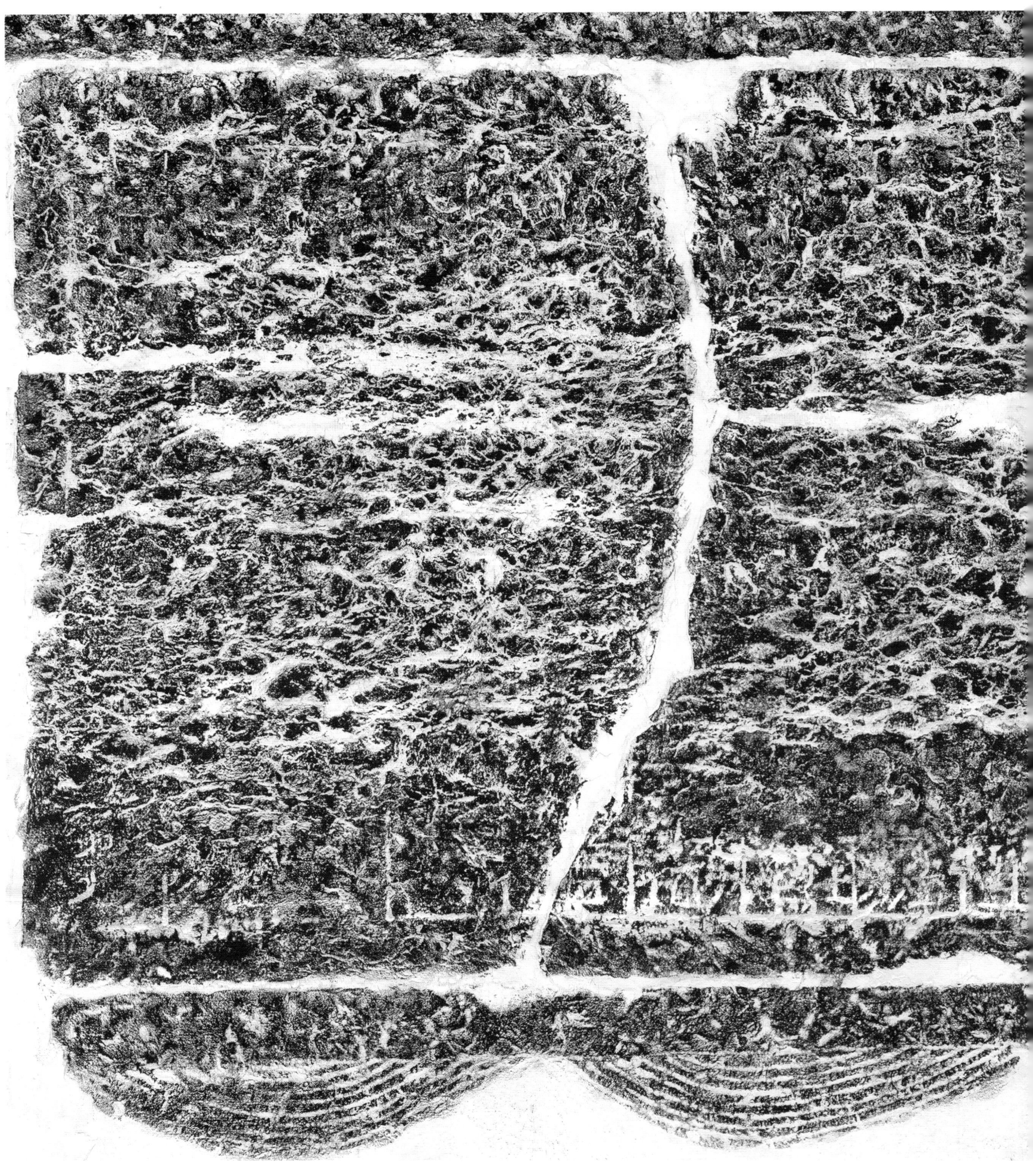

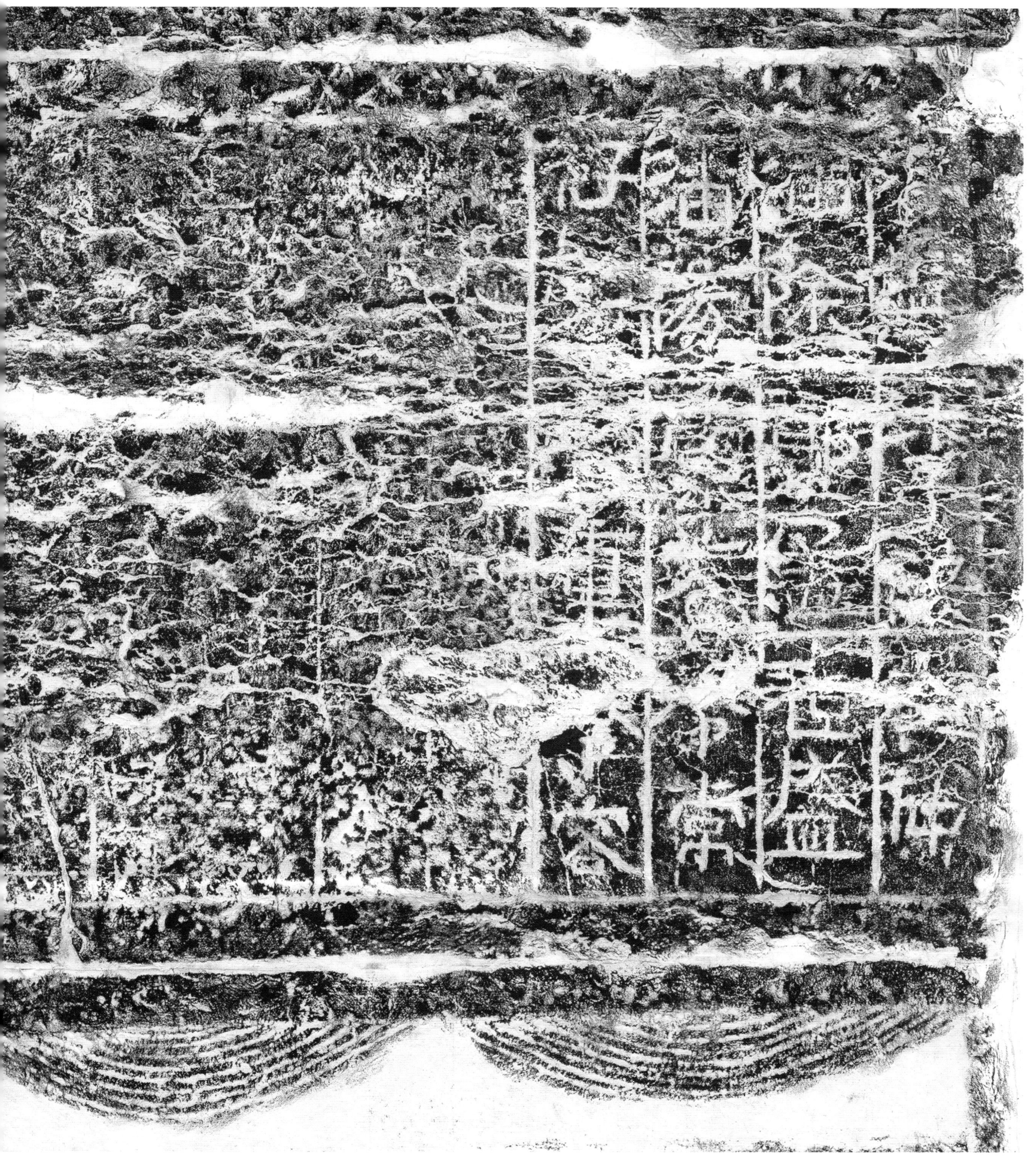

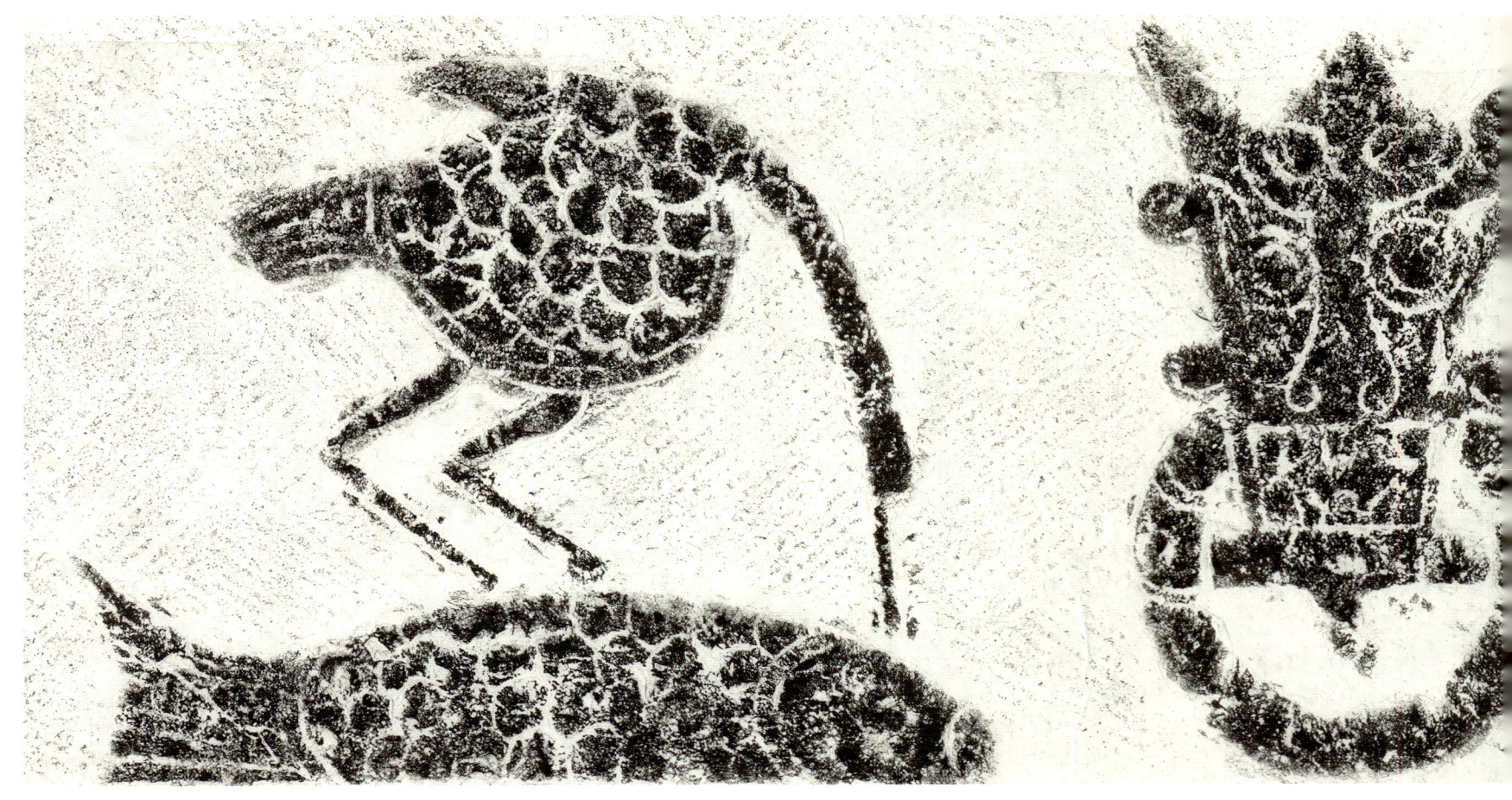

虎、羊头／少室阙东阙南面局部

水鸟啄鱼图／少室阙东阙南面局部

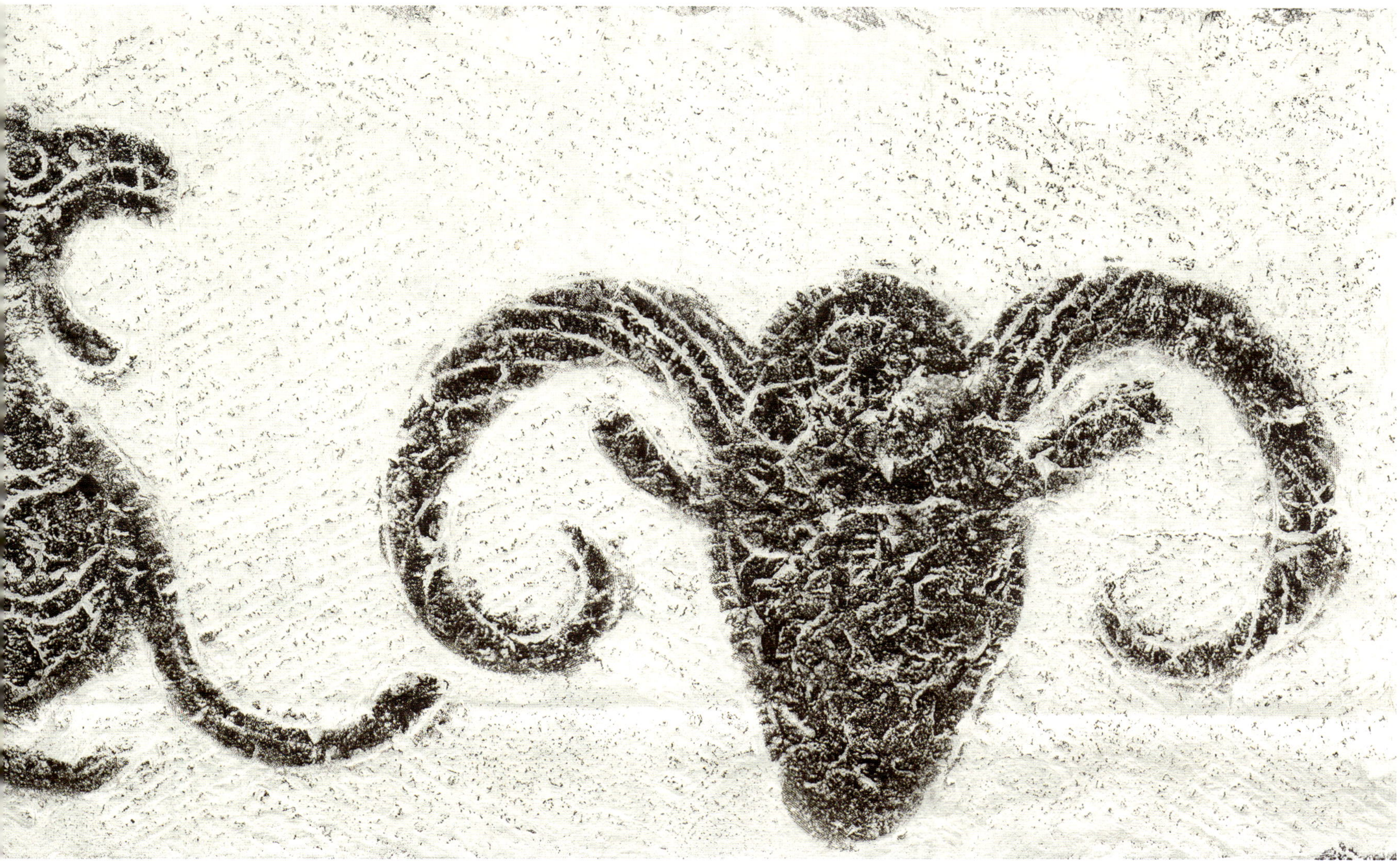

嵩山／东汉三阙／

龙／少室阙东阙南面局部

虎／少室阙东阙南面局部

李仁清传拓艺术

嵩山／东汉三阙／

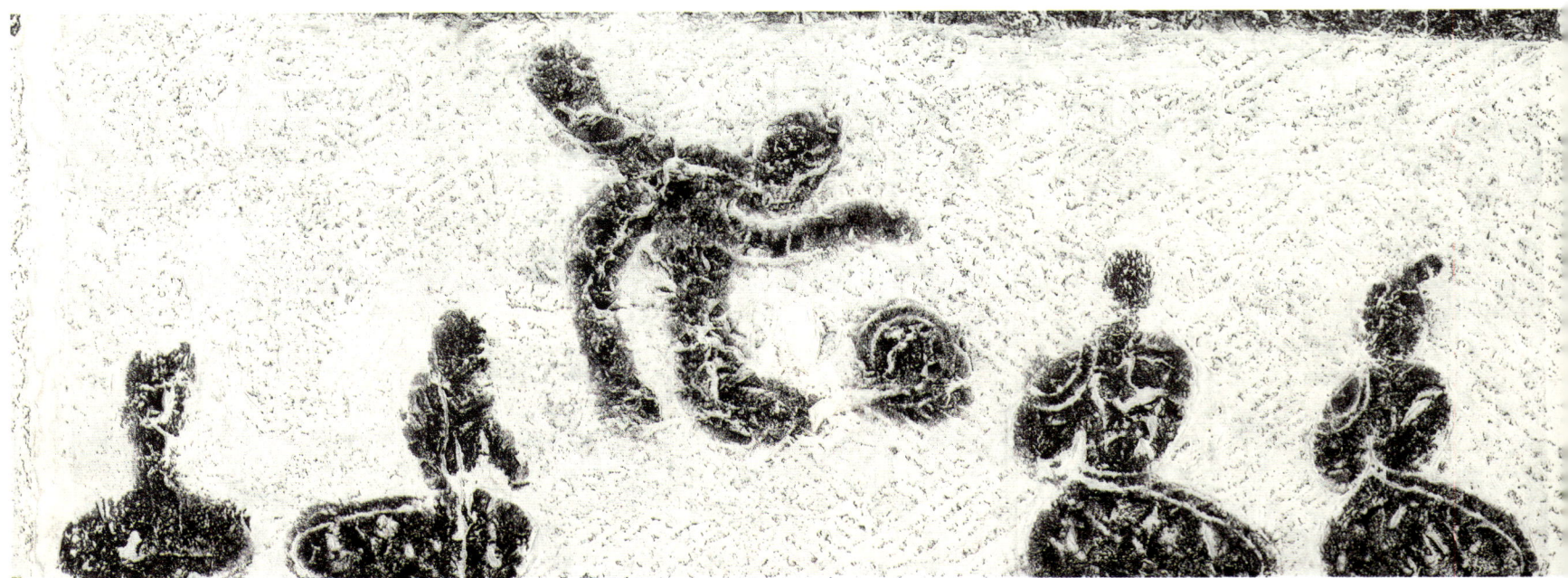

拜谒图／少室阙东阙南面局部

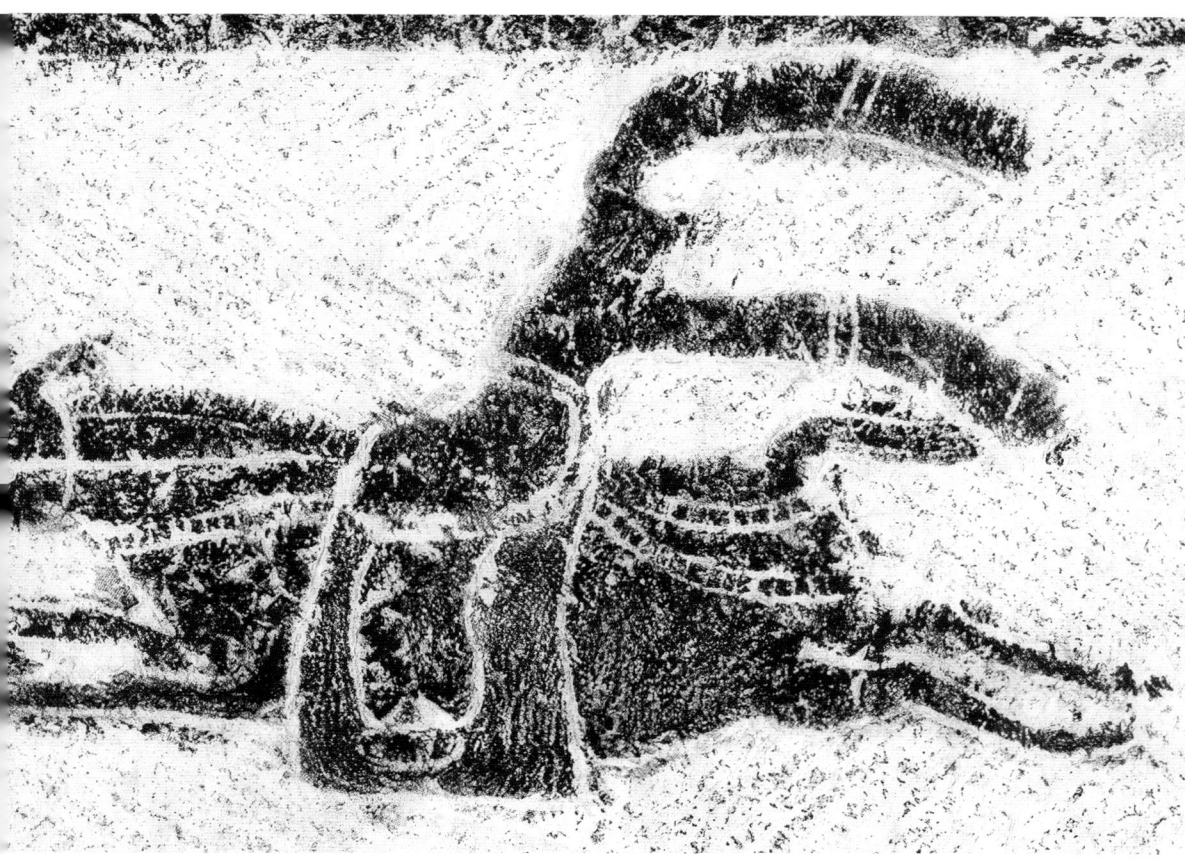

马戏／少室阙东阙南面局部

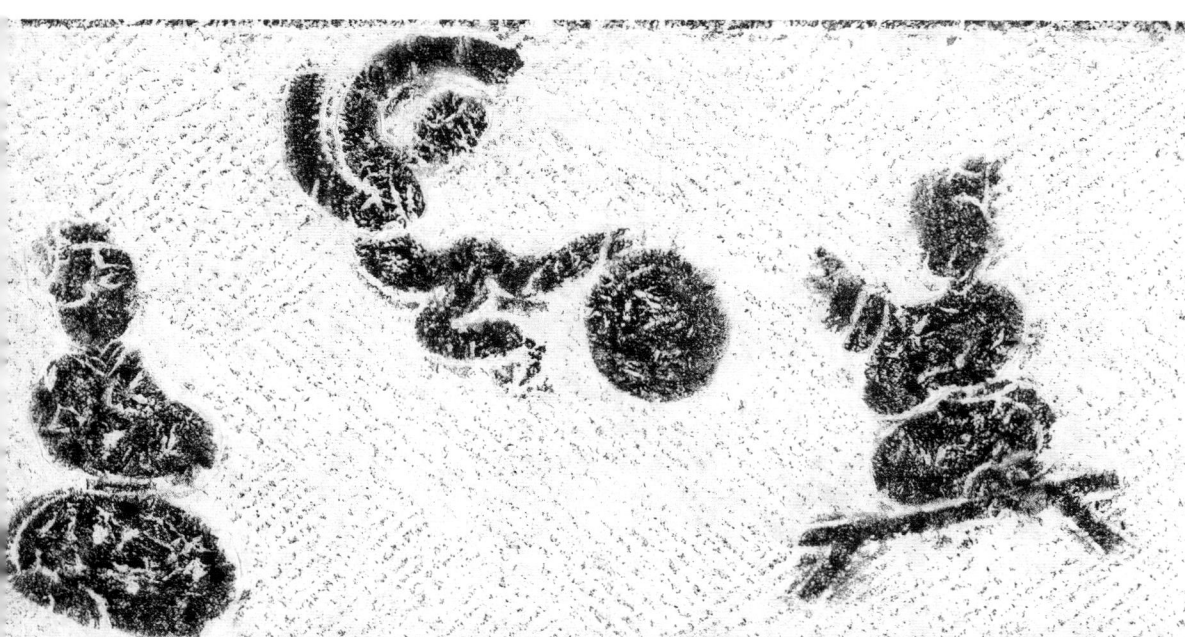

蹴鞠图／少室阙东阙南面局部

驯象图／少室阙东阙南面局部

车骑出行图／少室阙东阙南面局部

宴饮图／少室阙东阙北面局部

李仁清传拓艺术 LIRENQING CHUANTAYISHU

嵩山／东汉三阙／

043

斗鸡图／少室阙东阙北面局部

骑行图／少室阙东阙北面局部

嵩山／东汉三阙／

少室阙东阙东面：东汉元初五年（118）至延光二年（123）建，拓片高208厘米，宽69厘米，2008年天地之中历史建筑群申报世界文化遗产建档时拓印。东侧刻狐逐兔、人物、骑行、龙等画面。

East surface of the east part of the Shaoshi Que: Built between 118, the fifth year of the Yuanchu era of the Eastern Han dynasty, and 123, the second year of the Yanguang era of the dynasty. The rubbing, 208 cm tall and 69 cm wide, was made in 2008 during the application for the World Heritage Site inscription of the "The Centre of Heaven and Earth" historic monuments. On the surface are carved scenes of a fox chasing a rabbit, human figures, horse riding, dragons, etc.

少室阙东阙西面：东汉元初五年（118）至延光二年（123年）建，拓片高208厘米，宽79厘米，2008年天地之中历史建筑群申报世界文化遗产建档时拓印。西面刻龙、飞鸟、水鸟、人物等画面。

West surface of the east part of the Shaoshi Que: Built between 118, the fifth year of the Yuanchu era of the Eastern Han dynasty, and 123, the second year of the Yanguang era of the dynasty. The rubbing, 208 cm tall and 79 cm wide, was made in 2008 during the application for the World Heritage Site inscription of the "The Centre of Heaven and Earth" historic monuments. On the surface are carved images of dragons, flying birds, waterfowl, human figures, etc.

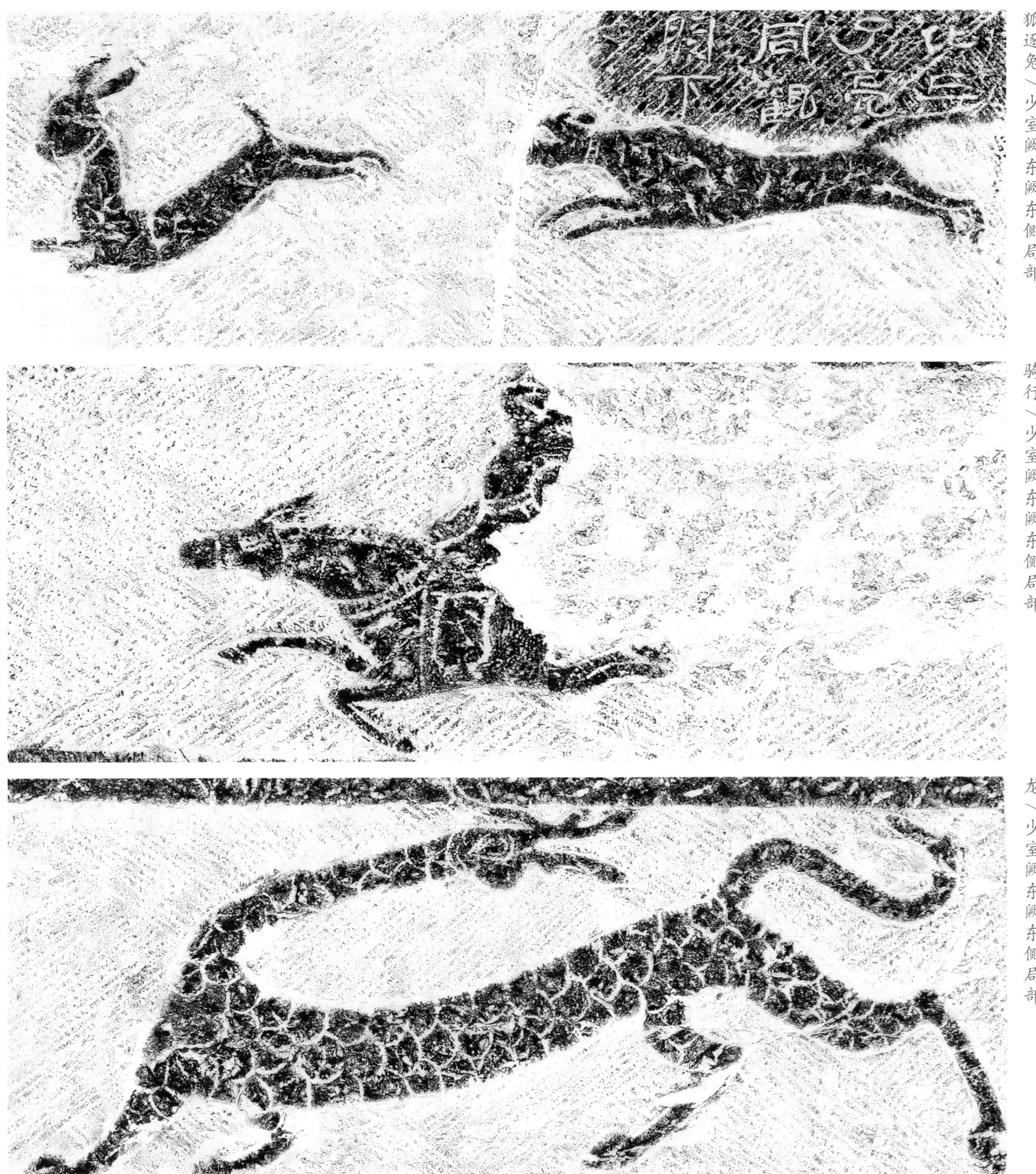

狐逐兔／少室阙东阙东侧局部

骑行／少室阙东阙东侧局部

龙／少室阙东阙东侧局部

水鸟／少室阙东阙西侧局部

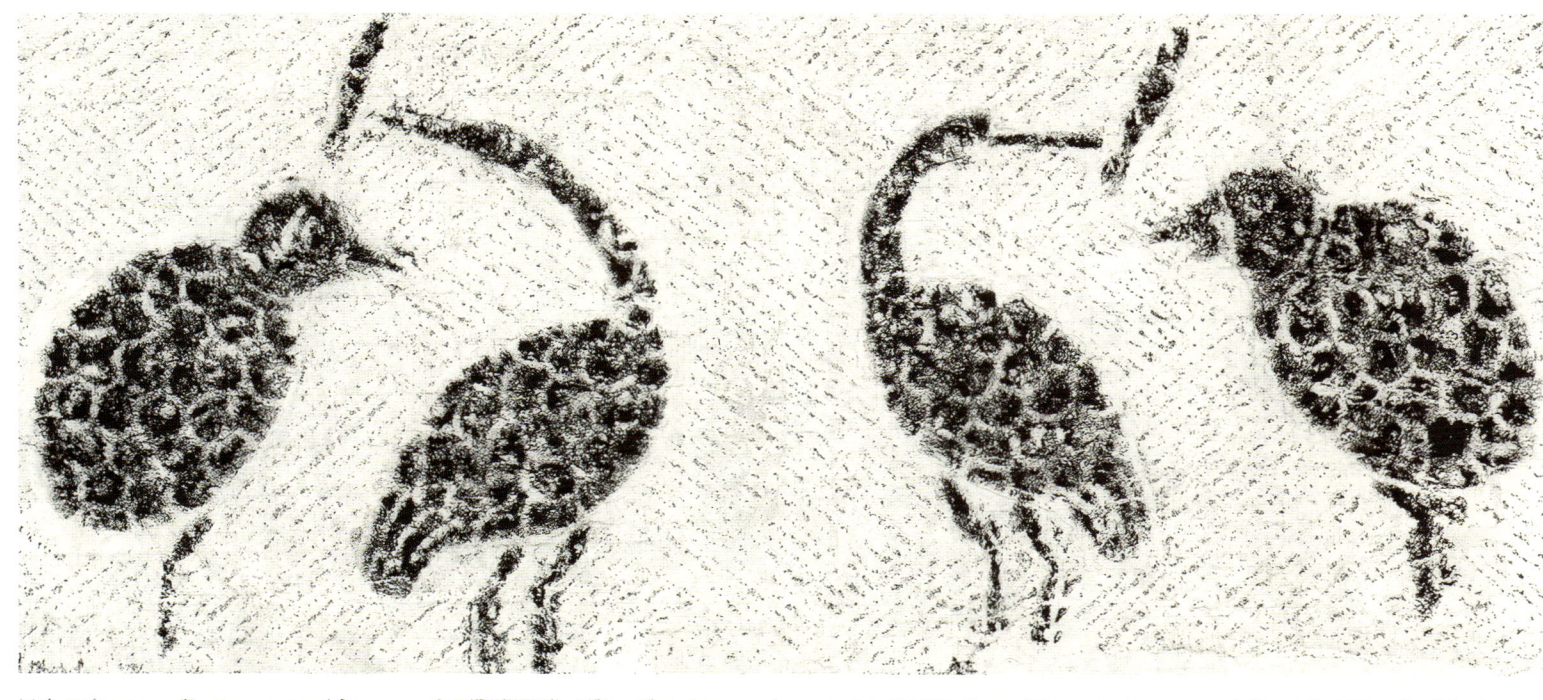

人物／少室阙东阙西侧局部

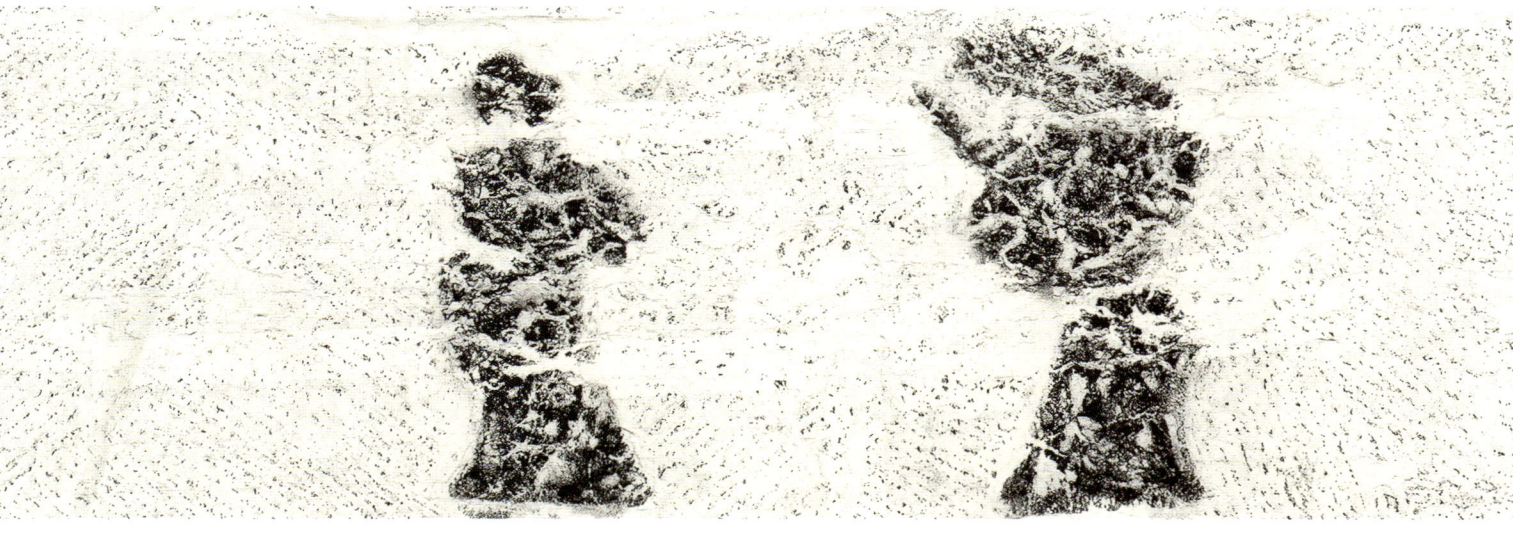

人物／少室阙东阙西侧局部

嵩山／东汉三阙

少室阙西阙南面：东汉元初五年（118）至延光二年（123）建，拓片高295厘米，宽250厘米，2008年天地之中历史建筑群申报世界文化遗产建档时拓印。西面上方刻"少室神道之阙"，阴刻篆书。阙铭下刻龙、虎、轺车出行和比翼鸟画面。

South surface of the west part of the Shaoshi Que: Built between 118, the fifth year of the Yuanchu era of the Eastern Han dynasty, and 123, the second year of the Yanguang era of the dynasty. The rubbing, 295 cm tall and 250 cm wide, was made in 2008 during the application for the World Heritage Site inscription of the "The Centre of Heaven and Earth" historic monuments. On the west upper part of the surface is engraved an inscription in seal script, "Shaoshi Shendao Zhi Que" (Gate Tower on the Divine Path to the Shaoshi), beneath which are carved images of dragons, tigers, carriages, and lovebirds.

少室阙西阙南面：东汉元初五年（118）至延光二年（123）建，拓片高295厘米，宽250厘米，2008年天地之中历史建筑群申报世界文化遗产建档时拓印。北面因画像风化严重，阙铭现存16行，篆书，每行4字，两行之间有阴刻竖界线，最后3行刻在西阙西面外。少室阙虽仅存阙铭19行篆书较完整，仍为历代金石学家所珍重。

South surface of the west part of the Shaoshi Que: Built between 118, the fifth year of the Yuanchu era of the Eastern Han dynasty, and 123, the second year of the Yanguang era of the dynasty. The rubbing, 295 cm tall and 250 cm wide, was made in 2008 during the application for the World Heritage Site inscription of the "The Centre of Heaven and Earth" historic monuments. The north surface of the gate tower is seriously weathered, and the remnant of the inscription carved in seal script is in 16 columns (the last 3 columns carved on the west surface), each containing 4 characters, and an engraved separating line between every two neighboring columns. The inscription to the Shaoshi Que, though with only 19 columns remaining quite intact, has been highly valued by epigraphers throughout the ages.

少室阙铭

少室阙铭

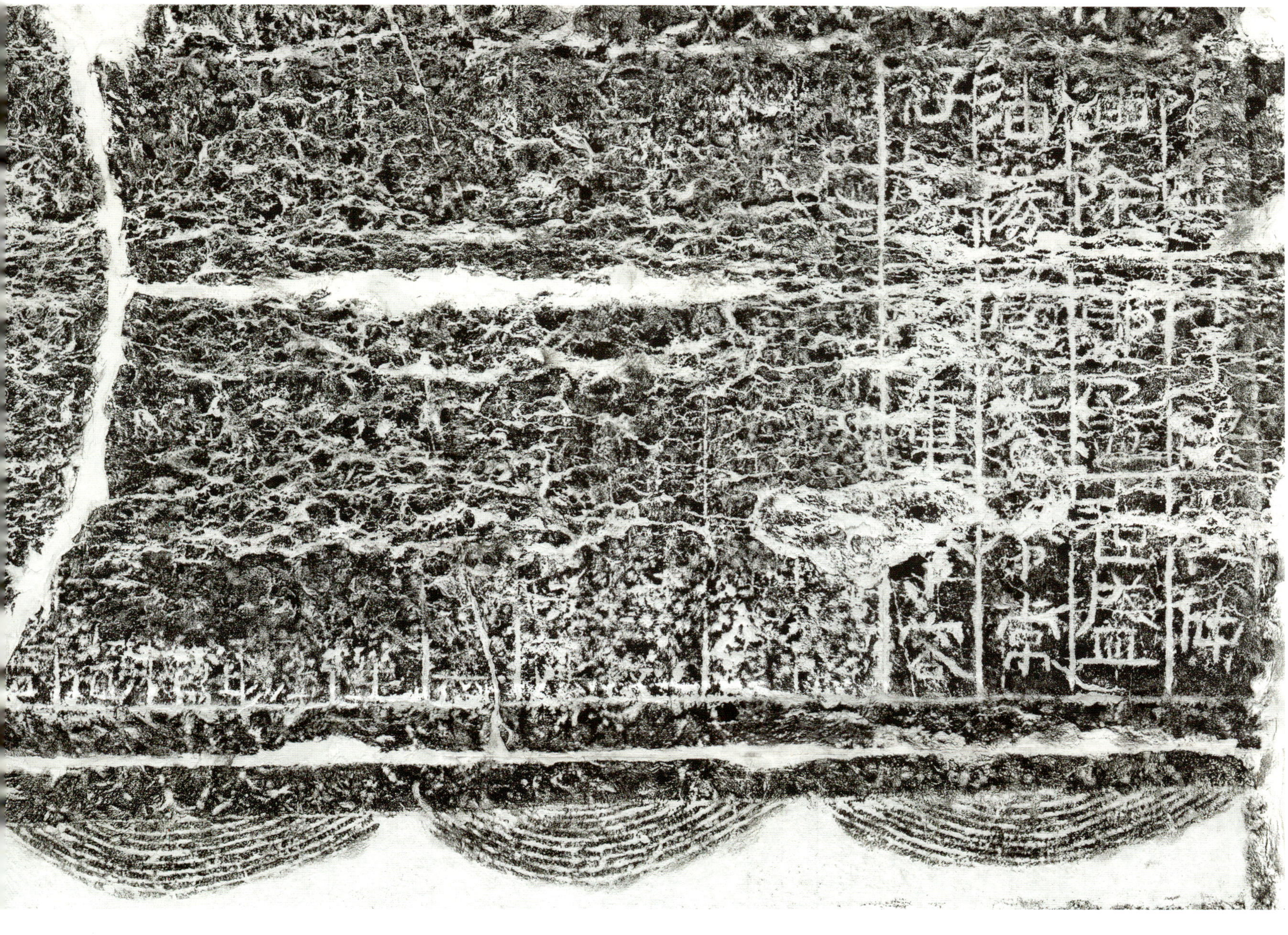

嵩山／东汉三阙／

轮车出行／少室阙西阙南面局部

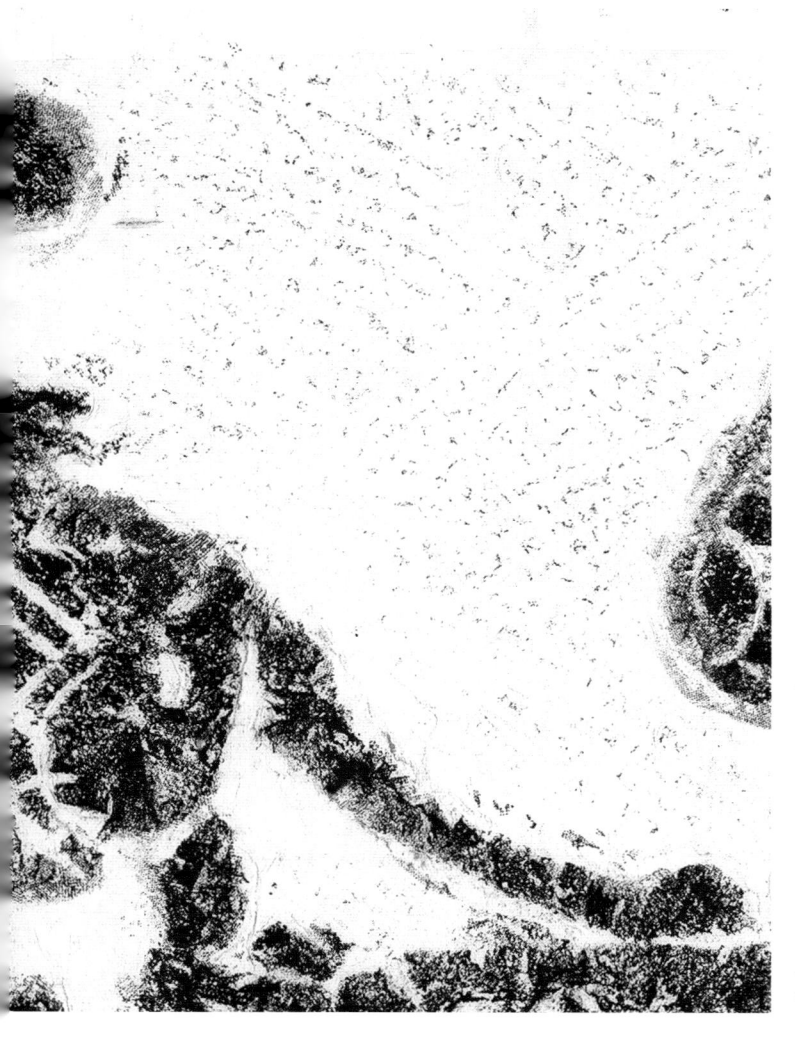

虎／少室阙西阙南面局部

嵩山／东汉三阙

比翼鸟／少室阙西阙南面局部

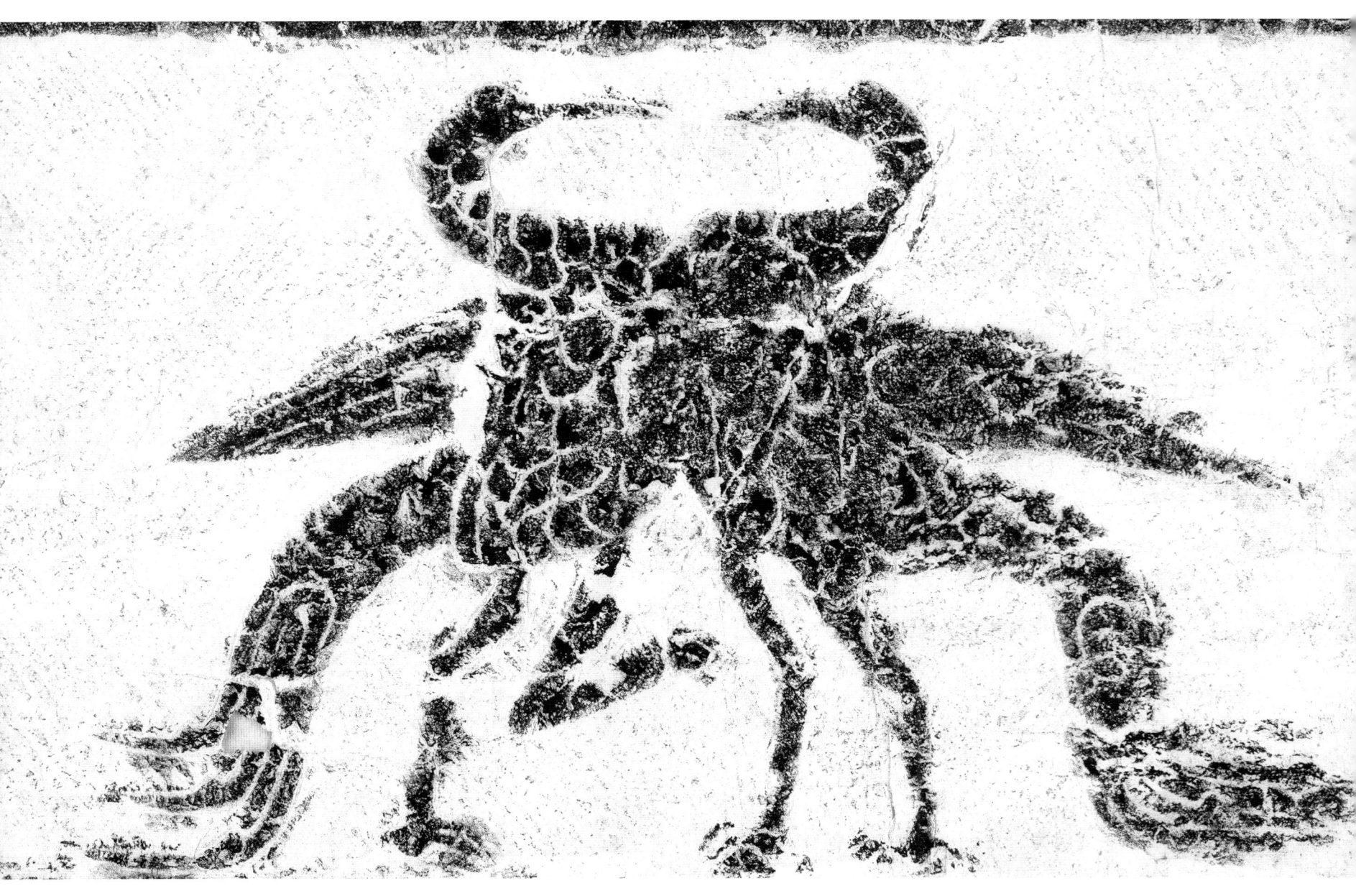

少室阙西阙东面：东汉元初五年至（118）延光二年（123）建，拓片高222厘米，宽69厘米，2008年天地之中历史建筑群申报世界文化遗产建档时拓印。东面残损严重，下方龙保存较完整。

East surface of the west part of the Shaoshi Que: Built between 118, the fifth year of the Yuanchu era of the Eastern Han dynasty, toand 123, the second year of the Yanguang era of the dynasty. The rubbing, 222 cm tall and 69 cm wide, was made in 2008 during the application for the World Heritage Site inscription of the "The Centre of Heaven and Earth" historic monuments. The surface is seriously damaged except for a well-preserved dragon image.

少室阙西阙西面：东汉元初五年（118）至延光二年（123）建，拓片高295厘米，宽70厘米，2008年天地之中历史建筑群申报世界文化遗产建档时拓印。上层月宫图和3行阙铭保存较完整，下6层残损严重。

West surface of the west part of the Shaoshi Que: Built between 118, the fifth year of the Yuanchu era of the Eastern Han dynasty, and 123, the second year of the Yanguang era of the dynasty. The rubbing, 295 cm tall and 70 cm wide, was made in 2008 during the application for the World Heritage Site inscription of the "The Centre of Heaven and Earth" historic monuments. A carved moon palace and the 3-column part of the inscription on the surface of the top layer are well preserved, and the surface of the lower six layers is seriously damaged.

龙〈少室阙东阙东侧局部

嵩山〈东汉三阙〉

月宫阙／少室阙西阙西侧局部

少室阙铭

启母阙东阙南面：东汉延光三年（124）建，拓片高283厘米，宽208厘米，2008年天地之中历史建筑群申报世界文化遗产建档时拓印。南面刻人物画像、幻术和马、骑马出行、交龙图、斗鸡、驯象、双蛇等图像。

South surface of the east part of the Qimu Que: Built in 124, the third year of the Yanguang era of the Eastern Han dynasty. The rubbing, 283 cm tall and 208 cm wide, was made in 2008 during the application for the World Heritage Site inscription of the "The Centre of Heaven and Earth" historic monuments. On the surface are carved human figures, scenes of sorcery and horseback tour, as well as images of intertwining dragons, fighting cocks, elephant training, twin snakes, etc.

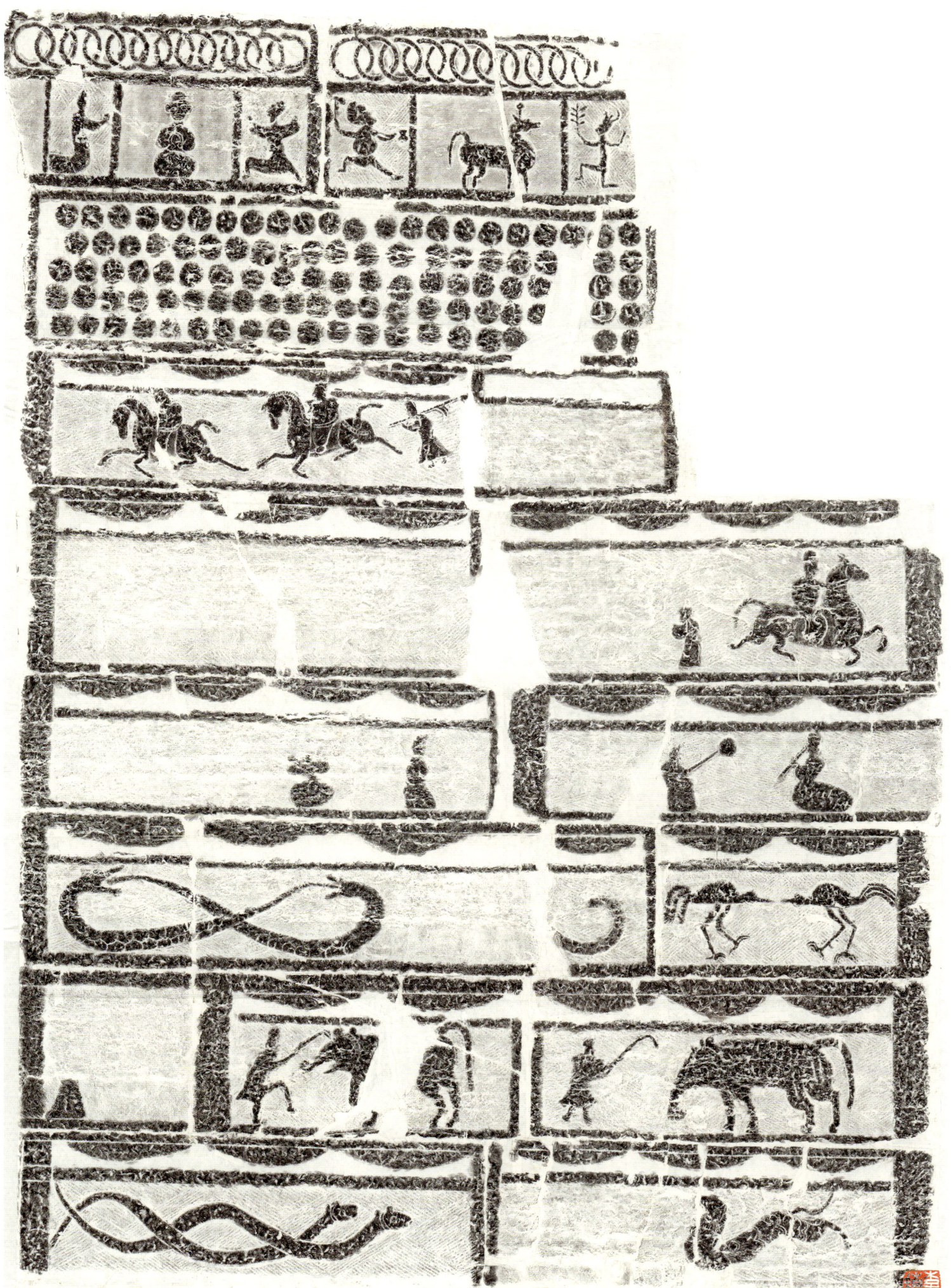

启母阙东阙北面：东汉延光三年（124）建，拓片高282厘米，宽210厘米，2008年天地之中历史建筑群申报世界文化遗产建档时拓印。北面刻骑行、吐火图、果下马、进谒、鹤叨鱼、虎和长青树等图案。

North surface of the east part of the Qimu Que: Built in 124, the third year of the Yanguang era of the Eastern Han dynasty. The rubbing, 282 cm tall and 210 cm wide, was made in 2008 during the application for the World Heritage Site inscription of the "The Centre of Heaven and Earth" historic monuments. On the surface are carved scenes of horse-riding, fire spiting, ponies, inferiors meeting with their superior, a crane pecking at a fish, as well as images of tigers, evergreen trees, etc.

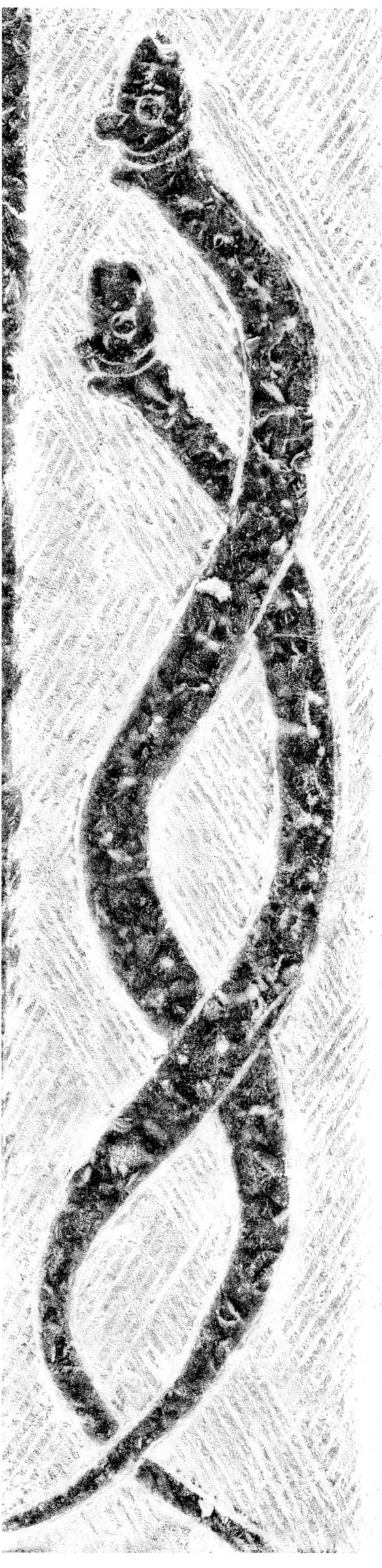

双蛟图／启母阙东阙南面局部

李仁清传拓艺术

嵩山／东汉三阙／

幻术、马／启母阙东阙南面局部

人物／启母阙东阙南面局部

嵩山／东汉三阙

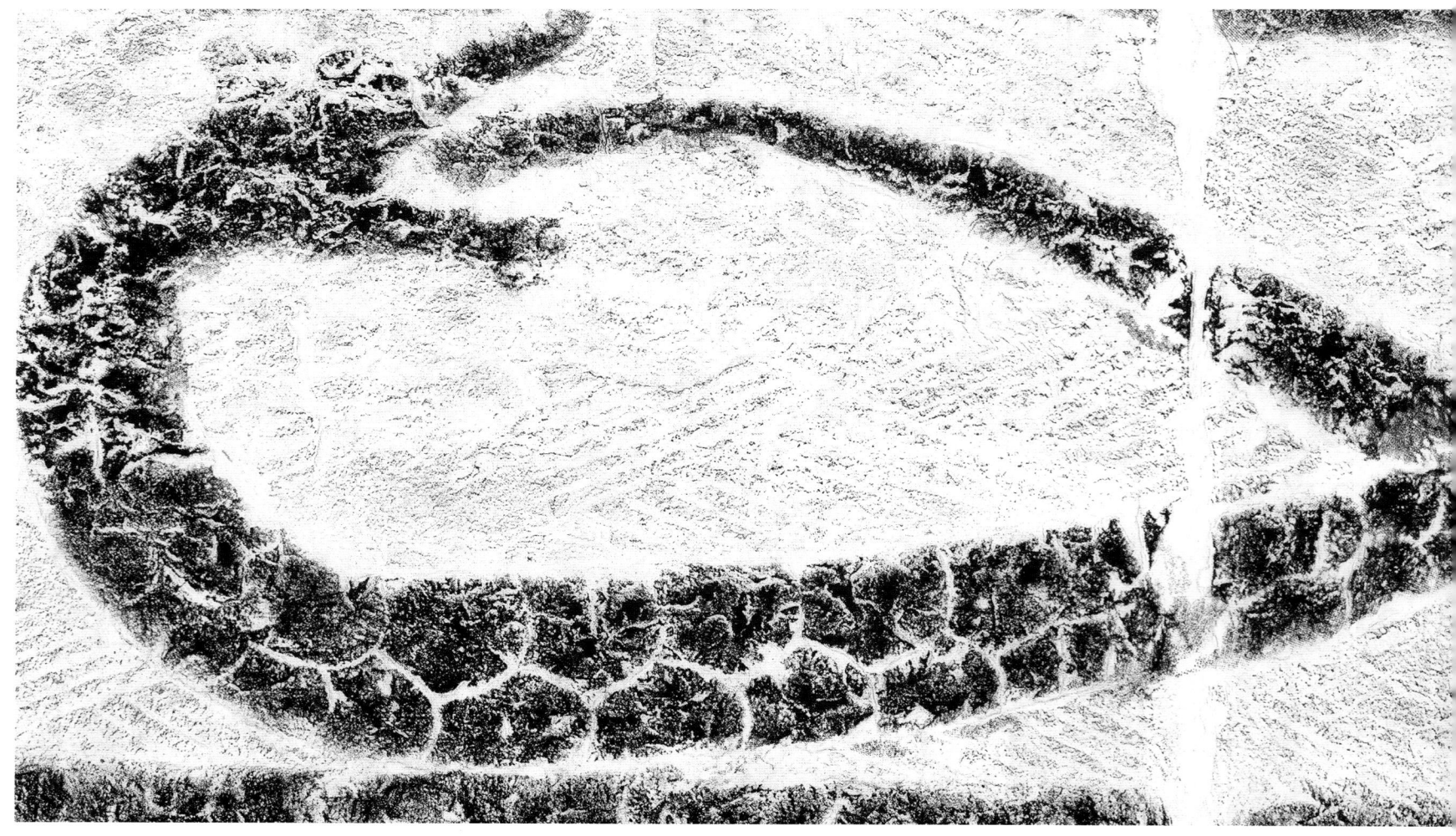

骑马出行／启母阙东阙南面局部

交龙图／启母阙东阙南面局部

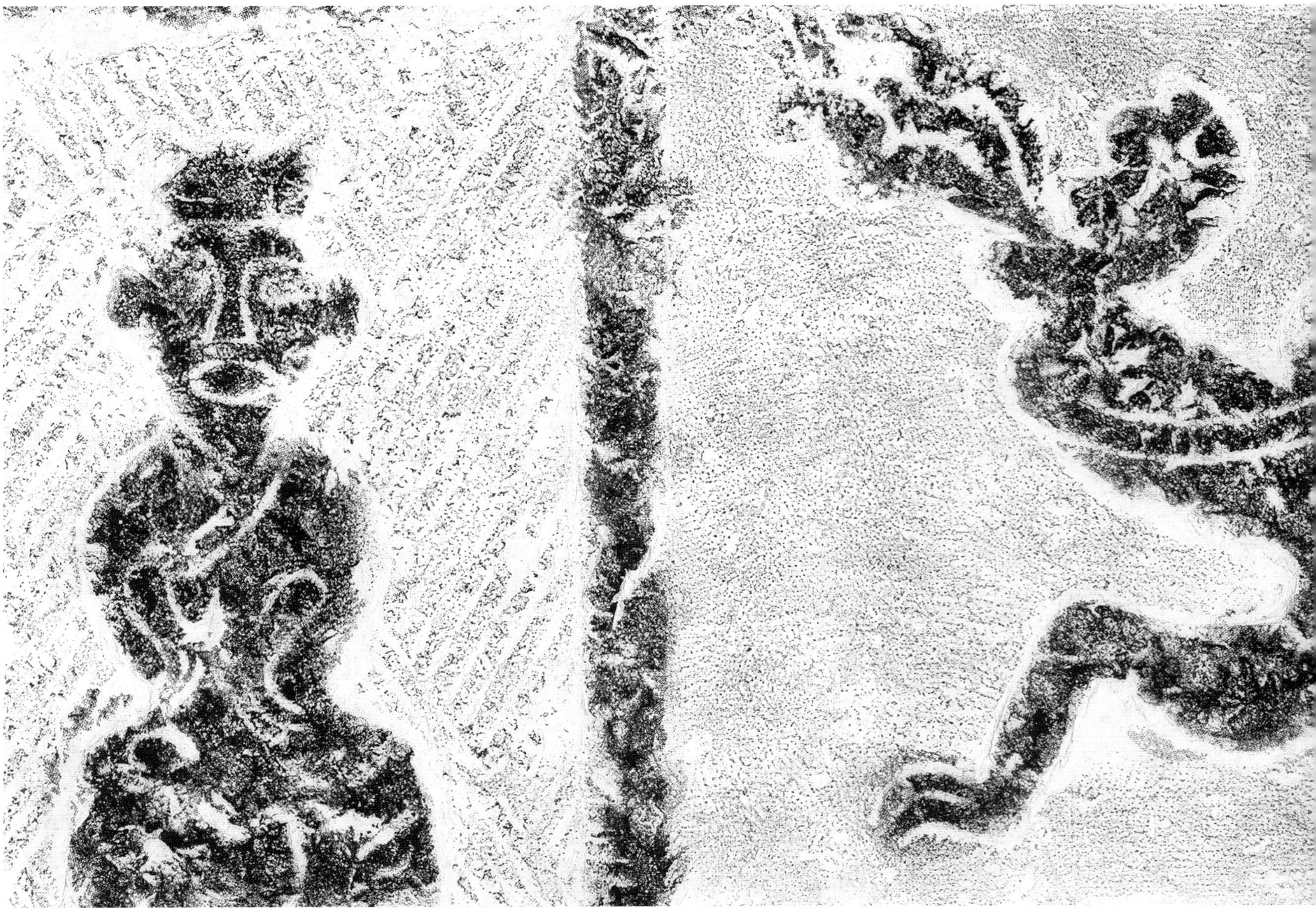

果下马／启母阙东阙北面局部

吐火图／启母阙东阙北面局部

嵩山／东汉三阙

水鸟啄鱼图／启母阙东阙北面局部

进谒图／启母阙东阙北面局部

嵩山／东汉三阙

东汉延光三年（124）建，拓片高175厘米，宽75厘米，2008年天地之中历史建筑群申报世界文化遗产建档时拓印。东面残损较重，仅存骑马出行、虎和长青树等图案。

Built in 124, the third year of the Yanguang era of the Eastern Han dynasty. The rubbing, 175 cm tall and 75 cm wide, was made in 2008 during the application for the World Heritage Site inscription of the "The Centre of Heaven and Earth" historic monuments. The east surface is seriously damaged except for the images of horseback tour, tigers, evergreen trees, etc.

东汉延光三年（124）建，拓片高280厘米，宽75厘米，2008年天地之中历史建筑群申报世界文化遗产建档时拓印。西面中部残缺，上下层刻马戏、猎兔、龙和长青树等图案。

Built in 124, the third year of the Yanguang era of the Eastern Han dynasty. The rubbing, 280 cm tall and 75 cm wide, was made in 2008 during the application for the World Heritage Site inscription of the "The Centre of Heaven and Earth" historic monuments. The middle part of the west surface is damaged, and on the surfaces of the upper and lower layers are carved images of circus, rabbit hunting, dragons, evergreen trees, etc.

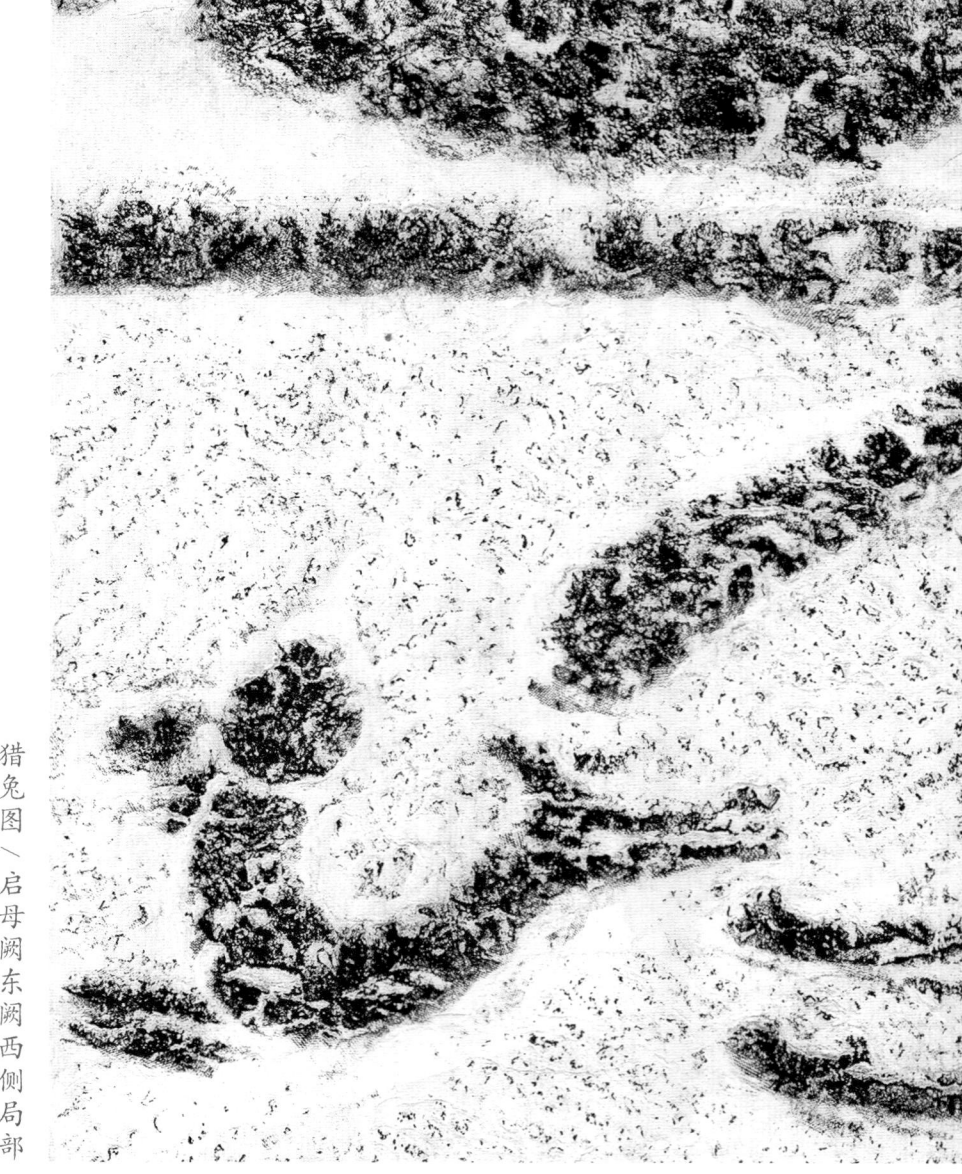

猎兔图＼启母阙东阙西侧局部

马戏图／启母阙东阙西侧局部

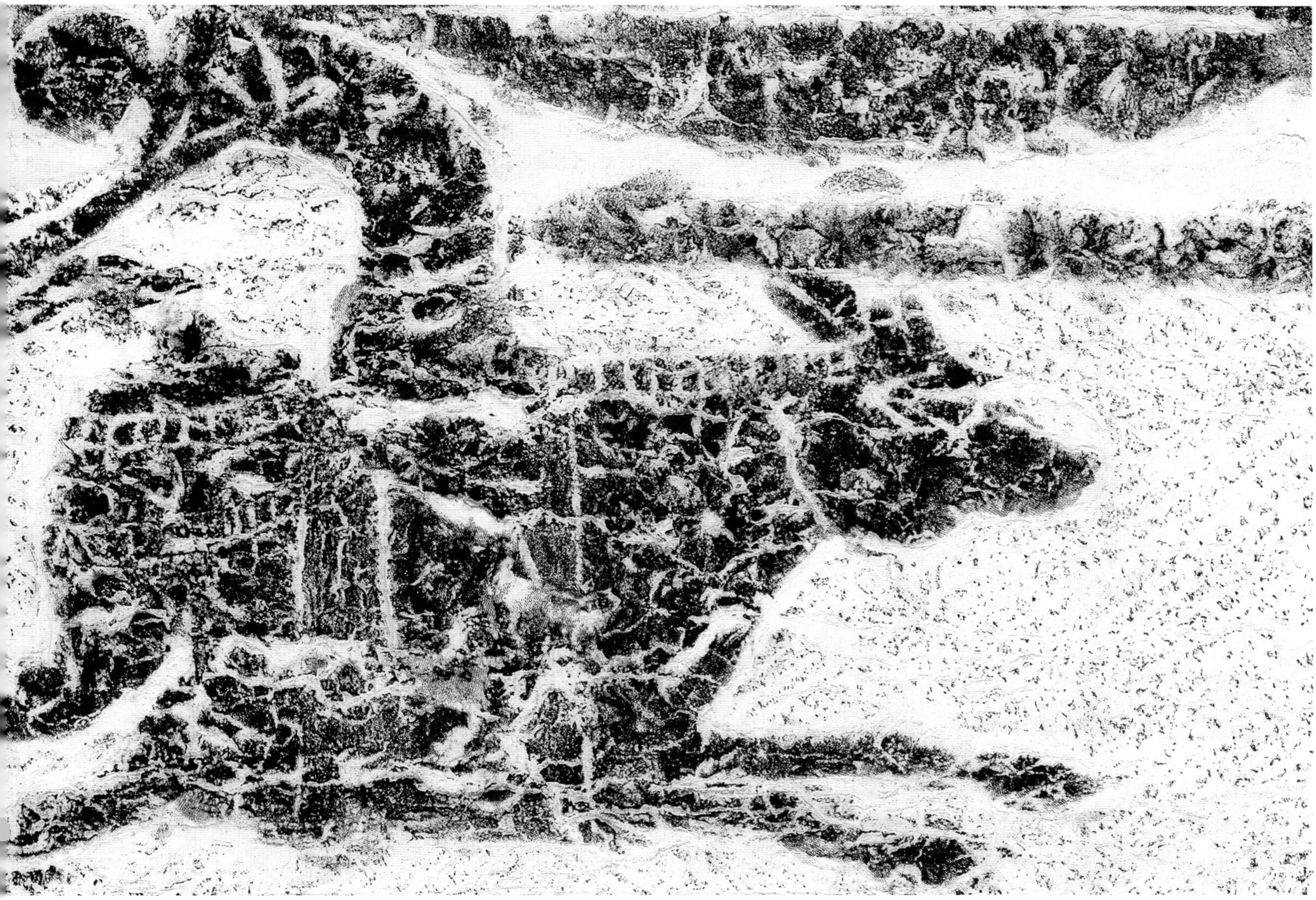

嵩山／东汉三阙／

李仁清传拓艺术

东汉延光三年（124）建，拓片高273厘米，宽207厘米，2008年天地之中历史建筑群申报世界文化遗产建档时拓印。南面刻蛟龙穿环、饮宴、龙、虎、象和骆驼、双马等图案。

Built in 124, the third year of the Yanguang era of the Eastern Han dynasty. The rubbing, 273 cm tall and 207 cm wide, was made in 2008 during the application for the World Heritage Site inscription of the "The Centre of Heaven and Earth" historic monuments. On the south surface are carved images of dragons winding through rings, feast, dragons, tigers, elephants, camels, twin horses, etc.

东汉延光三年（124）建，拓片高273厘米，宽209厘米，2008年天地之中历史建筑群申报世界文化遗产建档时拓印。北面有两方阙铭，一方为启母阙铭，另一方为堂溪典嵩高庙请雨铭。下面刻饮宴、蹴鞠、夏禹化熊、龙长青树、虎扑鹿和犬逐兔等画像。

Built in 124, the third year of the Yanguang era of the Eastern Han dynasty. The rubbing, 273 cm tall and 209 cm wide, was made in 2008 during the application for the World Heritage Site inscription of the "The Centre of Heaven and Earth" historic monuments. On the north surface are two inscriptions, one to the Qimu Que and the other on Tang Xidian's prayer at the Songgao Temple for rain. The lower part of the surface is carved with images of feast, ball game, Yu the Great changing into a bear, dragons, evergreen trees, a tiger springing at a deer, a dog chasing a rabbit, etc.

启母阙铭

启母阙铭

启母阙铭

嵩山／东汉三阙／

启母阙铭

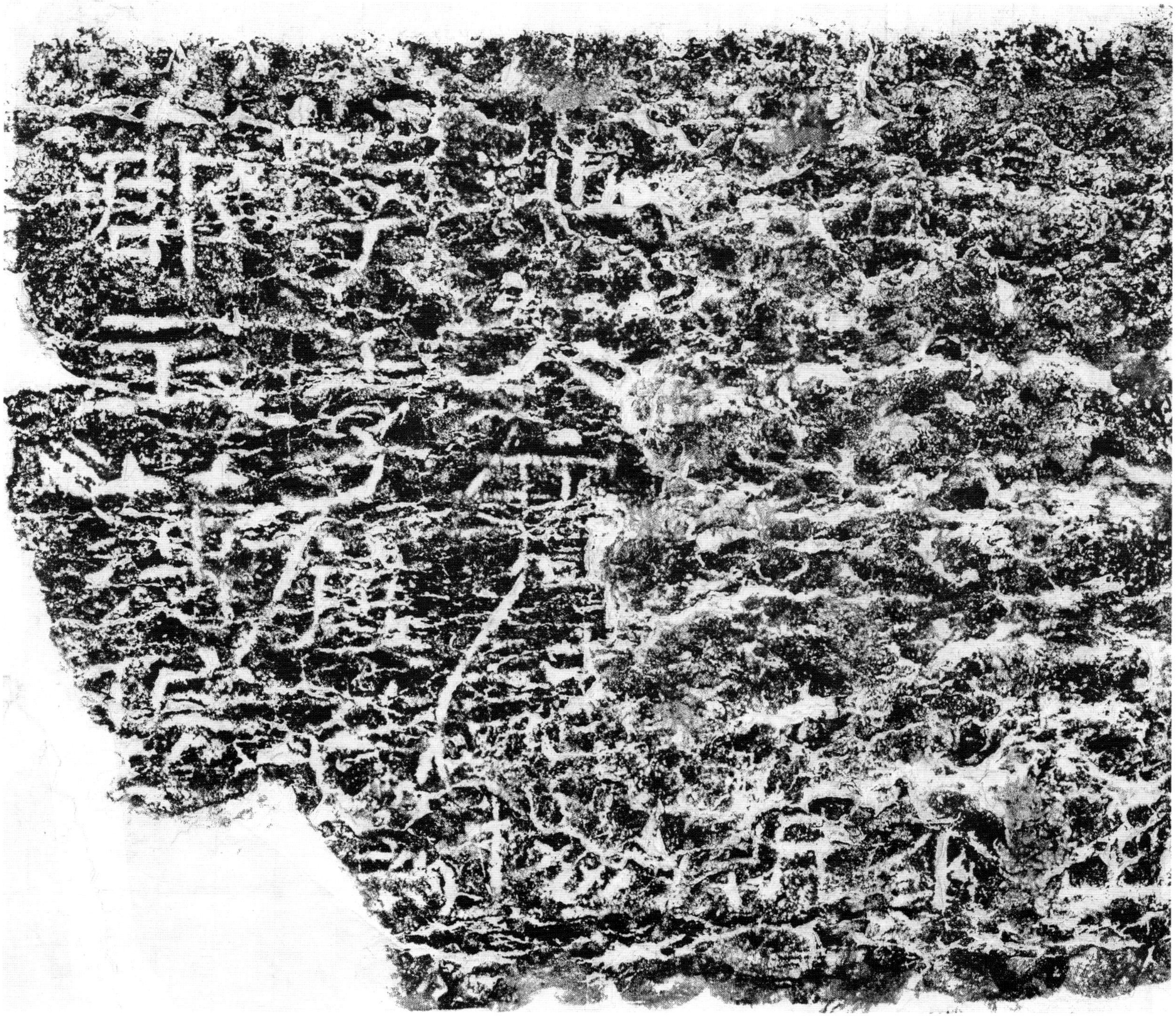

启母阙铭

嵩山／东汉三阙／

夏禹化熊图／启母阙西阙北面局部

蹴鞠图 / 启母阙西阙北面局部

嵩山 / 东汉三阙

双马图／启母阙西阙南面局部

象和骆驼／启母阙西阙南面局部

嵩山／东汉三阙

启母阙铭

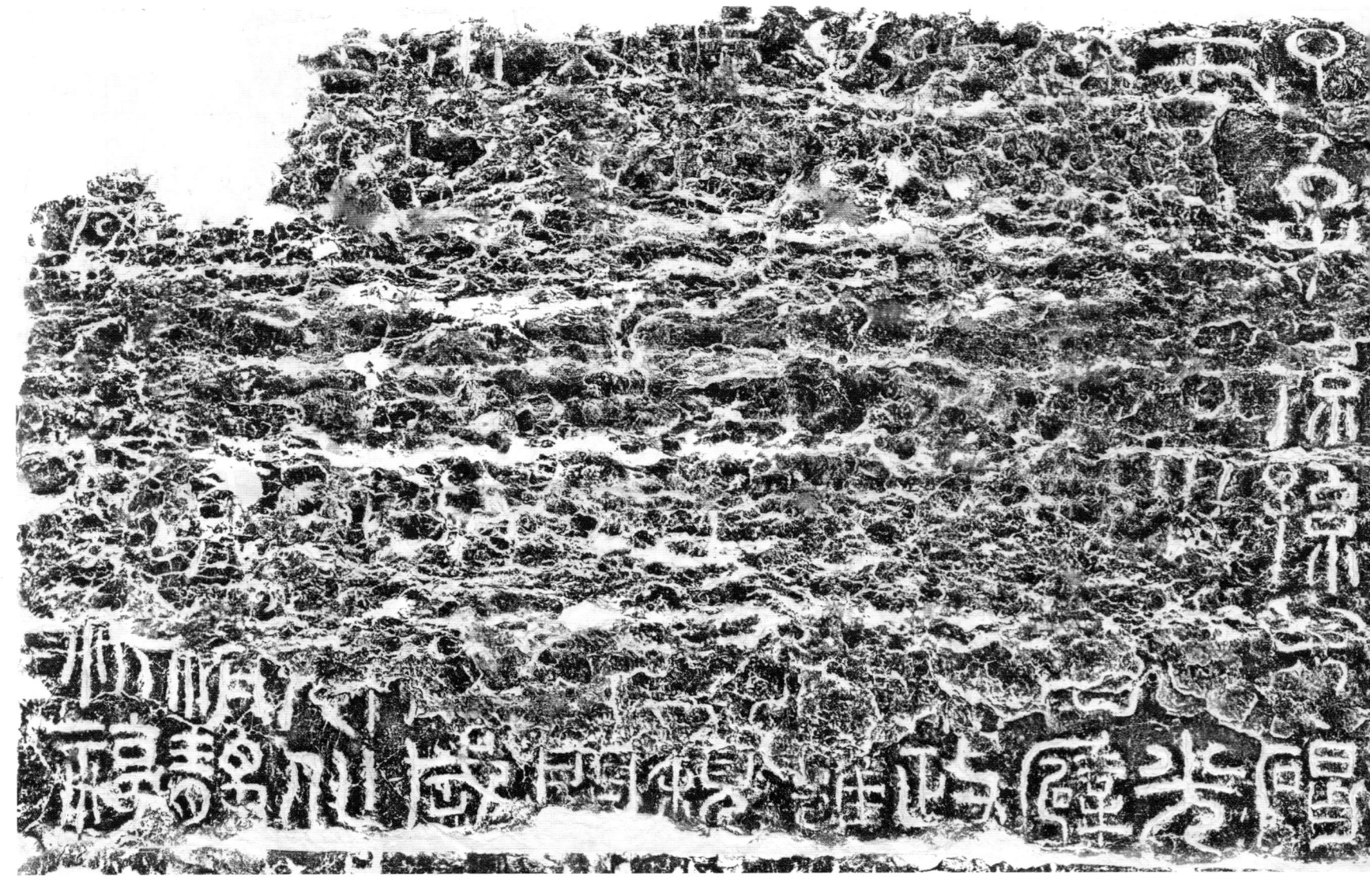

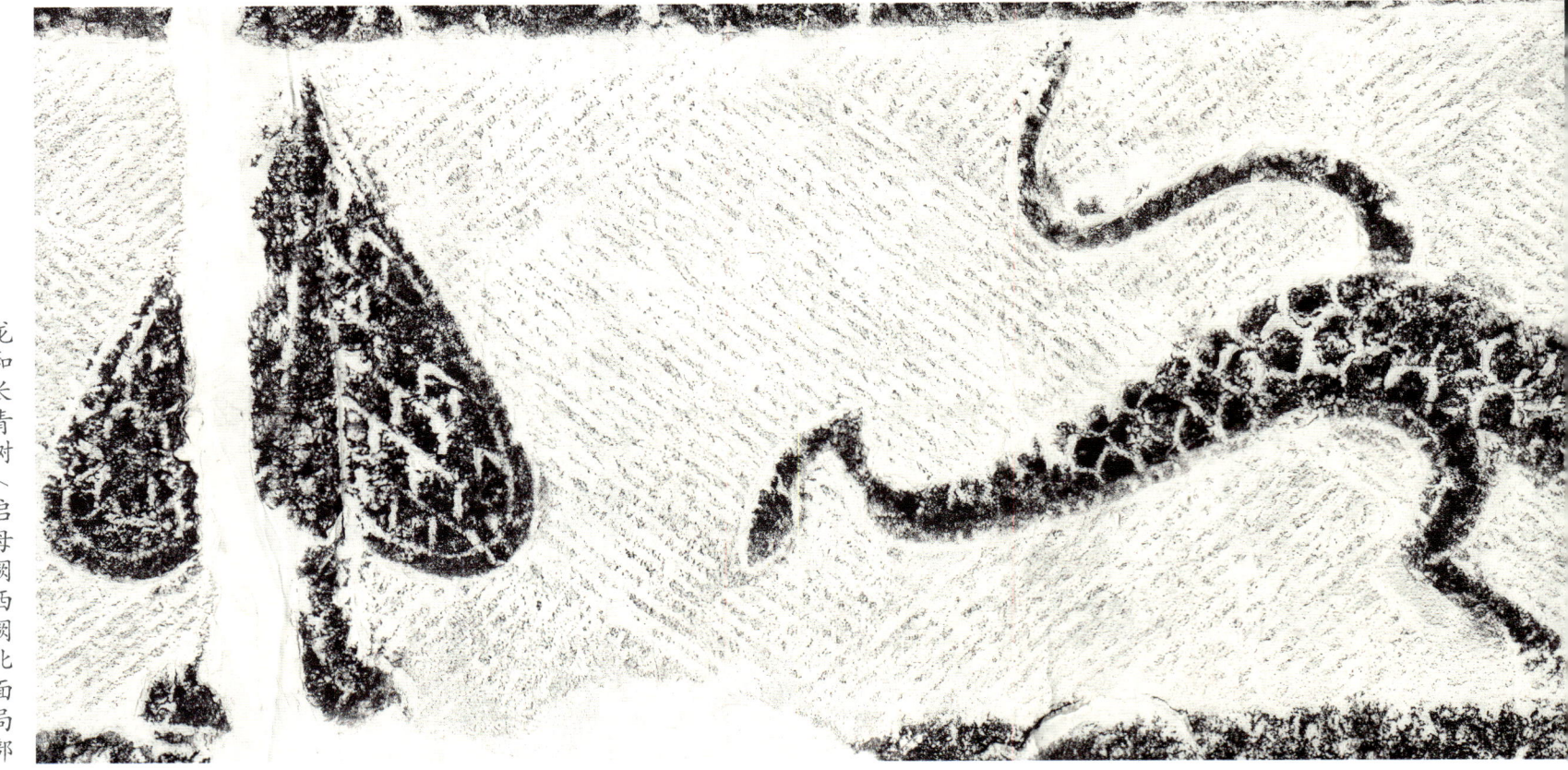
龙和长青树／启母阙西阙北面局部

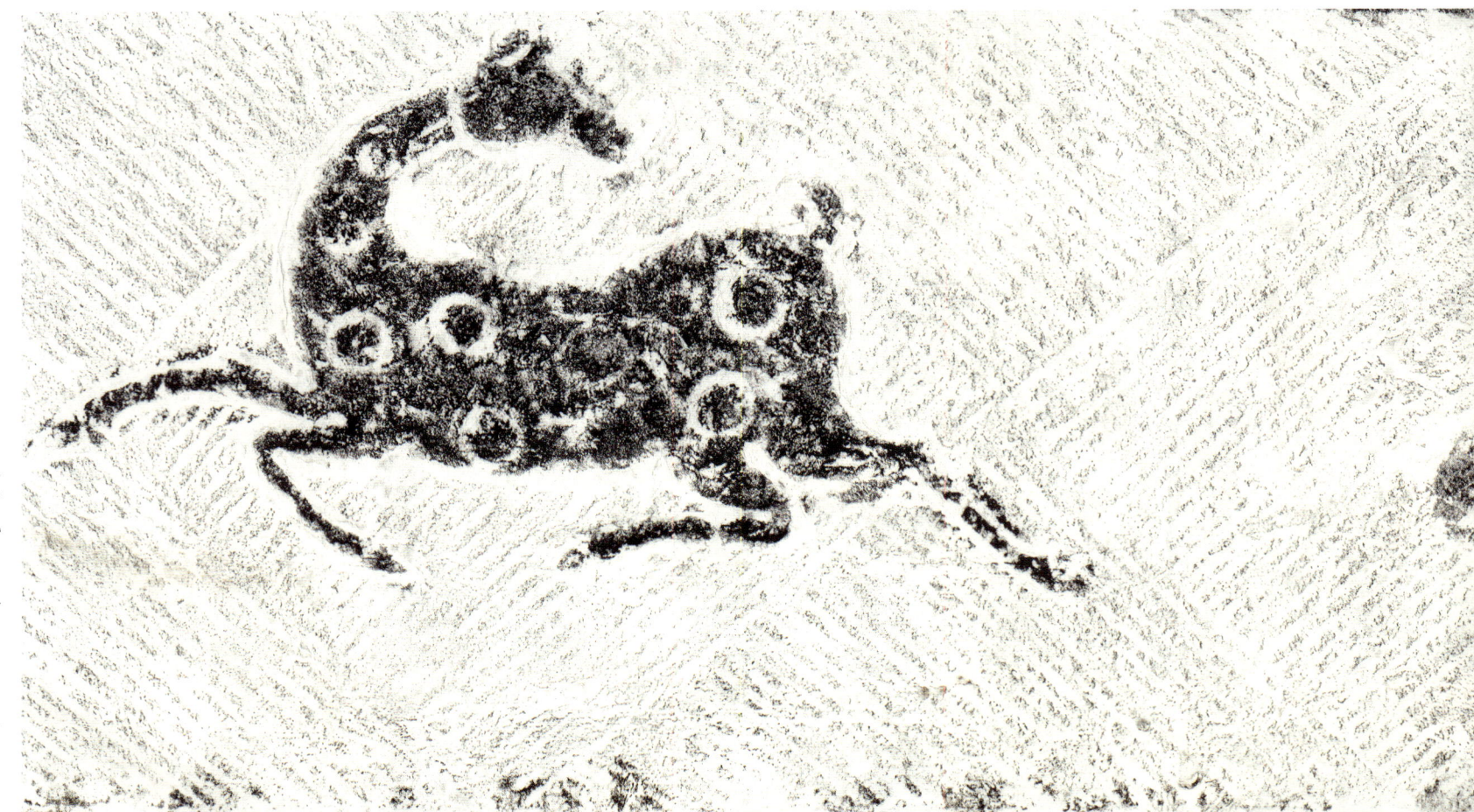
虎扑鹿／启母阙西阙北面局部

嵩山／东汉三阙

兔／启母阙西阙北面局部

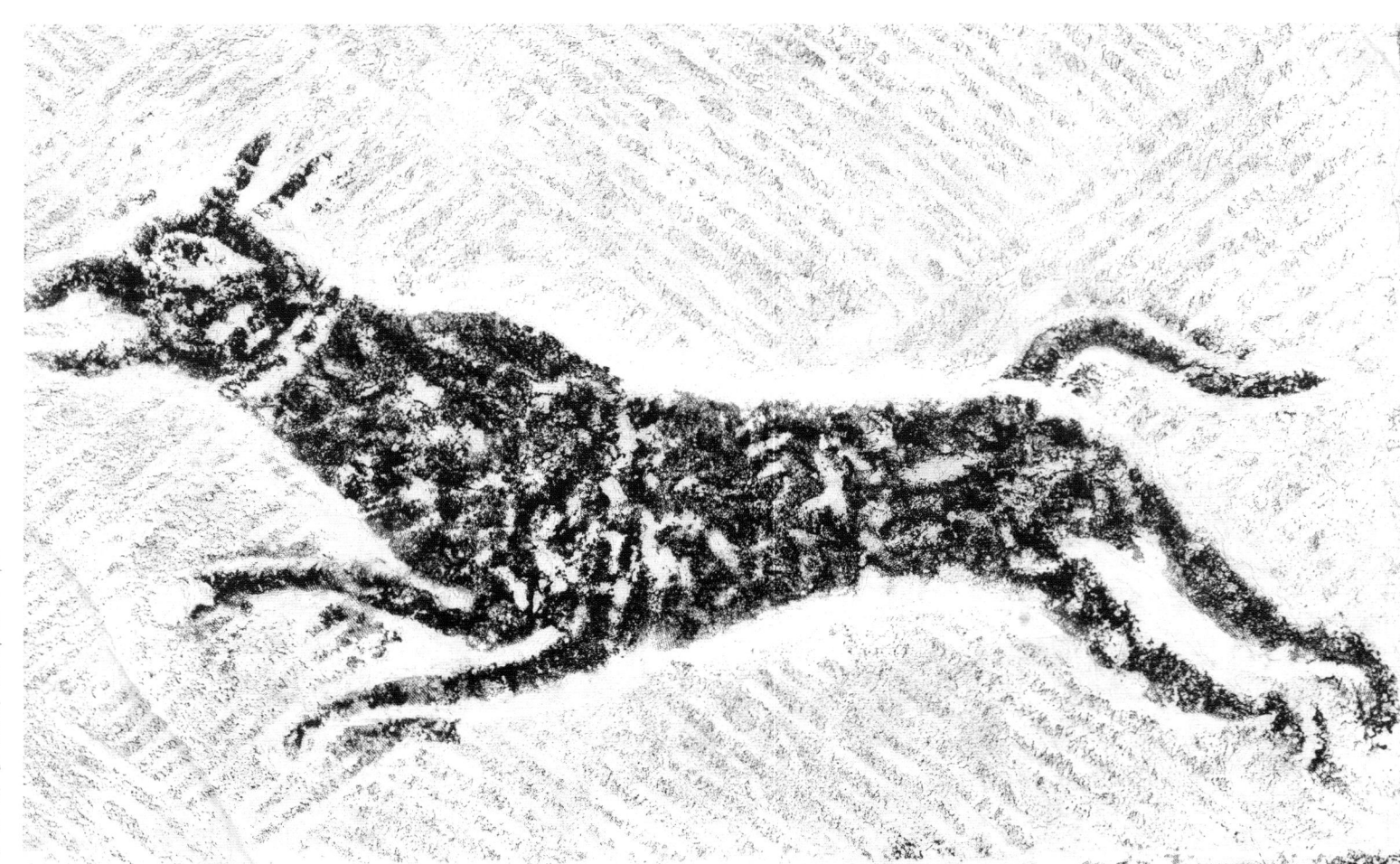

犬／启母阙西阙北面局部

东汉延光三年（124）建，拓片高278厘米，宽75厘米，2008年天地之中历史建筑群申报世界文化遗产建档时拓印。东面上刻铭记和月宫、狩猎、蛟龙等画像。

Built in 124, the third year of the Yanguang era of the Eastern Han dynasty. The rubbing, 278 cm tall and 75 cm wide, was made in 2008 during the application for the World Heritage Site inscription of the "The Centre of Heaven and Earth" historic monuments. On the east surface are carved images of an inscription, a moon palace, hunting, scaled dragons, etc.

东汉延光三年(124)建，拓片高184厘米，宽66厘米，2008年天地之中历史建筑群申报世界文化遗产建档时拓印。西面残损严重，仅存蛟龙较为完美。

Built in 124, the third year of the Yanguang era of the Eastern Han dynasty. The rubbing, 184 cm tall and 66 cm wide, was made in 2008 during the application for the World Heritage Site inscription of the "The Centre of Heaven and Earth" historic monuments. The west surface is seriously damaged except for the well-preserved images of scaled dragons.

阙铭乳丁纹

月宫图／启母阙西阙东侧

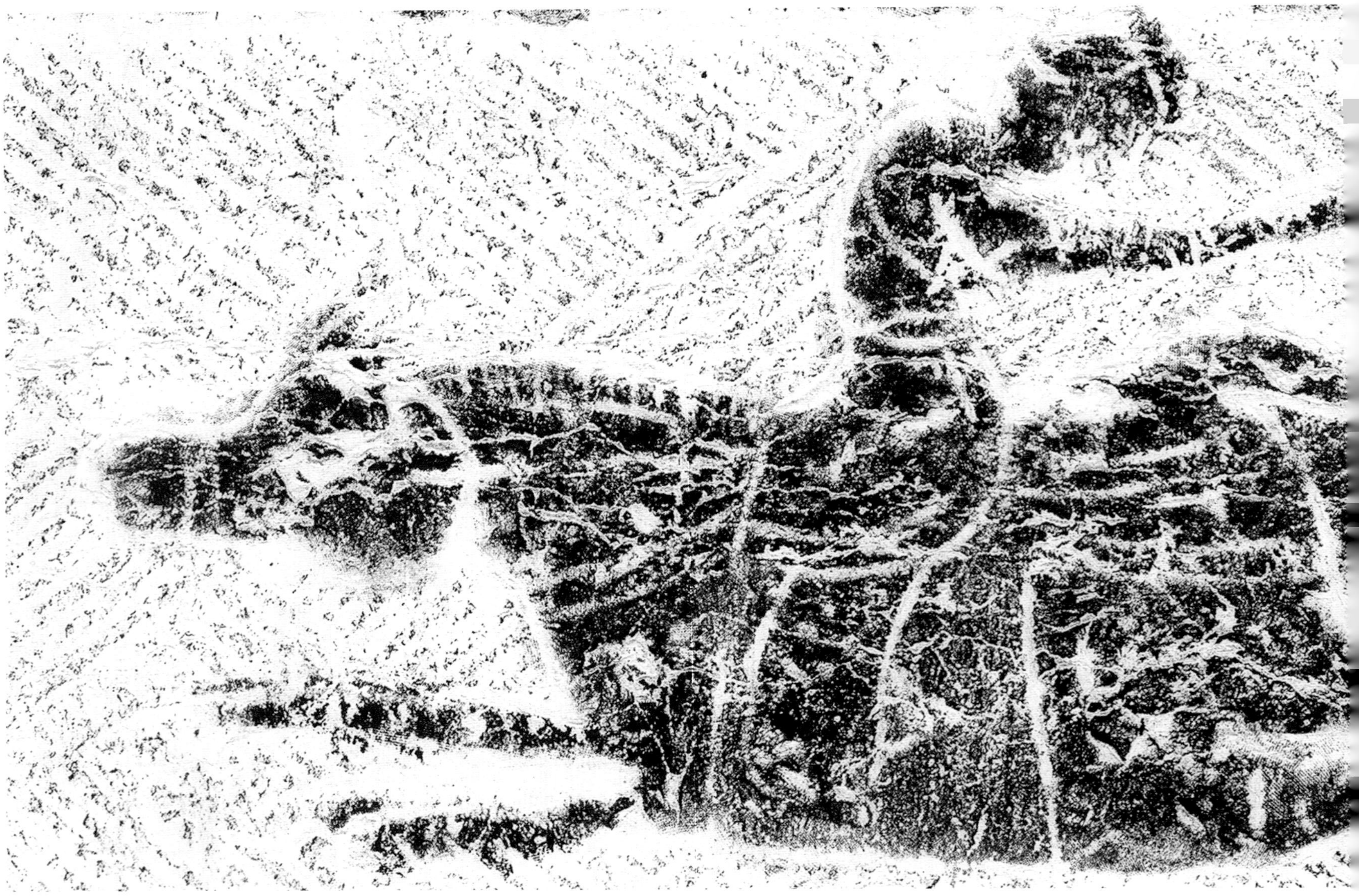

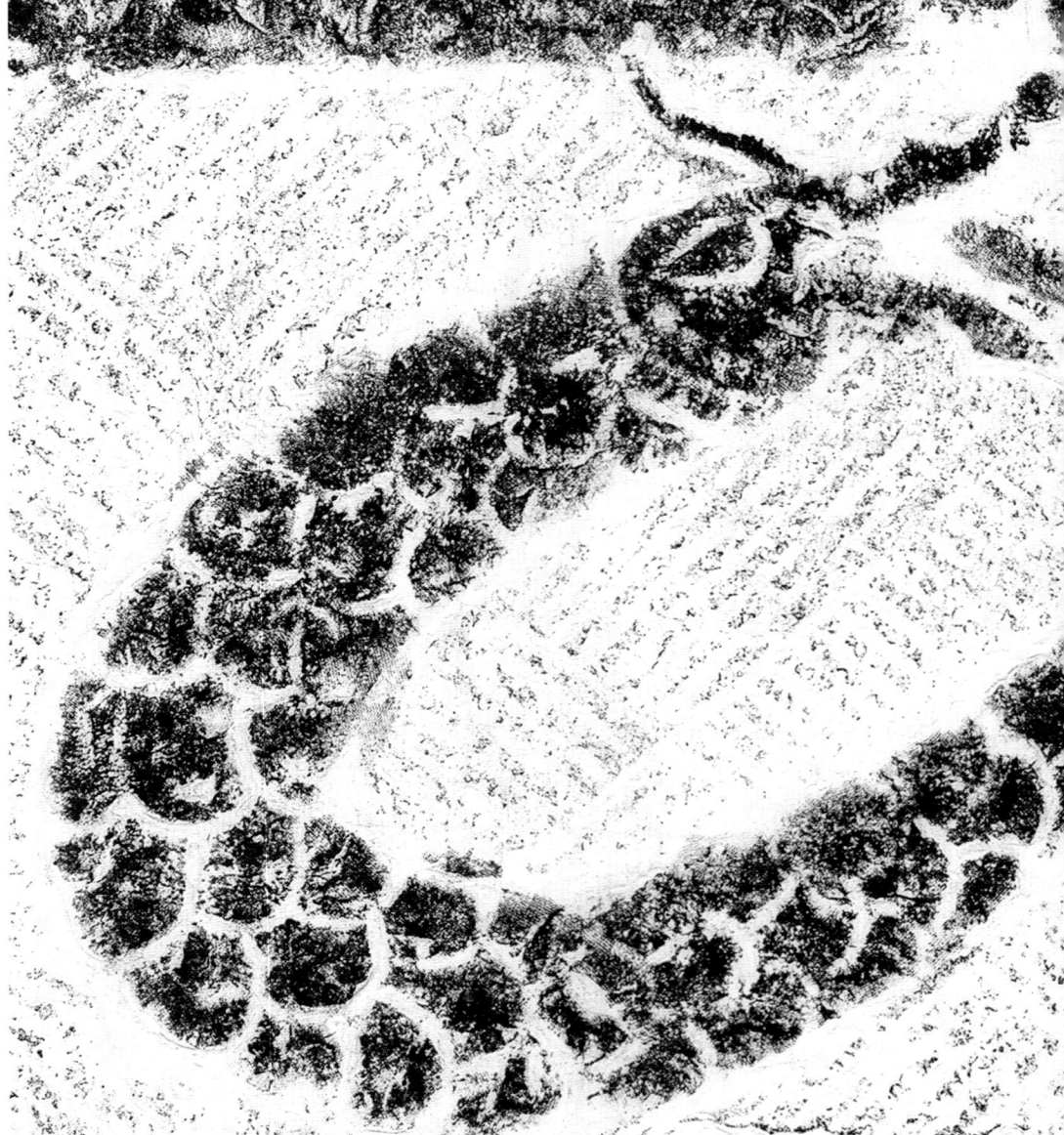

蛟龙图\启母阙西阙东侧局部

狩猎图／启母阙西阙东侧局部

李仁清传拓艺术

嵩山／东汉三阙／

北魏
巩义石窟寺

Shiku Temple, Gongyi,
Northern Wei

巩义石窟寺为全国重点文物保护单位。位于河南省巩义市（原巩县）东北9公里大力山下伊洛河北岸，始建于北魏孝文帝（471—503）时期。巩义石窟是继洛阳龙门石窟之后，北魏皇室开凿的另一座造像石窟。石窟寺初称"希玄寺"，唐改"净土寺"，宋称石窟寺。北魏宣武帝时，景明年间（500—503）已形成规模，后经东西魏、北齐及唐、宋时，又陆续刻一些小龛，连续400多年，形成壮观的石窟群。

巩义石窟寺造像是外来文化与本土文化融合的优秀艺术作品，是我国石窟浮雕艺术中的杰作，也是国内现存洞窟造像中保存较为完整的北魏浮雕造像。石窟寺开凿5个洞窟，1个千佛佛龛和北朝摩崖造像龛。除第五窟外，其他4窟都有中心方柱，造像内容非常丰富。

第一窟，为巩义石窟规模最大窟，高和四壁边长均约6米，方形窟，窟内中心方柱，方柱四面开凿佛龛，保存较完整，雕像十分威武。窟内门东西两侧各雕3层礼佛图，保存比较完整。皇帝礼佛图雕刻三列，第一列为三组，第一组共九人像，比丘像身着博带式袈裟为前导，后一菩提树，图像高大，戴通天皇冠，为皇帝像，其余八像略小的为侍从执事像。从第二列至第三列，比丘像为前导，每组除主像外，身后为侍从像。从总体结构分析，皇帝身后的主像，依次排列应为太子、王公贵族及重臣。皇后礼佛图与皇帝相辉照，仍以比丘尼为前导，首尾各刻一菩提树，第一列后几组和下二列主像应是公主妃嫔等像。皇帝、皇后礼佛图，创造出每幅画面在静穆中寓生动的活力。其他三壁雕文殊维摩诘和闭目冥思本尊，四壁脚刻有技乐、神王、力士和异兽等。窟门外东西两侧雕力士各一尊，东又有1摩崖大龛，龛内有尊高5.3米立佛和2菩萨。门西侧刻北朝造像龛、供养人和题记。

第二窟：北魏开凿，此窟为半成品，窟前壁无存，除窟内东壁刻一东魏佛龛外，东西壁和中心方柱还刻唐代造像10余龛，题记为唐龙朔年间（661—663）。二窟东后坑崖刻20余龛和北朝题记，蕴含着很高的艺术价值。

第三窟：北魏开凿，窟为方形，窟中心柱四面各雕一大龛，龛内各刻1佛2菩萨2弟子，中心方柱南壁上方刻1对供养飞天，她们头戴莲瓣冠，佩项圈，腕钏，一手捧供果，一手持莲花，身穿薄纱，飘带从头后绕过两肩，静细观赏，有引人入胜之精美感，实石窟雕塑艺术作品中之罕见者。窟藻井雕方格平棋，除东南角残损外其他较为完整。门东侧礼佛图残缺，西侧刻3层礼佛图。东西两壁中部各刻一龛，龛内1佛2菩萨2弟子，四周千佛，中心柱和四壁壁脚刻神王、力士、歌舞技乐人和异兽雕像也十分别致和生动。尤其中心柱基座西面双面神王像，怀抱婴儿，两面部紧连在一起，共享一只眼睛，用手遮住半面脸，都显示完整的人物画面。从发髻和表情上看，两个人物神态又有所不同，可以看出一面是男性面孔，而另一半又是女性面孔，充分表现出北魏工匠雕刻才艺。

第四窟：与第三窟形大小相似，北魏开凿，窟内为方形，藻井刻方格式平棋，保存完整，方格内刻供养飞天、莲花化生、忍冬和莲花等。构图生动，刻工细腻。中心柱四面各刻两层造像龛，中心柱东面上下层龛内各刻1佛2菩萨，柱基座刻4身神王像。南壁上龛内刻1佛2菩萨2弟子，下层1佛2菩萨，柱基座刻4身神王像。柱西壁上龛雕1佛2菩萨，下龛雕释迦多宝双佛并坐。柱北壁与东面相似。窟内东、西壁中部各刻1龛，东壁龛内刻1佛2菩萨和2弟子，西壁龛内雕1佛2菩萨2弟子保存比较完整，佛座左右刻两护法狮。窟南壁门东西两侧刻礼佛图，东侧4例，东侧上方残损过半，西侧两列，东西礼佛图壁脚雕4异兽。门西2层礼佛图下是1幅壁画，由于退色和烟熏，画面难辨。北壁中部雕1龛，龛内刻1佛2菩萨2弟子，东、西、北壁脚刻27歌舞伎乐人，19躯神王像，残损较为严重。

第五窟：该窟较小，没有中心方柱，窟高、长和宽约3米，窟顶雕高浮雕莲花藻井，环绕6身供养飞天，四角各刻莲花化生，地面刻圆形莲花，与藻井相对应，东壁1龛，北半部残缺，龛南半部上刻供养飞天，其下莲花化生和神王，佛龛下方刻1比丘。南壁上方刻7佛，窟门两侧各刻1立佛站在莲花座上，西壁与东壁相似，除龛内北侧菩萨被盗和主尊头像残损外，其他保存较完整，尤其龛两侧对应供养飞天和佛座下2比丘雕刻最为精细。北壁北魏和唐时期雕有大小龛，龛形两侧各刻1托山力士，龛座两侧刻1对护法狮。

巩义石窟有诸佛、礼佛图、歌舞伎乐人、神王、飞天、神兽、佛教故事、藻井图饰等。其中第一窟"帝后礼佛图"、第三窟"飞天"最为精美。此外，刻于各窟壁脚和中心方柱基座下层的歌舞伎乐人、神王浮雕像也十分别致和生动。

The Shiku Temple in Gongyi is a major cultural heritage site in China, located at the foot of the Dali Mountain 9 kilometers northeast of Gongyi City (former Gongyi County), Henan, on the north bank of the Yiluo River. First built during the reign of Emperor Xiaowen (471-503) of the Northern Wei dynasty, it is another Buddhist cave complex that the Norther-Wei imperial court initiated following the Longmen Caves in Luoyang. Originally called the Xixuan Temple, this temple was renamed the Jingtu Temple in the Tang dynasty before it got its current name. The temple had already become quite sizable by the Jingming era (500-503) during the reign of Emperor Xuanwu of Northern Wei, and, in more than 400 years, through the Eastern and Western Wei, Northern Qi, Tang and Song dynasties, evolved into a significant complex of Buddhist caves.

The statues at the Shiku Temple are fine works of art as a result of an integration of local and foreign cultures; they represent masterpieces of cave sculpture in China and are Northern-Wei statues well preserved among extant carve statues in the country. There are 5 caves, 1 Thousand-Buddha Niche, and cliff statues from the Northern dynasties. Except Cave 5, all other caves each have a central square column inside on which are carved a wide variety of things.

Cave 1: The biggest of the caves in Gongyi. It is a square cave, about 6 meters in height and in the side length of each of the four walls. Inside it is a square column in the middle, on each of whose four surfaces are carved niches with impressive statues. On the walls of both the east and the west sides of the opening to the cave inside are carved 3 layers of Buddha worshiping scenes, which are well preserved. The carved scenes of an emperor worshiping the Buddha are arranged in three columns. The first column comprises three groups of images. The first group of images contains nine figures: a bhikkhu in the lead wearing a robe with a wide girdle, behind him a bodhi tree; a tall figure of an emperor wearing a towering crown; and eight smaller figures of attendants. In the second and third columns, there are bhikkus in the lead, and main figures behind them are attendants. Judging by the overall composition, the main figures behind the emperor are presumably the crown prince, princes and dukes, and high-ranking officials. Echoing the emperor worshiping the Buddha, the scene of an empress worshiping the Buddha also has a bhikku leading a procession that begins and ends with a bodhi tree; main figures in the latter groups of the first column and in the second column below are presumably princesses, concubines, etc. Though still, the images of the emperor and empress worshiping the Buddha offer a sense of motion. On the three other walls are carved images of Manjushri and Vimalakirti and their yidams in meditation; at the foot of the four walls are carved images of flying apsaras, god-kings, guardians, and mystical creatures. On the walls on both the west and the west sides of the opening to the cave are carved statues of a guardian; on the east side there is also a colossal cliff niche that contains a 5.3-meter-tall standing Buddha and 2 Bodhisattvas. On the west side of the opening are carved niches from the Northern dynasties, donors and an inscription.

Cave 2: Dug out during the Norther Wei dynasty, this cave is an unfinished one. The frontal wall of the cave doesn't exist. In addition to a Northern-Wei niche carved in the east wall inside the cave, on the east and west walls and the central square column are caved more than 10 Tang-dynasty niches, as well as an inscription that dates back to the Longshuo era (661-663) of the Tang dynasty. In a pit behind, to the east of the cave, there are over 20 niches as well as Northern-dynasties inscriptions, and they have very high artistic value.

Cave 3: Dug during the Northern Wei dynasty, this cave is a square one. In the middle of the cave is a square column into each of the four surfaces of which is carved a big niche that contains a Buddha, two bodhisattvas and two disciples. On the upper south surface of the column is a pair of flying apsaras, each wearing a lotus petal-shaped crown, a necklace, bracelets, and a thin gown, fruit offerings in one hand and a lotus flower in the other, with a long ribbon on shoulders from behind the head; they are breathtakingly beautiful and rarely seen among cave structures. On the caisson are engraved checks, and the caisson is well preserved except its damaged southeast corner. On the east side of the doorway is carved a scene of a Buddhist ceremonial which has parts missing, and on the west side three layers of scenes of Buddhist ceremonials. In the middle of both the east and the west walls is a niche that contains one Buddha, two bodhisattvas and two disciples, and around the niche are a multitude of Buddha statues. On the central column and at the bottom of the four walls, there are vivid statues of god-kings, guardians, performers, and mythical creatures. In particular, on each of the four surfaces of the column base, there is a statue of a two-faced god-king with a baby in the arm; the two faces adjoin one another and share one eye, and when either face is covered with a hand, it is a complete figure. Judging by hair and expression, the two faces have different countenance, and it is not hard to see that one face is a man's face and the other is a woman's, showing the ingenuity of Northern-Wei artisans.

Cave 4: Dug during the Northern Wei dynasty, this cave is similar to Cave 3 in shape and size. Squire inside, the cave has a caisson carved in checks, and within the checks are caved images of flying apsaras making offerings, rebirth from the lotus, honeysuckle, lotus flowers, etc. These carvings are vivid and exquisite. Into each of the four surfaces of the central column are carved two niches, one over the other. The niches on the east surface of the column both contain a Buddha and two bodhisattvas, and on the surface of the column base are carved four god-kings. The upper niche on the south surface of the column contains one Buddha, two bodhisattvas and two disciples, the lower one contains one Buddha and two bodhisattvas, and on the surface of the column base are carved four god-kings. The upper niche on the west surface of the column contains one Buddha and two bodhisattvas, and in the lower niche are Gautama Buddha and Prabhutaratna Buddha sitting next to one another. Carvings on the north surface of the column are similar to those on the east surface. On both the east and the west walls of the cave inside, there is a niche; in the east niche are carved a Buddha, two bodhisattvas and two disciples, and in west east niche are one Buddha, two bodhisattvas and two disciples, as well as two guardian lions on the left and right sides of the throne. On the south wall of the cave, on the east and west sides of the doorway are carved scenes of Buddhist ceremonials, four on the east side - over half of them damaged, and two on the west side; at the bottom of the wall, beneath the Buddhist ceremonials on both sides are four mythical creatures. Beneath the two scenes of Buddhist ceremonials on the wall to the west of the doorway, there is a mural that is unrecognizable due to discoloration and sootiness. In the middle of the north wall of the carve is carved a niche which contains one Buddha, two bodhisattvas and two disciples. At the bottom parts of the east, west and north walls are carved 27 performers and 19 god-kings, all seriously damaged.

Cave 5: This cave is small in size, about 3 meters in height, length and width, without a central square column inside. It has a caisson with lotus flowers carved in high relief, around which are 6 figures of flying apsaras making offerings, with rebirth from lotus images in the four corners. On the floor there is a carved round lotus flower corresponding to the caisson. On the east wall is a niche, the north half of it damaged; in the south half is carved flying apsaras beneath which are images of rebirth from lotus and god-kings. Beneath this niche is carved a bhikkhu. In the upper part of the south wall are carved 7 Buddhas, and on either side of the doorway is a carved figure of the Buddha standing on a lotus throne. The west wall is similar to the east one, and except the north part of the niche where the bodhisattva is stolen and the Buddha's head is damaged, all other parts are well preserved, most notably the flying apsaras and the two bhikkhus beneath the throne. On the north wall are a big niche dug during the Northern Wei dynasty, and a small one dug during the Tang dynasty; on either side of the niche is carved a mountain-bearing guardian, and on each side at the bottom is carved a guardian lion.

The caves in Gongyi contain statues of Buddhas, performers, flying apsaras, god-kings and mythical creatures, carved scenes of Buddhist ceremonials and tales, as well as caisson sculptures. The most exquisite of them are the Empress Worshiping the Buddha in Cave 1 and the flying apsaras in Cave 3. The performers at the bottom of the walls inside the caves, and the god-kings carved in relief on the lower parts of the column bases, are also quite impressive.

第一窟中心方柱东龛：拓片高430厘米，宽278厘米，创自北魏孝文帝至宣武帝景明年间（471—503年），2009—2010年拓印。龛内右侧一菩萨已佚，仅存两飞天。左侧保存完整，龛壁脚雕7身神王。雕刻十分生动。

East niche on the central square column in Cave 1: Dug and carved in 471-503 during the reigns of Emperors Xiaowen and Xuanwu of Northern Wei. The rubbing, made in 2009-2010, is 430 cm high and 278 cm wide. A bodhisattva on the right inside the niche is lost, and there are only two flying apsaras left. The left part is well preserved, with 7 god-kings carved at the bottom of the niche. The carvings are quite vivid.

飞天

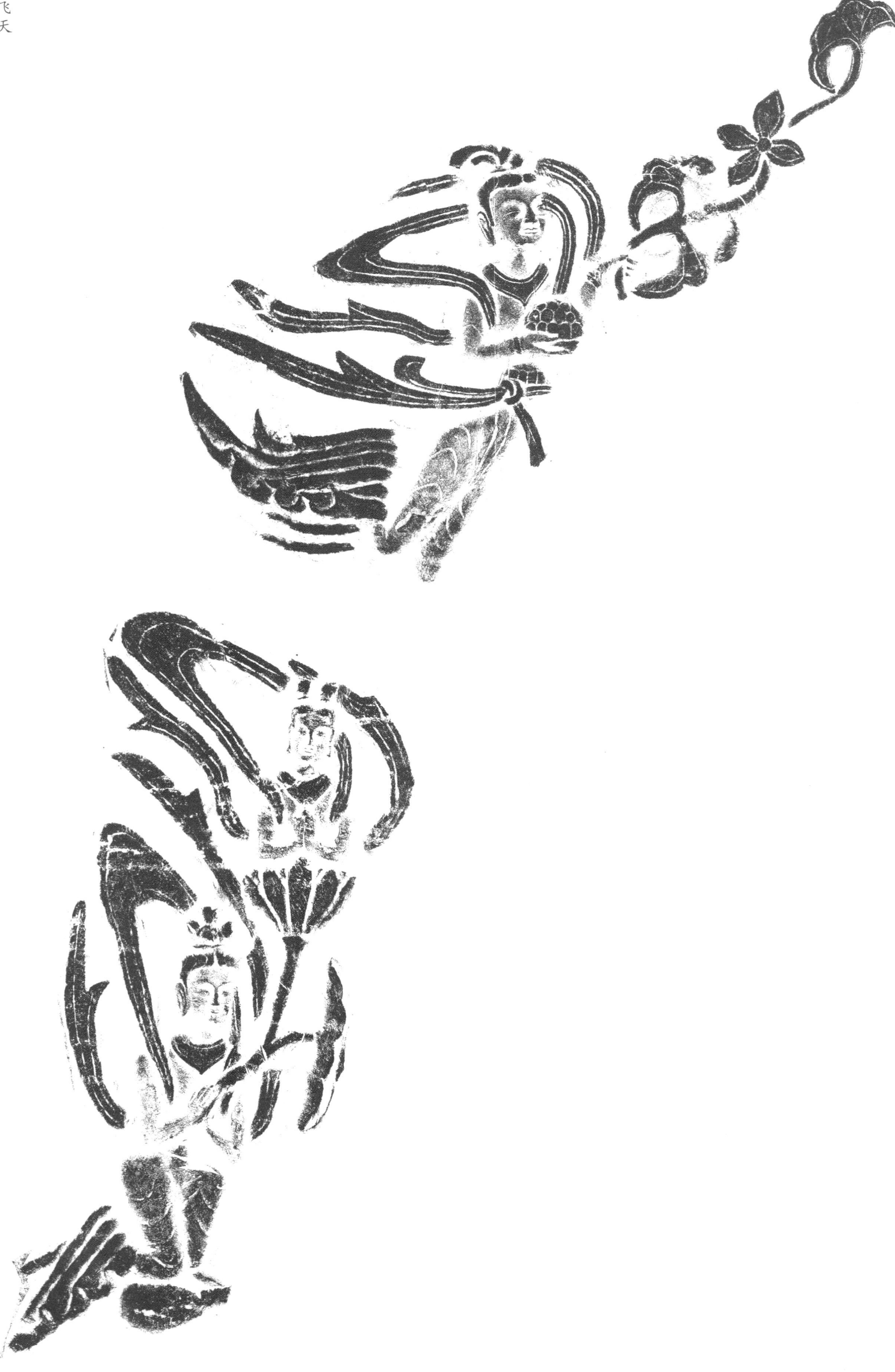

飞天

李仁清传拓艺术
LIRENQING
CHUANTAYISHU

/北魏/
/巩义石窟寺/

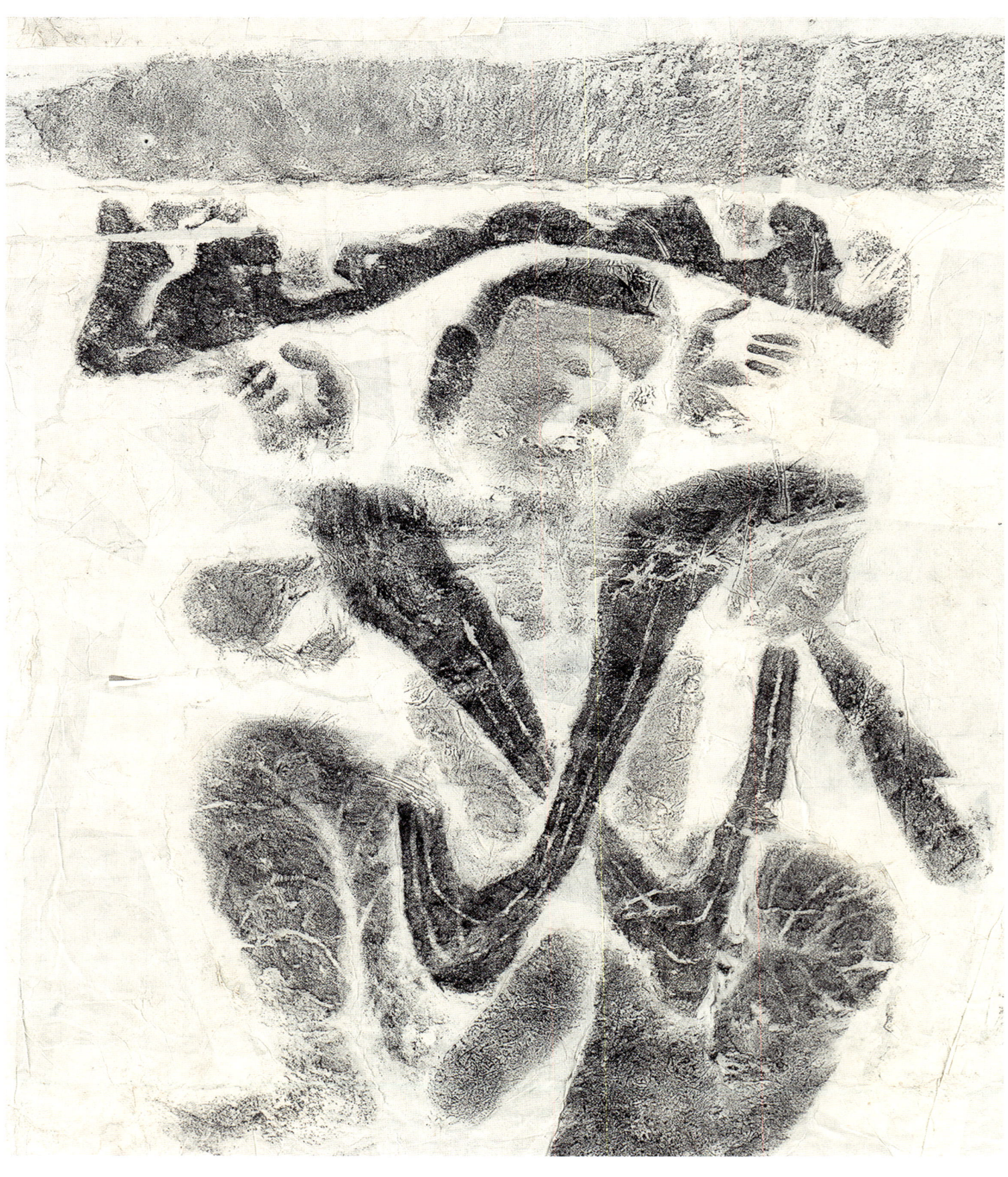

神王像

神王像

/北魏/巩义石窟寺/

菩萨

菩萨

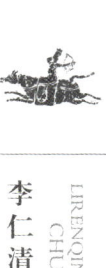

李仁清传拓艺术
LIRENQING
CHUANTAYISHU

/北魏/
/巩义石窟寺/

West niche on the central square column in Cave 1: Dug and carved in 471-503 during the reigns of Emperors Xiaowen and Xuanwu of Northern Wei. The rubbing, made in 2009-2010, is 422 cm high and 278 cm wide. The niche is well preserved except for two bodhisattvas whose heads are damaged. Different than other three ones, this niche contains a flying apsara carved in the upper part of it.

第一窟中心方柱西龛：拓片高422厘米，宽278厘米，创自北魏孝文帝至宣武帝景明年间（471—503），2009—2010年拓印。除龛内两菩萨头像残缺外，其他保较完好，与其它三龛不同的是其上方各雕一身伎乐飞天。

伎乐天

/北魏/ /巩义石窟寺/

第一窟中心方柱南龛：拓片高 423 厘米，宽 310 厘米，创自北魏孝文帝至宣武帝景明年间（471—503），2009—2010 年拓印。南龛是中心柱四面造像保存比较完整的窟龛，龛两侧下面雕有唐代小龛。

South niche on the central square column in Cave 1: Dug and carved in 471-503 during the reigns of Emperors Xiaowen and Xuanwu of Northern Wei. The rubbing, made in 2009-2010, is 423 cm high and 310 cm wide. This niche is well preserved in comparison with others. There are small niches dug during the Tang dynasty below it, on both sides.

供养天

/北魏/ /巩义石窟寺/

菩萨

菩萨

菩萨

〔北魏〕
〔巩义石窟寺〕

North niche on the central square column in Cave 1: Dug and carved in 471-503 during the reigns of Emperors Xiaowen and Xuanwu of Northern Wei. The rubbing, made in 2009-2010, is 420 cm high and 280 cm wide. This niche is structurally similar to the south one.

第一窟中心方柱北龛：拓片高 420 厘米，宽 280 厘米，创自北魏孝文帝至宣武帝景明年间（471—503），2009—2010 年拓印。北龛与南龛布局大致相同。

供养天

／北魏／
／巩义石窟寺／

皇帝礼佛图：拓片高230厘米，宽210厘米，创自北魏孝文帝至宣武帝景明年间（471—503），2009—2010年拓印。皇帝礼佛图雕刻三列，第一列为三组，第一组共九像，比丘像身着博带式袈裟为前导，后一菩提树，图像高大，戴通天皇冠，为皇帝像，其余八像略小的为侍从执事像。从第二列至第三列，比丘像为前导，每组除主像外，身后为侍从像。

Statue of the emperor worshiping the Buddha: Dug and carved in 471-503 during the reigns of Emperors Xiaowen and Xuanwu of Northern Wei. The rubbing, made in 2009-2010, is 230 cm high and 210 cm wide. The carved scenes of an emperor worshiping the Buddha are arranged in three columns. The first column comprises three groups of images. The first group of images contains nine figures: a bhikkhu in the lead wearing a robe with a wide girdle, behind him a bodhi tree; a tall figure of an emperor wearing a towering crown; and eight smaller figures of attendants. In the second and third columns, there are bhikkus in the lead, and main figures behind them are attendants.

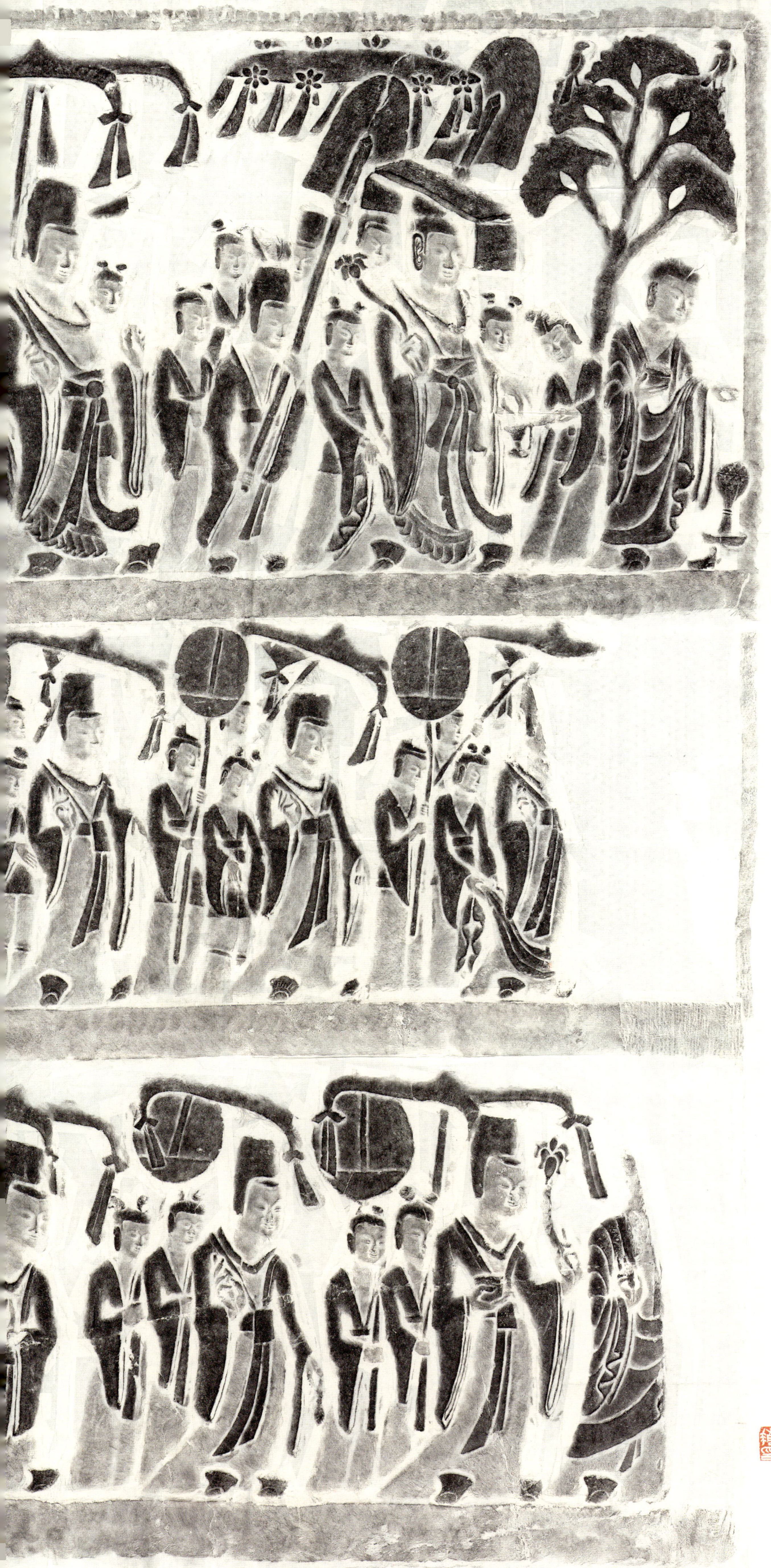

李仁清传拓艺术

北魏 巩义石窟寺

119

李仁清传拓艺术

/北魏/
/巩义石窟寺/

皇后礼佛图：拓片高230厘米，宽210厘米，创自北魏孝文帝至宣武帝景明年间（471—503），2009—2010年拓印。皇后礼佛图与皇帝相辉照，仍以比丘尼为前导，首尾各刻一菩提树，第一列后几组和下二列主像应是公主妃嫔等像。

Statue of the empress worshiping the Buddha: Dug and carved in 471-503 during the reigns of Emperors Xiaowen and Xuanwu of Northern Wei. The rubbing, made in 2009-2010, is 230 cm high and 210 cm wide. Echoing the emperor worshiping the Buddha, the scene of an empress worshiping the Buddha also has a bhikku leading a procession that begins and ends with a bodhi tree; main figures in the latter groups of the first column and in the second column below are presumably princesses, concubines, etc.

李仁清传拓艺术

/北魏/ /巩义石窟寺/

124

〔北魏〕〔巩义石窟寺〕

第三窟南壁西礼佛图：拓片高310厘米，宽165厘米，创自北魏孝文帝至宣武帝景明年间（471—503），2009—2010年拓印。礼佛图雕刻三列，第一列残缺过半，第二、第三列和壁脚技乐人保存较好。

Statue of worshiping the Buddha on the south wall of Cave 3: Dug and carved in 471-503 during the reigns of Emperors Xiaowen and Xuanwu of Northern Wei. The rubbing, made in 2009-2010, is 310 cm high and 165 cm wide. This includes three scenes; the first scene is half missing, and the other two scenes as well as the images of performers at the bottom are soundly preserved.

伎乐人

伎乐人

第三窟中心柱南龛：拓片高321厘米，宽218厘米，创自北魏孝文帝至宣武帝景明年间（471—503），2009—2010年拓印。龛内一佛二菩萨，龛楣刻一对飞天，均以弧形忍冬纹相托，体态轻盈，衣裙下摆上举张扬的幅度甚大，加强了飞动的节奏感。

South niche on the central square column in Cave 3: Dug and carved in 471-503 during the reigns of Emperors Xiaowen and Xuanwu of Northern Wei. The rubbing, made in 2009-2010, is 321 cm high and 218 cm wide. The niche contains one Buddha and two bodhisattvas. At the top part of it is a carved pair of flying apsaras, each above a curved honeysuckle pattern, who appear graceful and full of motion with their gowns floating up.

菩萨像

李仁清传拓艺术

/北魏/
/巩义石窟寺/

飞天

飞天

第四窟平棊：拓片高430厘米，宽438厘米，创自北魏孝文帝至宣武帝景明年间（471—503），2009—2010年拓印。保存完整，平棊内8身供养飞天和8身莲花化生，是研究北魏雕刻艺术史的重要实物资料。

Caisson of Cave 4: Dug and carved in 471-503 during the reigns of Emperors Xiaowen and Xuanwu of Northern Wei. The rubbing, made in 2009-2010, is 430 cm high and 438 cm wide. Well preserved, on the caisson are carved 8 flying apsara making offerings and 8 images of rebirth from lotus, which are crucial materials for research on the Northern-Wei history of sculpture.

李仁清传拓艺术

北魏
巩义石窟寺

飞天

莲花

莲花化生

李仁清传拓艺术

莲花

/北魏/巩义石窟寺/

供养天

莲花

莲花化生

忍冬

/北魏/
/巩义石窟寺/

供养天

莲花

莲花化生

莲花化生

供养飞天

莲花

供养飞天

莲花

北魏 巩义石窟寺

供养天

供养天

供养天

莲花化生

李仁清传拓艺术

/北魏/巩义石窟寺/

四窟西礼佛图：拓片高290厘米，宽162厘米，创自北魏孝文帝至宣武帝景明年间（471—503），2009—2010年拓印。西侧礼佛图上刻两层，其下平面为一幅壁画，壁脚雕两异兽，其下平面是巩义石窟仅存的一幅壁画。

West statue of worshiping the Buddha in Cave 4: Dug and carved in 471-503 during the reigns of Emperors Xiaowen and Xuanwu of Northern Wei. The rubbing, made in 2009-2010, is 290 cm high and 162 cm wide. It comprises two Buddha worshiping scenes, one upon the other. Beneath it is a mural - the sole one left in the caves in Gongyi, and at the bottom there are two mythical creatures.

异兽

李仁清传拓艺术

/北魏/
/巩义石窟寺/

四窟东礼佛图：拓片高305厘米，宽167厘米，创自北魏孝文帝至宣武帝景明年间（471—503），2009—2010年拓印。雕刻四列，第一列残存过半，下雕两异兽。

East statue of worshiping the Buddha in Cave 4: Dug and carved in 471-503 during the reigns of Emperors Xiaowen and Xuanwu of Northern Wei. The rubbing, made in 2009-2010, is 305 cm high and 167 cm wide. It comprises four Buddha worshiping scenes, the top one largely damaged. Below are carved two mythical creatures.

异兽

/北魏/巩义石窟寺/

四窟中心方柱南龛：拓片高333厘米，宽164厘米，创自北魏孝文帝至宣武帝景明年间（471—503），于2009—2010年拓印。分上下两龛，上龛雕刻一佛二菩萨二弟子、左右各一供养飞天。下龛一佛二菩萨，左右各一供养飞天。

South niches on the central square column in Cave 4: Dug and carved in 471-503 during the reigns of Emperors Xiaowen and Xuanwu of Northern Wei. The rubbing, made in 2009-2010, is 333 cm high and 164 cm wide. There are two niches, one upon the other. The upper one contains a Buddha, two bodhisattvas and two disciples, with a flying apsara on each side. The lower one contains a Buddha, two bodhisattvas and two disciples, with a flying apsara on each side.

佛像

李仁清传拓艺术

/北魏/巩义石窟寺/

一佛二弟子二菩萨像

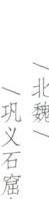

李仁清传拓艺术

/北魏/
/巩义石窟寺/

155

第五窟藻井：拓片高274厘米，宽290厘米，创自北魏孝文帝至宣武帝景明年间（471—503），于2009—2010年拓印。为方型藻井，中心雕高浮雕莲花，周围环绕6身飞天，四角雕忍冬和莲花化生，给人一种繁盛崇高的审美感觉。

Caisson of Cave 5: Dug and carved in 471-503 during the reigns of Emperors Xiaowen and Xuanwu of Northern Wei. The rubbing, made in 2009-2010, is 274 cm high and 290 cm wide. It is a square caisson. In the middle is carved a lotus in high relief, around which are 6 flying apsaras, with images of honeysuckle and rebirth from lotus at each of the four corners, giving a sense of prosperity and loftiness.

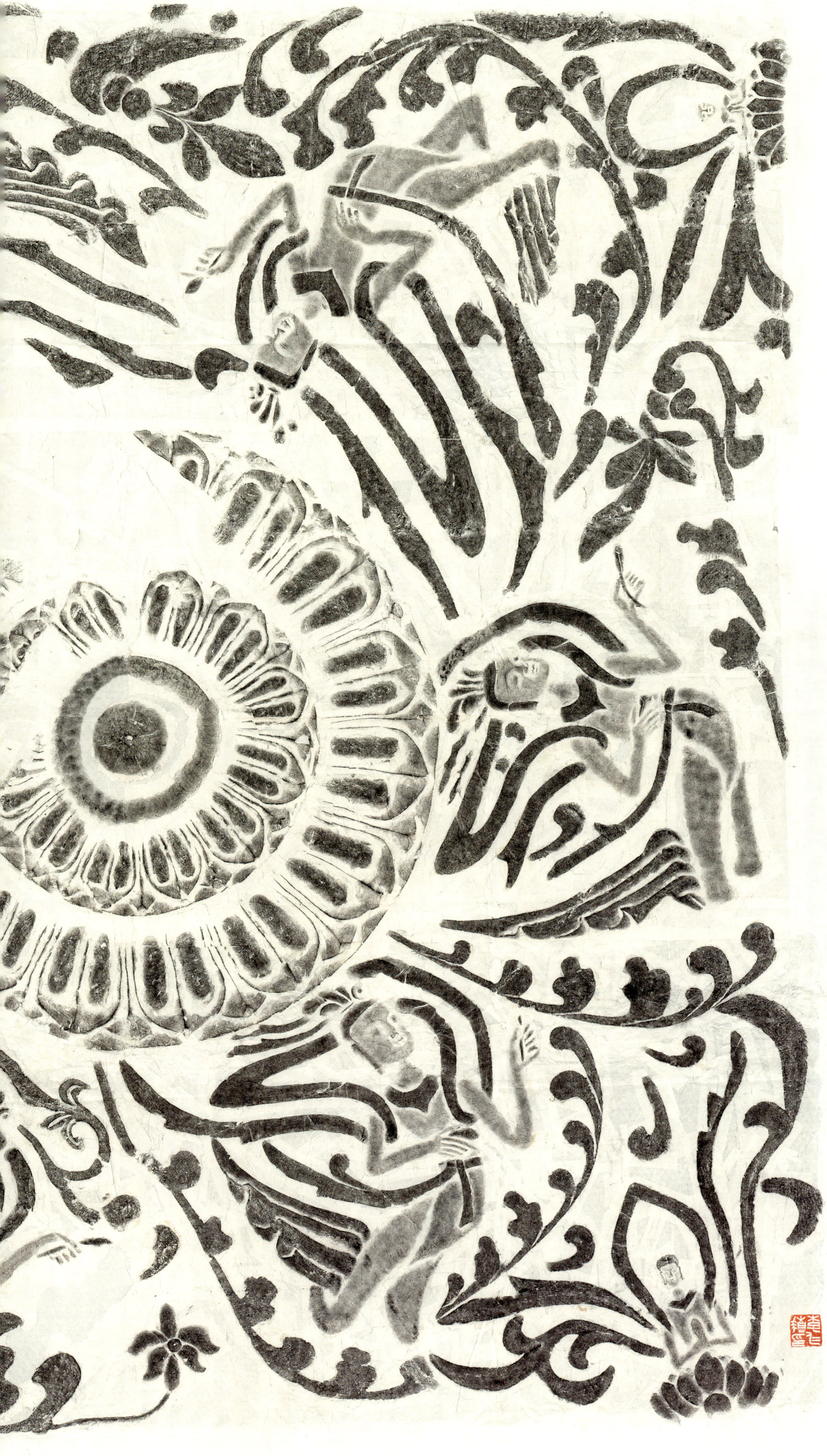

李仁清传拓艺术
LIRENQING CHUANTAYISHU

/北魏/
/巩义石窟寺/

供养天

供养天

/北魏/
/巩义石窟寺/

供养天

供养天

立佛：拓片高 280 厘米，宽 303 厘米，创自北魏孝文帝至宣武帝景明年间（471—503），于 2009—2010 年拓印。南壁门楣刻 5 尊坐佛，两侧卷草纹，窟门东、西各有一尊立佛，站在莲花座上。

Buddhas: Dug and carved in 471-503 during the reigns of Emperors Xiaowen and Xuanwu of Northern Wei. The rubbing, made in 2009-2010, is 280 cm high and 303 cm wide. On the lintel of the south wall are carved 5 sitting Buddhas with a coiled grass pattern on either side, and on both the east and the west sides of the doorway is a Buddha standing on a lotus throne.

立佛：拓片高 280 厘米，宽 303 厘米，创自北魏孝文帝至宣武帝景明年间（471—503），于 2009—2010 年拓印。南壁门楣刻 5 尊坐佛，两侧卷草纹，窟门东、西各有一尊立佛，站在莲花座上。

Buddhas: Dug and carved in 471-503 during the reigns of Emperors Xiaowen and Xuanwu of Northern Wei. The rubbing, made in 2009-2010, is 280 cm high and 303 cm wide. On the lintel of the south wall are carved 5 sitting Buddhas, and on both the east and the west sides of the doorway is a Buddha standing on a lotus throne.

北朝石刻造像

Stone Sculptures of the Northern Dynasties

北魏 释迦牟尼佛
Sculpture of Gautama Buddha, Northern Wei

此像为河南博爱县出土，现藏河南博爱博物馆。由碑身和碑座组成，未见发愿文及年款。依风格似北魏（386—534）时期作品。

拓片高272厘米，宽108厘米，是典型的莲瓣背屏，背屏刻三躯歌舞伎乐飞天和七佛，中下部雕一佛二菩萨二弟子像，座两侧各刻一护法狮。造像雕刻精美细腻，线条流畅。主佛与两侧胁侍菩萨间还有线刻僧人像，体甚小。主佛与两侧菩萨皆赤足脚踏莲台，主佛高肉髻，垂耳短颈，慈眉善目，面方圆，身平直。穿褒衣博带式通肩大衣，内着僧祇支，手施无畏、与愿印。主佛头后有头光，背屏上方刻精美的火焰纹，背屏上方左右各刻一歌舞乐伎天，体态轻盈，长裙彩带，飘曳飞舞。

Discovered in Boai County, Henan, and preserved at the Henan Boai Museum, the stele consists of a stele body and a base on which the body rests, and on its surface is inscribed neither a vow nor the year of its completion. It appears in style to be a work dating back to the Northern Wei (286-534).

The rubbing is 272 cm tall and 108 cm wide. It is a typical lotus petal-shaped back screen carved with three flying apsaras and seven Buddhas. In the middle and lower parts are one Buddha, two bodhisattvas and two disciples, and there is a guardian lion on each side of the throne. The sculpture is exquisite with flowing lines. Between the main Buddha and the attendants on both sides are small engraved Buddhist figures. The main Buddha and the bodhisattvas all stand on lotus thrones in bare feet. Lop-eared and short-necked, the main Buddha has a head crowned with a tall topknot, and a broad face, looking kind and amiable; standing straight, he wears a loose one-piece robe outside the saṃghāti, his hand in an abhaya mudra. There is a halo around the main Buddha's head. The upper part of the back screen is a pattern of flames, and on each side is a flying apsara in a graceful long robe.

Sculpture of Gautama Buddha, 280 cm × 115 cm, 2004.
释迦摩尼像／2004年／280厘米×115厘米

李仁清传拓艺术
LIRENQING CHUANTAYISHU

／北魏／
／释迦牟尼佛／

167

右菩萨像

右弟子像

李仁清传拓艺术

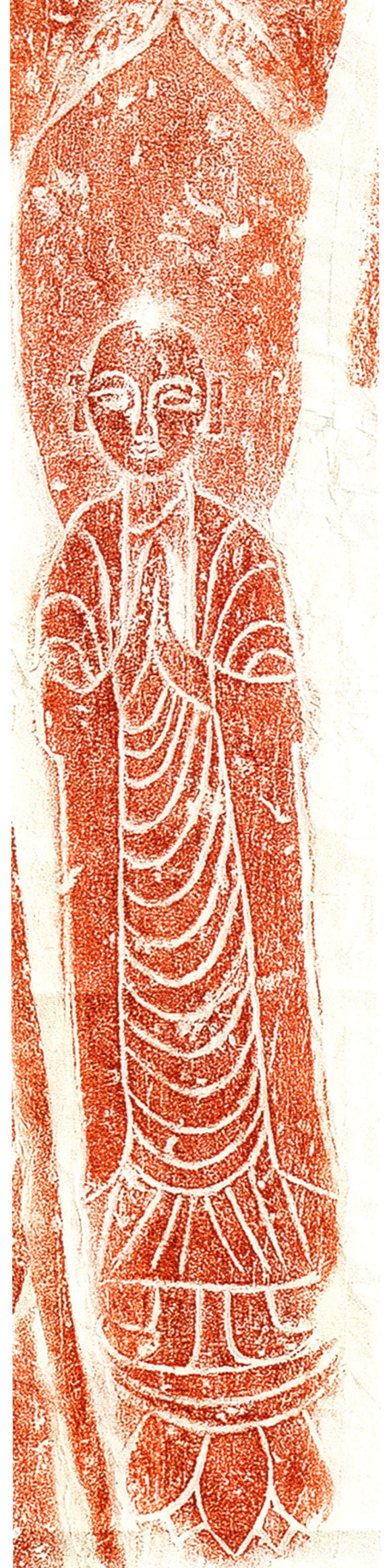

/北魏/
/释迦牟尼佛/

左弟子像

左菩萨像

李仁清传拓艺术

〈北魏〉释迦牟尼佛

东魏 嵩阳寺造像碑
Buddhist Stele at Songyang Temple, Eastern Wei

中岳嵩阳寺造像碑：东魏天平二年（535）雕造，拓片高370厘米，宽96厘米，2008年天地之中历史建筑群申报世界文化遗产建档时拓印。

碑阳：碑分碑首、碑身和碑座三部分组成，碑首为六龙盘绕，中部篆书阳刻"嵩阳寺伦统碑"。碑身造像残损严重，仅存一尊佛龛，下半部刻隶书撰写"中岳嵩阳寺碑铭序"，主要介绍雕刻造像经过。

碑阴：碑首为六龙盘绕，中部刻一佛龛。碑身镌刻88尊佛和6方造像龛。碑侧刻盘绕龙纹。碑趺四面刻神王与花卉，图案颇为精致，为中原石刻艺术中的精美之作。

Buddhist stele at the Songyang Temple, Mount Song: Completed in 535, the second year of the Tianping era of the Eastern Wei. The rubbing of the stele, 370 cm tall and 96 cm wide, was made in 2008 during the application for the World Heritage Site inscription of the "The Centre of Heaven and Earth" historic monuments.

Front surface: The stele comprises three parts: the head, the body, and the base. The head is six intertwining dragons, and in the middle is an engraved inscription that reads "Songyang Si Luntong Bei" (Stele of Ethnic Principles of Songyang Temple). In the body which has been seriously damaged, there is only one Buddhist niche left, below which is a text engraved in clerical script - "Preface to the Stele of the Songyang Temple at Mount Song" which is an introduction to the sculpture.

Back surface: The head is six intertwining dragons, and in the middle is a Buddhist niche. There are 88 Buddhas and 6 niches carved in the body. On the side surfaces are engraved patterns of intertwining dragons. On the four side surfaces of the stele base are carved god-kings and flowers representative of stone sculpture in the Central Plains.

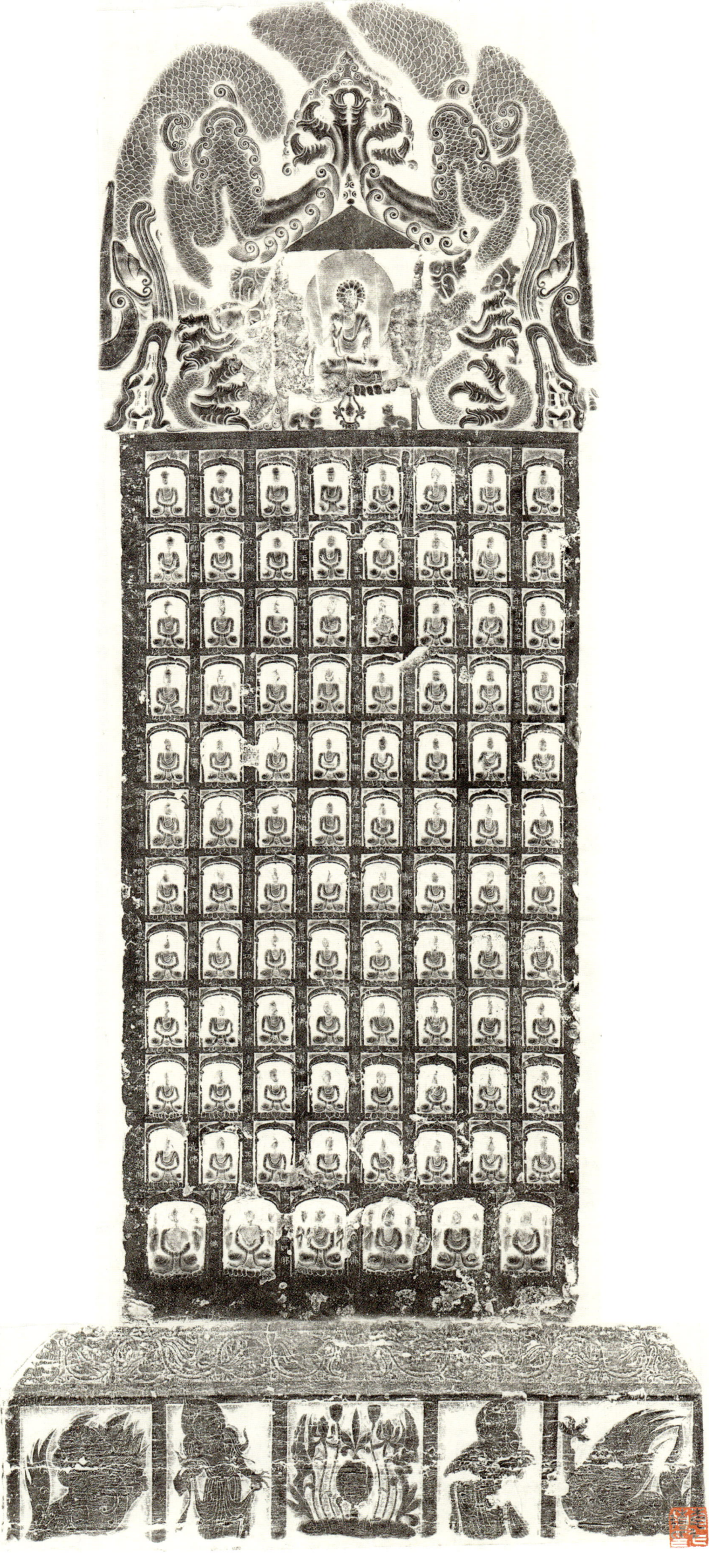

嵩阳寺造像碑／2008年／363厘米×150厘米

Songyang Temple Stele, 263 cm × 150 cm, 2008.

／东魏／嵩阳寺造像碑／

碑阳

174

右侧面　　左侧面

李仁清传拓艺术　LIRENQING CHUANTAYISHU

/东魏/嵩阳寺造像碑/

175

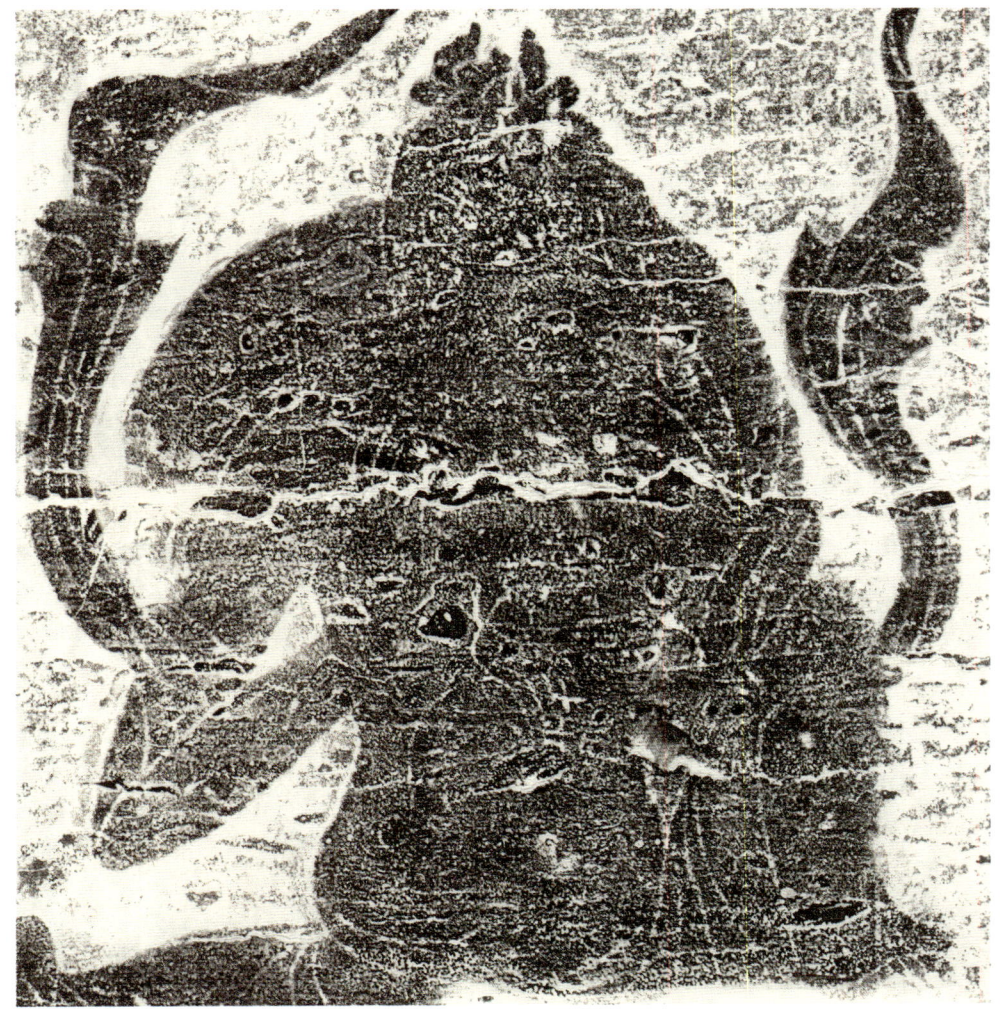

神王像

博山炉

神王像

博山炉

/东魏/嵩阳寺造像碑/

碑阴

李仁清传拓艺术

/东魏/ /嵩阳寺造像碑/

力士像

博山炉

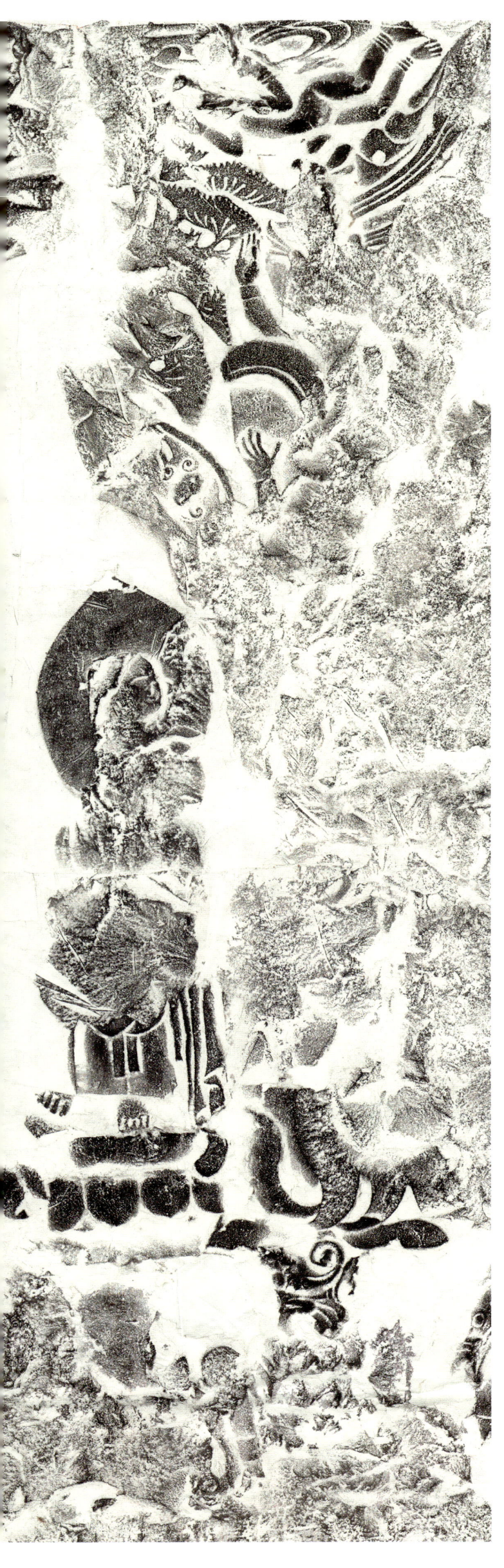

碑阳大龛

/东魏/
/嵩阳寺造像碑/

章儀無量億[illegible]金[illegible]相表王城家現[illegible]
燦丹彩絢煥色[illegible]光輝宇宙異須彌[illegible]之
層[illegible]龍勇樺[illegible]何[illegible]現達閣通[illegible]所[illegible]
廊重複[illegible]何[illegible]迤[illegible]有者階[illegible]充各則[illegible]寶[illegible]泉
四道甘菓柳裊長條松聲圓音[illegible]效[illegible]果紅輝儀成瑤[illegible]
異禽巡獸飲啄相鳴碩學名賢鍾武相望[illegible]是[illegible]誦列館法[illegible]共[illegible]
應真四集與響八飛香煙[illegible]霧[illegible]禪[illegible]六時靡輟方為眾[illegible]安[illegible]之靈
場八輩十方三世之苑圖也[illegible]平二年四月八日備[illegible]二統九[illegible]樹[illegible]
雕鑄尊像贊貽嘉福顯彰聖儀高足大沙門統遵法師是懷體[illegible]珠族
絜仁緒明般若宇汪洋開妙思於三空之表顯真如於四邑之外引群
生丹飛巨海率諸邑義[illegible]王天宮勉循嚴震兼造白玉像一軀者屬侍郎
剎廟鐫磨妙匠精巧三十二相八十好圓色[illegible]靈光暉[illegible]像書
仰資皇帝聖曆無窮國境寧泰大后德[illegible]永保仁齡禎[illegible]景[illegible]含
我淨若見若聞等一常樂備盡邊塵[illegible]來除感鍾此福與詞[illegible]
明明大聖皎皎無著至[illegible]至妙澄[illegible]常樂無像無言形名應世[illegible]年
播宣苦諦聲光振動濯我塵滯化息[illegible]林終歸實際金儀[illegible]像勒興
香尊避坐三寶誦昇為模為指永劫[illegible]維大沙門權機[illegible]傳葉風秀[illegible]
弘通常住道德芳烈帝后欽裕搆造靈基朝野傾務遽慕妙善近先秖[illegible]
唯聖唯賢爰依爰附億兆來賴天龍[illegible]仰城齊千空止其無[illegible]
[illegible]日庚申從高陽觀移來會善寺立

嵩阳寺碑铭序

夫至理空净北大始无名寄其言以身毒家
框於軍敬之国布怒奢悋之身骨□重牛□闍之
召洞蓮岸善埴金弗將優□□□□□□□□
然乃遺形八□還舉慧頂□□□□□□□□
布世控三皇帝所凝□東□□□□□□□□
普蕉乃□車永□召□□□□□□□□□□
□挟引四王□佛資□□□□□□□□□□
□□□王心□師□□□□□□□□□□□
和□□□次甲之□□□□□□□□□□□
□□□□心子建□□□□□□□□□□□
□□□□屬展民藍□□□□□□□□□□
□□國□寺麻並□□□□□□□□□□□
□中緣老中檀既□□□□□□□□□□□
始咸七毅魂緣主本從□□□□□□□□□
□戚□旁絶頹七頼卒□□□□□□□□□
巍巖□名逕中層□□□□□□□□□□□
□□□□□匠佛之□□□□□□□□□□
遠攀□□□骸法次□□□□□□□□□□
□□□思陰先也□□□□□□□□□□□
□□盞其遺興則□□□□□□□□□□□
□□□績泳禾□□□□□□□□□□□□
□□□□□禪師□□□□□□□□□□□
□□□繼師□□□□□□□□□□□□□
□□□軒中侍律□□□□□□□□□□□
□□□□壹万文改□□□□□□□□□□
□□□副師頴朱□□□□□□□□□□□
□□□□巧共其□□□□□□□□□□□

北齐 刘碑寺造像碑

Buddhist Stele at Liubei Temple, Northern Qi

刘碑寺造像碑，简称"刘碑寺碑"，位于河南省登封市东南刘碑村，是河南现存体量最大的造像碑。北齐天保八年（557）豫州刺史刘碑等人刻立。后人因碑兴建佛寺，因名"刘碑寺"，村落沿其名曰刘碑村。1963年河南省人民政府公布其为省级文物保护单位，2006年批准为第六批全国重点文物保护单位。

刘碑寺造像碑由碑首、碑身、碑座三部分组成，碑首与碑身连为一体，用整块石材雕成。通高398厘米，宽146厘米，厚50厘米。碑首雕6条盘龙，碑身造像3列，上下共4层，雕刻内容丰富，有人物、菩提树、狮子、山石以及莲花等。碑阴面上方开龛刻佛像7尊，中刻18躯供养人，下方刻造像发愿文及造像供养人题名，字体楷隶兼书。碑两侧上方雕1佛2弟子立像，侧身刻精巧的盘绕龙纹。碑座正面和两侧雕10躯高浮雕力士，后面刻浅浮雕山林射猎图，画面有手执刀、执叉和执弓的骑士，还有狮、猛虎、猎犬、兔等动物，是一幅颇为最精美之作。

刘碑寺碑年代确切，内容丰富，雕工极为精湛，是中原地区北齐时期造像中的精品，与"敬史君造像碑"似出同一人之手，对于研究北齐造像风格、佛教题材以及书法艺术都具有重要意义。

The Buddhist stele at the Liubei Temple, called "Liubei Temple Stele" for short, is the largest extant stele in Henan, located in Liubei Village, southern Dengfeng, Henan Province. It was completed in 557, the eighth year of the Tianbao era of the Northern Qi dynasty, by Governor of Yu Prefecture Liu Bei among others. A temple was then built by virtue of the stele, called the Luibei Temple after which the village nearby was also named. The temple was proclaimed a provincial-level cultural heritage site by the Provincial People's Government of Henan in 1963, and made on the sixth list of major historical and cultural sites protected at the national level in 2006.

The stele comprises three parts: the head, the body, and the base, with the head and the body carved out of a whole mass of stone. It is 398 cm tall from the top to the bottom, 146 cm wide, and 50 cm think. On the head surface are six intertwining dragons; on the body surface, there are three columns of statuettes which are in four rows, including human figures, bodhi trees, lions, rocks, lotus flowers, etc. Carved into the upper part of the back of the body are seven niches which each contain a Buddhist statuette, in the middle part are statuettes of 18 donors related to the stele, and in the lower part are a Buddhist vow and the donors' names engraved in either regular or clerical script. On either side surface are one Buddha and two disciples, all of them in a standing posture, and beneath the statuettes is an exquisite pattern of intertwining dragons. On the front and side surfaces of the stele base are 10 guardians carved in high relief, and on the back surface is a spectacular mountain hunting scene carved in low relief - including horseback riders wielding a saber, a fork or a bow and arrow, as well as animals like lion, tiger, hunting dog, and rabbit.

Rich in content and superb in sculpture, the Liubei Temple Stele represents one of the best statues from the Northern Qi dynasty in the Central Plains, and it appears to have been created by the same artisan who sculpted the Jing Shijun Stele. And both steles are of great importance to research on the style of sculpture, Buddhism, painting and calligraphy during the Northern Qi.

碑阳　Front surface of the stele

李仁清传拓艺术　LIRENQING CHUANTAYISHU

/北齐/刘碑寺造像碑/

187

碑阳大龛

碑座正面

〔北齐〕〔刘碑寺造像碑〕

碑阴

Back surface of the stele

碑座背面

李仁清传拓艺术
LIRENQING
CHUANTAYISHU

/北齐/
/刘碑寺造像碑/

碑阴上部

〔北齐〕〔刘碑寺造像碑〕

金山遠求名匠奇思窂聞巧殊世
外四挾靈巋之顯西思窂聞巧殊陽世
派流瀍澗建之一區櫺王舍之殊
騰霄月真容凝像然之化者流無基三泉首陽
十方空空遍滿視之化者流無尋光曜首
觀之者我心寂滅師為皇祉中花生
寧輔顯上登以此家果緣福鍾境
世頗顧使神興紫宮開昇妙表心見僧永七
艺管攲子孫相位景九坐超生才妙
来栖道跡注注逢賢慶處遇聖蠶詰

夫妙静虚凝圣辙难言寻恍怕无相
非有慈悲心内腹知虽刑言幽绝诞迹无二三
而千晓悲潜情喻三欲济免扶苦诞迹应二
归空群神真境然车笃以运诸佛子擢十迹
碑河潜人宝爞唐笃信佛弟子应
袭踵前濒王衣冑代资佛基漢劉緒
柯嵩尢此也善衾因官瓊佛子汉刘
慕募乡耶首领识珠独晓皆是五紫芳
姬妓蘖英裹之孤挺晋魏九域磐轩
根之楔棟骰眪皇朝飞聲齊室故

僧	見	心	歡	聖	遊	辟	空	欽	望	護	儵	俗	道	士	俄	寧	珪	毃	晈	鏤
在	六	諸	蠢	濟	日	妙	隨	若	坐	金	寒	肩	場	上	俄	三	璋	黻	金	布
邑正	清淨	香火柱	邑子 戴始	邑子 戴成	邑子 劉空	邑子 戴雲	邑子 陳客	邑子 戴含	邑子 曹迴	邑子 劉顥	邑子 劉晱	邑子 劉挑	邑子 劉伍	邑子 劉小	邑子 劉貴	邑子 劉廣	邑子 張明	邑子 劉閏	邑子 劉方	邑子 曹邾	邑子 戴惠	邑子 劉荣
邑子 王羅	邑子 張始	邑子 劉興	邑子 劉僧	邑子 趙義	邑子 王䎱	邑子 王譽	邑子 陳傷	邑子 張進	邑子 趙遠	邑子 李要	邑子 朱銀	邑子 戴英	邑子 陳道	邑子 張雙	邑子 趙妙	邑子 陽郭	邑子 孫貴	邑子 譚賢	邑子 戴妃	邑子 盧蜜
	邑子 陳伏	邑子 陳榮	邑子 陳念	邑子 陳還	邑子 曹秩	邑子 曹伏	邑子 曹定	邑子 曹雙	邑子 陳顥	邑子 徐貴	邑子 魯兔	邑子 徐雅	邑子 焦興	邑子 李摩	邑子 許轉	邑子 許敬	邑子 許伏	邑子 陽男	邑子 楊姬	邑子 田桃	邑子 趙歸	邑子 歐陽
	邑子 陳眼	邑子 馬陳	邑子 馬桃	邑子 張清		邑子 王傷	邑子 王通	邑子 王琛	邑子 司馬	邑子 司馬	邑子 司馬	邑子 陽舍	邑子 陽迴	邑子 馮和	邑子 陽顥	邑子 席慶	邑子 龍賈	邑子 龍僧	邑子 陳雅	邑子 郭涂	邑子 陽和	邑子 王妃
	邑子 陳黑	邑子 劉次	邑子 曹敬	邑子 曹子	邑子 曹國	邑子 曹道	邑子 曹明	邑子 曹世	邑子 曹方	邑子 曹承	邑子 曹景	邑子 陽黑	邑子 郭顥	邑子 杜實	邑子 王始	邑子 王元		邑子 曹清	邑子 曹業	邑子 謝進	邑子 戴思	邑子 李景
	邑子 張妃	邑子 王黑	邑子 劉光	邑子 曹先	邑子 曹貴		邑子 曹國	邑子 曹世	邑子 曹延	邑子 曹高	邑子 曹景	邑子 郭貴	邑子 法進		邑子 王紹	邑子 王輔	邑子 王䎱	邑子 曹純	邑子 曹賈	邑子 趙敦	邑子 劉羅	邑子 姚胡

碑阴题名

光泉之殊揉室域是五爵漢子擢十迹無
曜首陽世石故磬軒業芳緒劉應二三相

大邑師僧和唯邢陽顥明唯邢曹元康唯邢戴
唯邢曹伏顥邑子戴奴
都邑主劉始興邑子劉伏興邑子
都邑主戴恭興邑子戴万邑子韓思明
都邑主劉巨當邑子趙顥德邑子戴禮
都邑主劉貴宗邑子郭黑帝邑子戴養
唯邢戴桃扶邑子戴小慶邑子劉道
唯邢成充邑子戴副祑邑子劉歡因
唯邢司馬莫引邑子劉眾愛邑子解
唯邢陳龍空邑子劉永進邑子陳羔司
唯邢曹舍問邑子戴方伯邑子陳稠周
唯邢女買邑子戴成傷邑子劉永和邑子陳稠女
唯邢陳充邑子戴惠邑子李義邑子戴紫雲
唯邢左樹生邑子戴紫雲邑子張托
唯邢陽延傷邑子劉聞臺邑子郭智
唯邢曹伏顥邑子郭貴買
邑子陽領孫
邑子陽子元
邑子陽伯生
邑子陽稠但
邑子陽司周
邑子陽欲因
邑子陽道
邑子韓帝
邑子陽始伏
邑子曹乞生
邑子曹匡生
邑子曹先
邑子曹業
邑子曹敬速
邑子曹毛穆
邑子劉子
邑子李清
邑子王太和
邑子程惠
邑子戴思興
邑子戴景暑
邑子戴景
邑子李景
邑子崔老
邑子郭景

右側面

202

右侧面上部龛像

李仁清传拓艺术

/北齐/刘碑寺造像碑/

203

碑座右侧面

李仁清传拓艺术

/北齐/
/刘碑寺造像碑/

205

碑身右侧面

刘碑寺造像碑左侧面 / 2008年 / 277厘米 × 124厘米

Left side surface of the Liubei Temple Stele, 277 cm × 124 cm, 2008.

李仁清传拓艺术
LIRENQING CHUANTAYISHU

/ 北齐 / 刘碑寺造像碑 /

左側面上部龕像

左侧面碑身

李仁清传拓艺术

/北齐/ /刘碑寺造像碑/

隋唐

灵泉寺洞窟

Grottoes at Lingquan Temple, Sui and Tang Dynasties

位于河南安阳善应镇南平村南的灵泉寺，原名宝山寺，东魏武定四年（546），由高僧道凭法师所创。591年隋文帝杨坚诏请该寺僧灵裕法师到长安，封为全国最高僧官"国统"，统管全国寺院僧尼，宝山寺改为灵泉寺。唐时仍为全国佛教中心，号称"河朔第一古刹"。

由寺院向东西方向延伸的宝山沟，又称万佛沟，有石窟247座，多为隋唐开凿，有中原"莫高窟"之誉。灵泉寺洞窟有造像、刻经、偈言、佛名、佛号等，其中大住圣窟和大留圣窟最负盛名。位于寺西的大住圣窟，开凿于隋开皇八年（589），窟门外两旁刻迦毗罗神王、那罗延神王浮雕像守卫，像身披铠甲，手持法器，脚踏牛羊，威然挺立，极为精美。窟外壁上遍凿佛龛及刻经。窟内雕释迦、弥勒等佛像。窟顶为宝相莲花藻井，周围环绕飞天。以两窟为中心，周边山崖隋至宋时期浅龛塔像密布，塔主来自灵泉寺及豫北各大寺院。此地乃全国最大的浮雕塔林，被称为"宝山塔林"。1996年灵泉寺及周边文物被定为全国文物重点保护单位。

Located south of Nanping Village in Shanying Town, Anyang, Henan, the Lingquan Temple, originally known as the Baoshan Temple, was founded by the eminent Buddhist master Daoping in 546, the fourth year of the Wuding era of the Eastern Wei dynasty. In 591, the Emperor Wen of Sui, Yang Jian, summoned the temple's Buddhist master Lingyu to Chang'an, and appointed him the country's highest Buddhist official called "Guotong", charged with managing all Buddhist monks and nuns countrywide; the temple was subsequently renamed the Lingquan Temple. During the Tang dynasty, the Lingquan Temple still remained the Buddhist center of the country, hailed as the "Top Old Temple of Heshuo".

Along the Baoshan Valley, also known as the 10,000-Buddha Valley, which stretches east to west from the temple, there are 247 grottoes, most of them dug out during the Sui and Tang dynasties, and these grottoes are noted as the "Mogao Caves" of the Central Plains. In the grottoes there are statues, engraved sutras and hymns, Buddhist names and pseudonyms, among other things. The best known of these grottoes are the Dazhu Holy Grotto and the Daliu Holy Grotto. Dug in 589, the eighth year of the Kaihuang era of the Sui dynasty, to the west of the temple, the Dazhu Holy Grotto is guarded at the entrance by the statues of the god-kings Kapila and Narayana, both armored, holding implements in hands and stepping on an ox and sheep, looking impressively solemn. The exterior wall of the grotto is dotted with niches and engraved scriptures. Inside the grotto are statues of Gautama Buddha, Maitreya among other Buddhas. The grotto has a caisson ceiling ornamented with lotus patterns around which there are flying apsaras. Around the aforesaid two grottoes, there are densely distributed shallow niches with high-relief pagodas which were carved in cliffs during the period from the Song to the Tang dynasty; the pagodas are largely modeled on those at the Lingquan Temple and major temples in northern Henan. This is the biggest forest of pagoda sculptures in relief, called the "Baoshan Pagoda Forest". The Lingquan Temple and the monuments around were designated as a major historical and cultural site protected at the national level in 1996.

神王像：位于安阳灵泉寺西的大住圣窟，隋开皇九年（589）开凿。拓片高237厘米，宽305厘米，于2003年拓印。窟门所雕迦毗罗和那罗延神王有护法之论。那罗延神王 头戴战盔，两颊长须垂飘于胸前，灰带自肩随风向上翻卷，左手持剑，右手握一长柄钢叉。迦毗罗神王头戴战盔，盔带自两肩垂下，左手握一长柄钢叉，右手持宝剑。两像头略偏向左肩，双目微闭，足踏卧式牛羊，威然挺立。神王上方刻"大隋开皇九年己酉岁敬造"。

God-king sculptures: At the entrance to the Dazhu Holy Grotto to the west of the Lingquan Temple in Anyang, dug in 589, the ninth year of the Kaihuang era of the Sui dynasty. The rubbing, made in 2003, is 237 cm tall and 305 cm wide. God-kings Kapila and Narayana carved at the entrance to the grotto appear poised to defend the Dharma. Narayana wears a helmet with ties curved up by wind, his long beard hanging down before his chest; he wields a sword in the left hand and a long-handled fork in the right hand. Kapila also wears a helmet with ties hanging down his shoulders, and holds a long-handled fork in the left hand and a sword in the right hand. Their heads tilt slightly towards their left shoulders, their eyes are half closed, and their feet step on an ox and sheep; they stand straight and solemnly. Above them is an engraved inscription that reads "Created with Respect in 589, the Ninth Year of Kaihuang, Great Sui".

李仁清传拓艺术 | LIRENQING CHUANTAYISHU

大住聖窟題記

大住圣窟题记

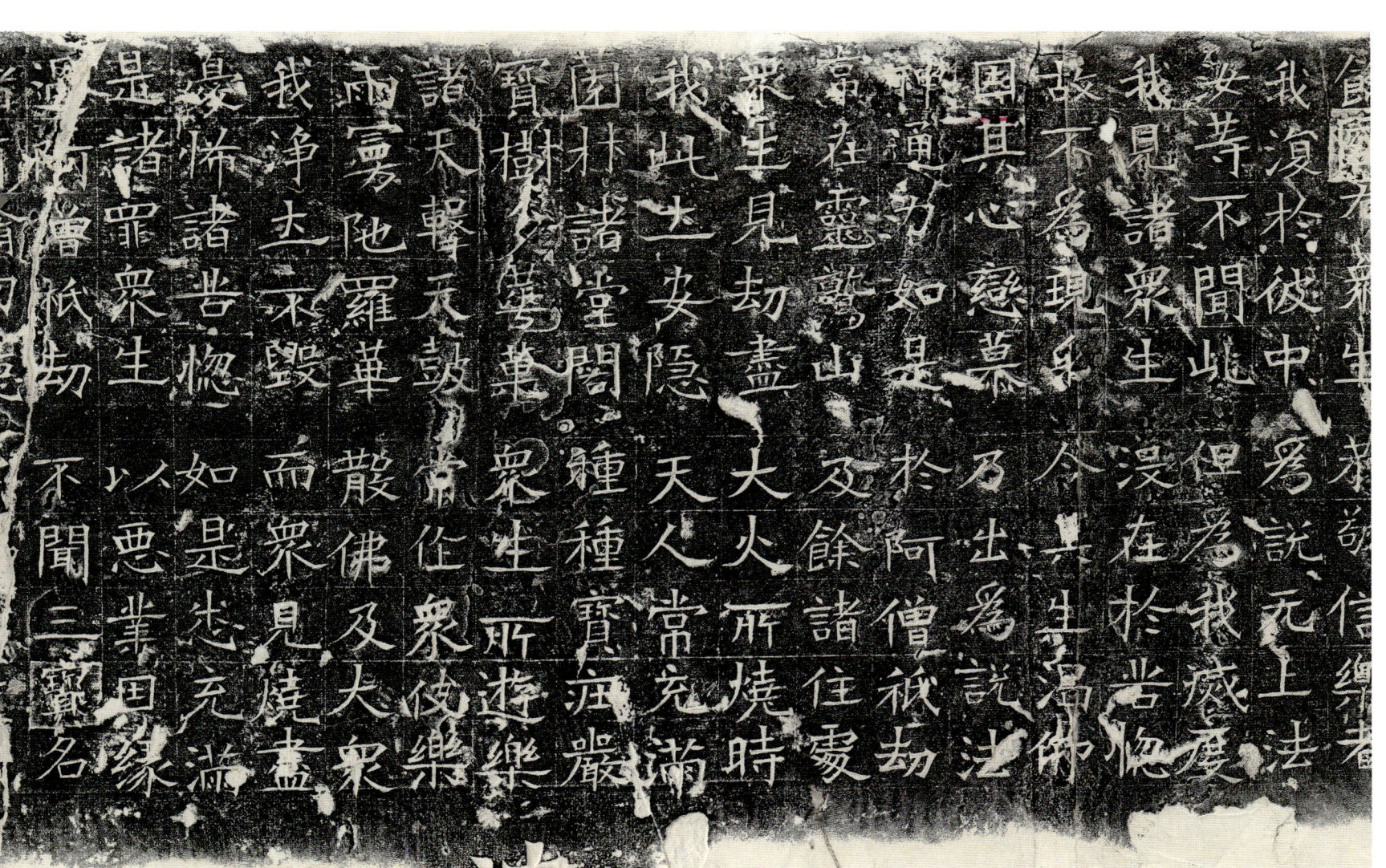

/隋唐/灵泉寺洞窟/

迦毗羅神王

216

隋唐 / 灵泉寺洞窟

佛名造像记：位于安阳灵泉寺西的大住圣窟西壁，隋开皇九年（589）开凿。拓片高240厘米，宽330厘米，于2003年拓印。上方刻妙法莲华经，其下刻六品刻经及佛名，分别为大集月藏经、二十五佛名、三十五佛名、五十三佛名和忏悔文。中部为唐代造像龛。

Engraved Names of Buddhas Record: On the west wall of the Dazhu Holy Grotto west of the Lingquan Temple in Anyang, dug in 589, the ninth year of the Kaihuang era of the Sui dynasty. The rubbing, made in 2003, is 240 cm tall and 330 cm wide. The upper part of it is the engraved Lotus Sutra; in the lower part are engraved six sutras as well as the names of Buddhas, and they are the Candragarbha Sutra, the Names of Twenty-five Buddhas, the Names of Thirty-five Buddhas, the Names of Fifty-three Buddhas, and the Repentances. In the middle is a niche caved in the Tang dynasty.

/隋唐/灵泉寺洞窟/

妙法莲华经分别功德品

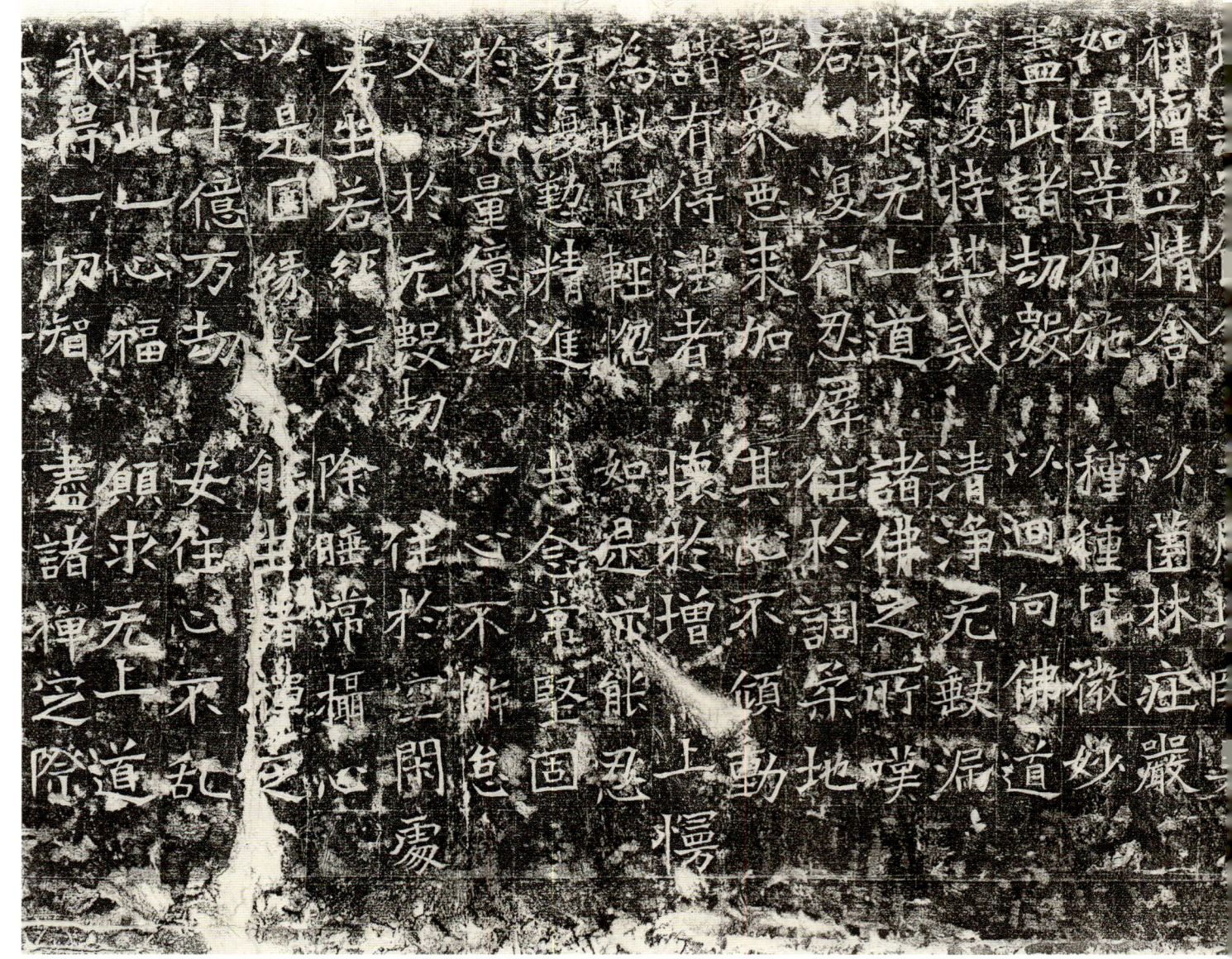

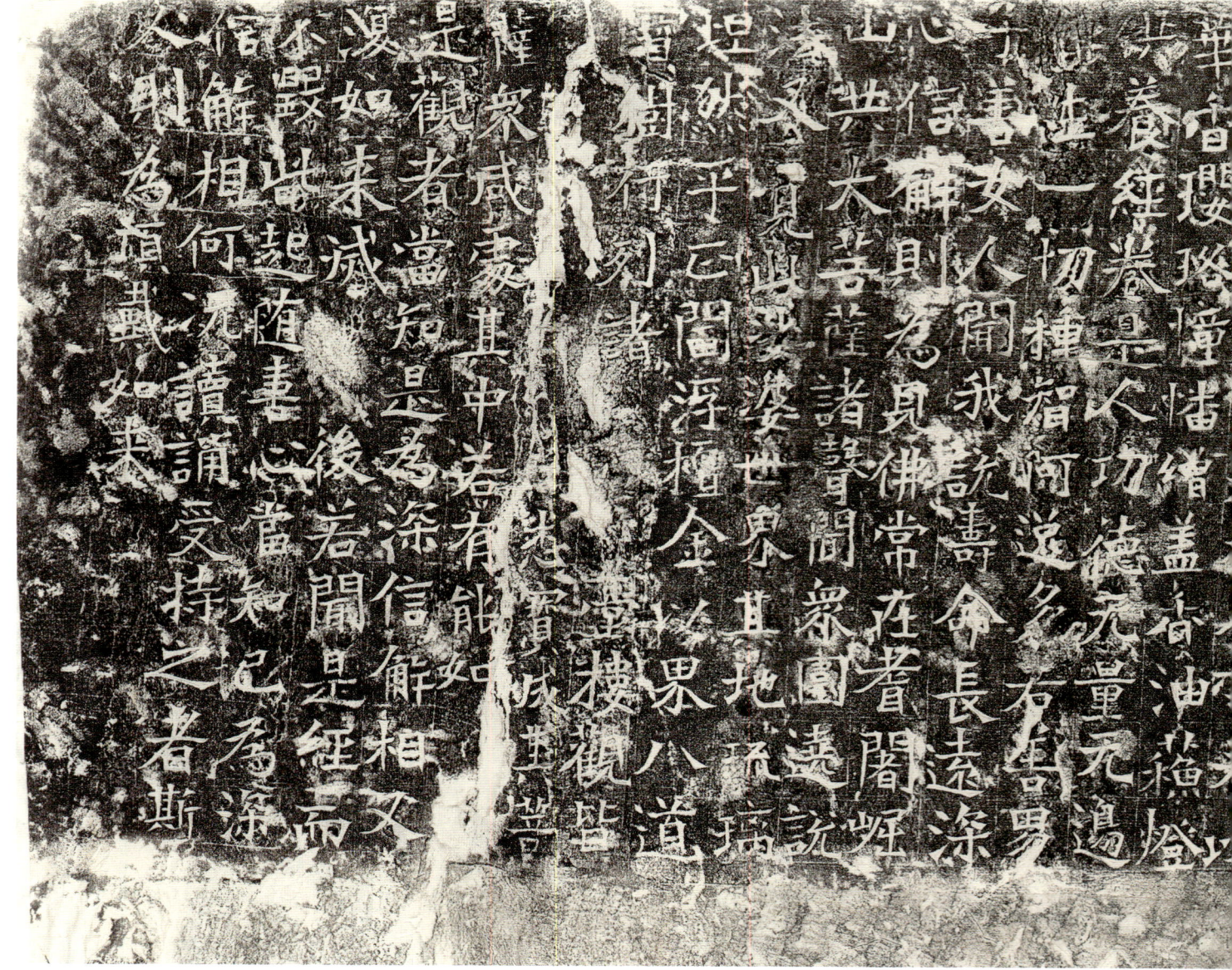

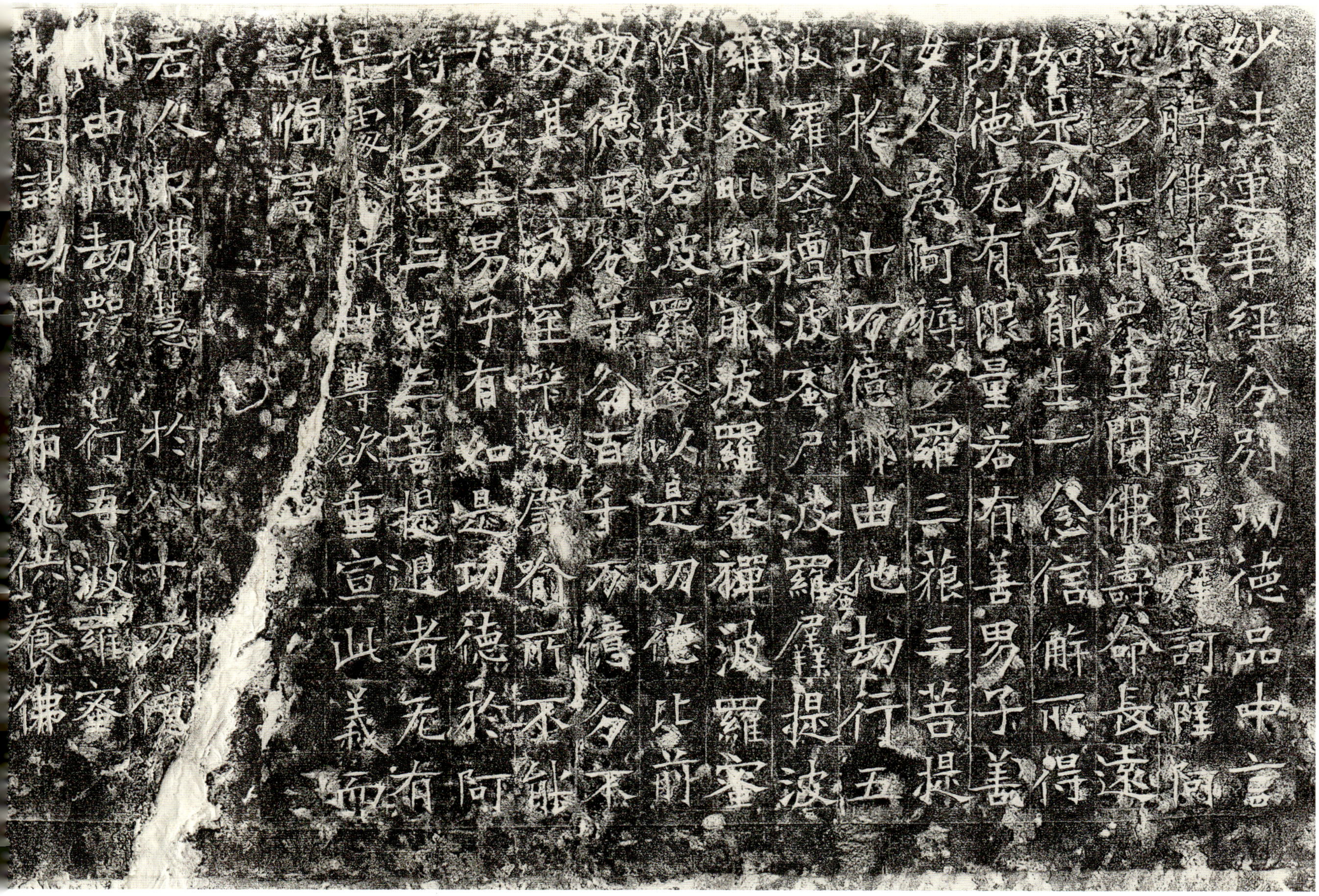
妙法蓮華經分別功德品中言
爾時佛告彌勒菩薩摩訶薩阿
逸多其有衆生聞佛壽命長遠
如是乃至能生一念信解所得
功德无有限量若有善男子善
女人為阿耨多羅三藐三菩提
故於八十万億那由他劫行五
波羅蜜檀波羅蜜尸波羅羼提波
羅蜜毗梨耶波羅蜜禪波羅蜜
除般若波羅蜜以是功德比前
功德百分千分百千万億分不
及其一乃至筭數譬喻所不能
知若善男子有如是功德於阿
耨多羅三藐三菩提退者无有
是處爾時世尊欲重宣此義而
說偈言
若人求佛慧 於八十万
億那由他劫數 行五波羅蜜
於是諸劫中 布施供養佛

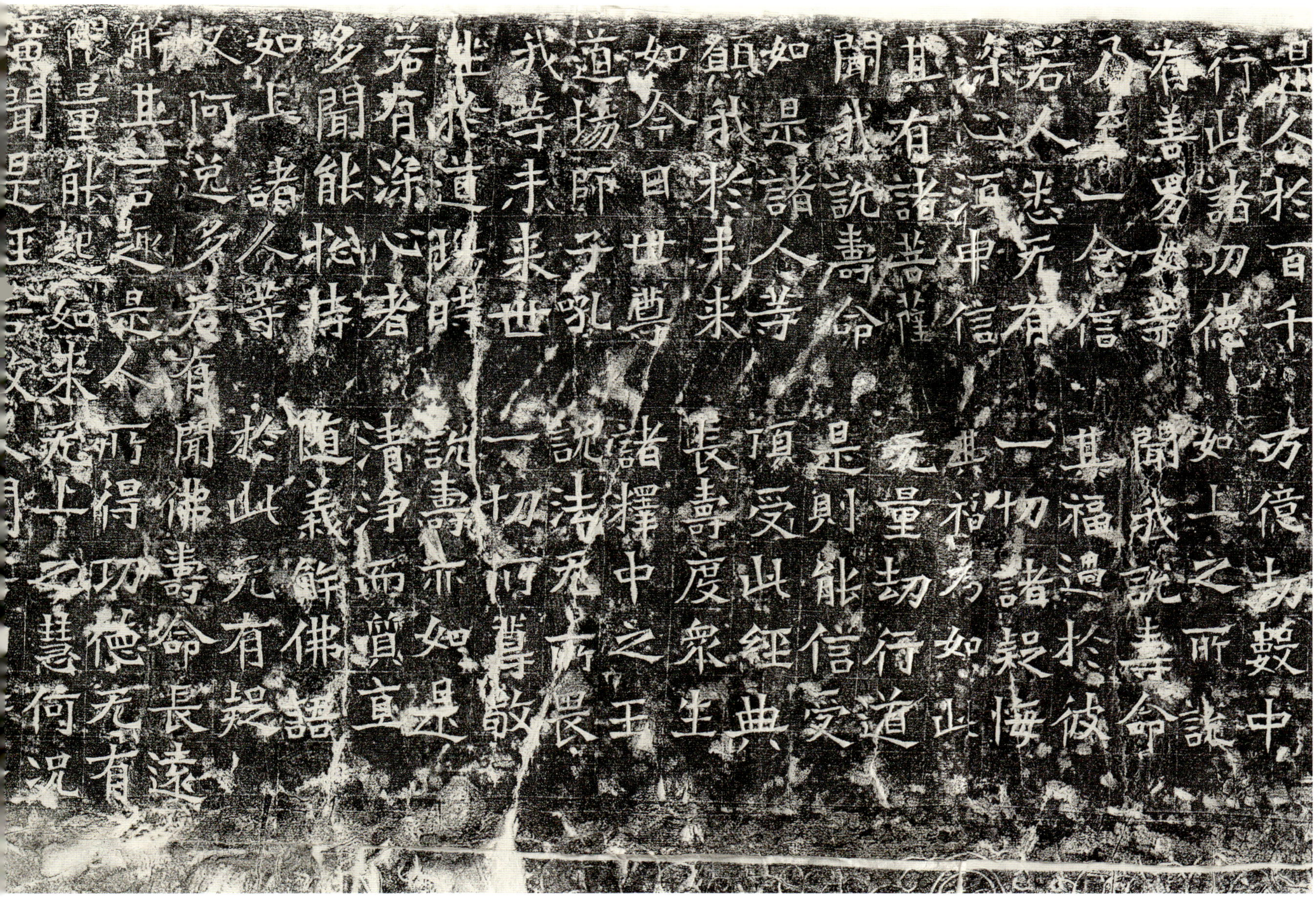
是人於百千 万億劫數中
行此諸功德 如上之所說
有善男女等 聞我說壽命
乃至一念信 其福過於彼
若人悉无有 一切諸疑悔
深心須臾信 其福為如此
其有諸菩薩 无量劫行道
聞我說壽命 是則能信受
如是諸人等 頂受此經典
願我於未來 長壽度衆生
如今日世尊 諸釋中之王
道場師子吼 說法无所畏
我等未來世 一切所尊敬
坐於道場時 說壽亦如是
若有深心者 清淨而質直
多聞能總持 隨義解佛語
如是諸人等 於此无有疑
又阿逸多 若有聞佛壽命長遠
解其言趣 是人所得功德无有
限量能起如來无上之慧何況
廣聞是經

观此希有慈悲士 raise迦大仙尊导师
普告一切声闻者 当作是可护持
一切刹头偷袈裟 当不非器勿与之
体是思已诸恶病 痰增亦令当护持
如众生昔未见闻 诸精气速能非时
一切来不随三种 诸精气增亦念护持
余众生慈悲念希有 能趣后大风世执闹雨
言佛慈悲无余 余众生速能趣向大世闻害
此道师诫后佛已 法眼 量广能持己法久住
彼佛灭后法慜住 山灭坚然久住
彼云已梵不究竟 恶轮法人烦眼惚魔住
彼此等国缘得二宝 究竟成就恶
断除烦恼午三尊 是故闻自速能作诸恶
悯一切众生故告 世闻自速能作趣

二十五佛名

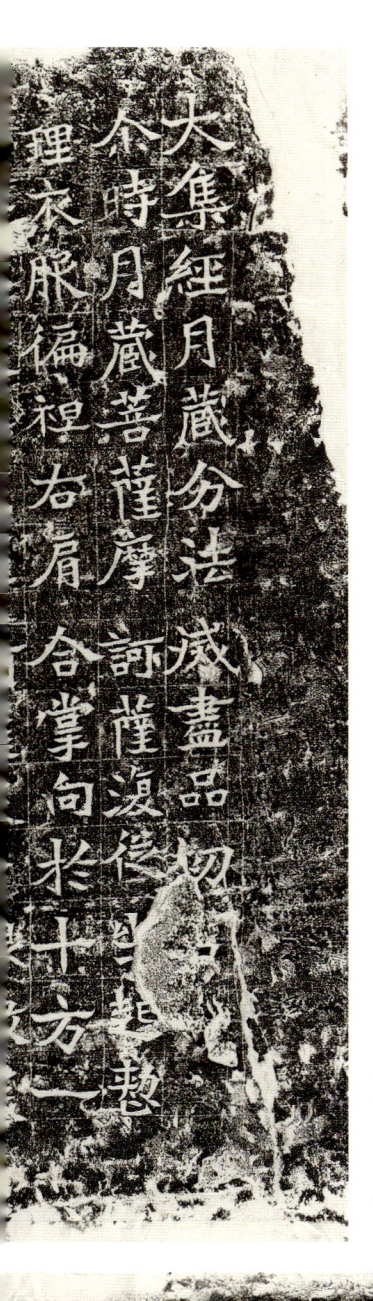

大集经月藏分法灭尽品

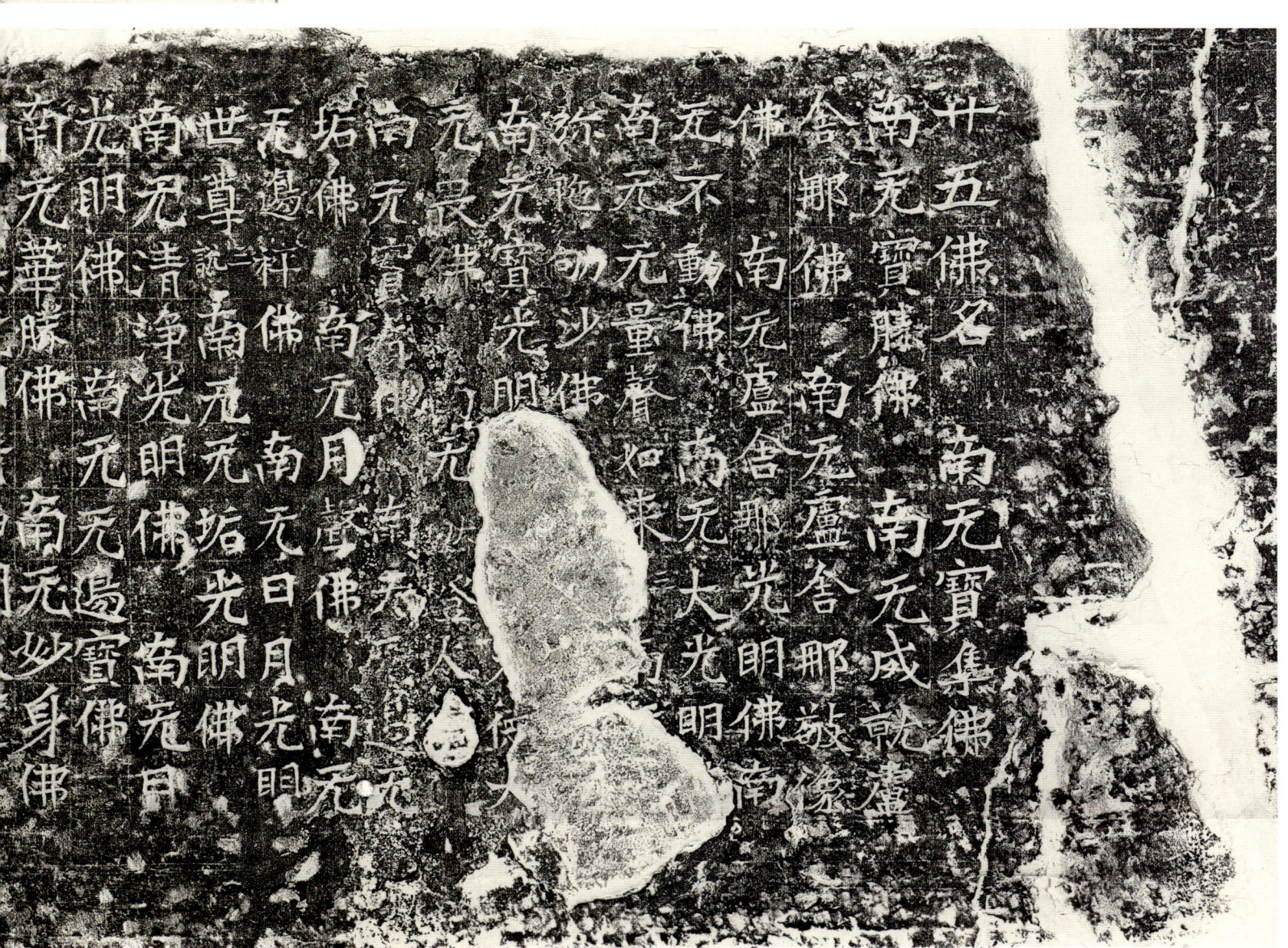

五十三佛名

三十五佛名

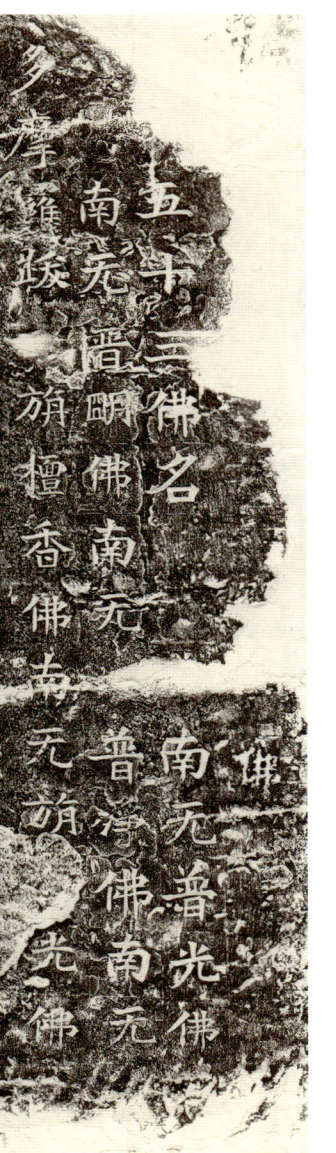

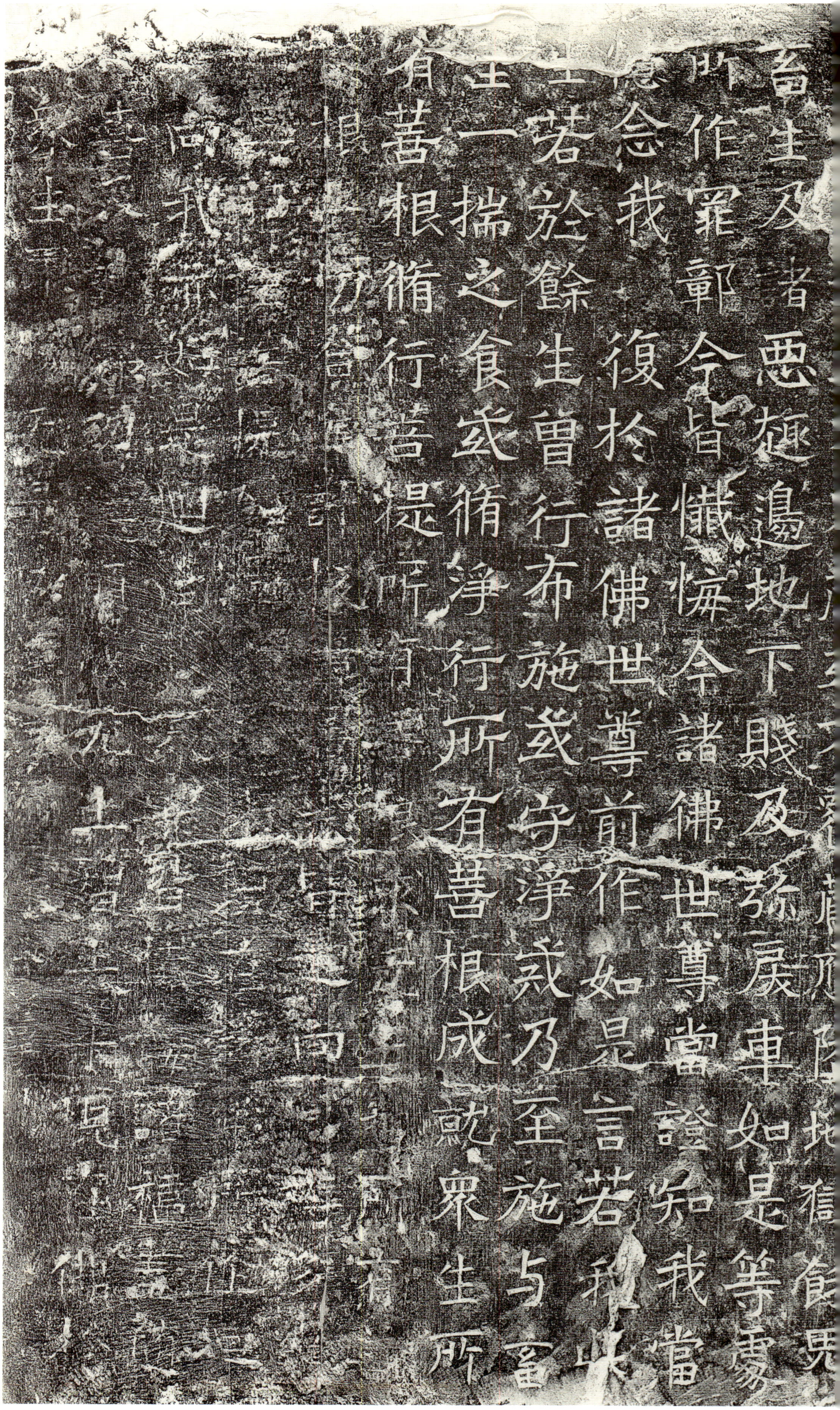

昔所作惡業　　
皆悉及今諸佛世尊當證知我等當
念作罪障今皆懺悔今諸佛世尊
一若我此餘復於諸佛世尊前作如是言若
菩於之生曾行布施戒乃
根循食或循淨行所有善根成就
力行菩提淨行所有善根

大住圣窟藻井：位于安阳灵泉寺西的大住圣窟西壁，隋开皇九年（589）开凿。拓片高207厘米，宽248厘米，于2003年拓印。大住圣窟藻井为方型藻井，中心雕莲花，周围环绕8身飞天，窟门上方飞天残损，现存6身飞天保存较完整。

Caisson of the Dazhu Holy Grotto: On the west wall of the Dazhu Holy Grotto west of the Lingquan Temple in Anyang, dug in 589, the ninth year of the Kaihuang era of the Sui dynasty. The rubbing, made in 2003, is 207 cm tall and 248 cm wide. The caisson is square with a lotus flower carved in the middle, around which are eight flying apsaras - six of them preserved quite well and the others above the grotto gate damaged.

/隋唐/
/灵泉寺洞窟/

飞天

飞天

北齐 林州洪谷寺塔龛
Pagodas at Honggu Temple in Linzhou, Norther Qi

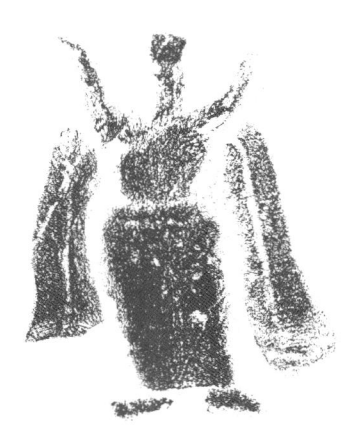

位于河南林州市合涧镇西部山中的洪谷寺，始建于北齐天保初。唐时有高僧挂锡此寺，宋改名宝岩院，后仍名为洪谷寺。洪谷寺现存文物以古塔著称，洪谷寺赖公禅师塔始建于唐，为七级密檐式砖塔，塔内中空，塔外为叠涩檐，顶部有宝瓶式塔刹。1986年公布为河南省文物保护单位。

灵泉寺及石窟、塔林、洪谷古塔，对研究古代建筑、塔式沿革、石刻艺术、佛教史都是不可多得的珍贵资料。

First built in the early years of the Tianbao era of the Northern Qi dynasty, the pagodas are located at the Honggu Temple in the mountains west of Hejian Town, Linzhou, Henan. During the Tang dynasty, eminent monks dwelt in this temple which in the Song dynasty was renamed first the Baoyan Temple and later the Honggu Temple. The temple is noted for its extant pagodas. Situated at this temple, the Pagoda of Zen Master Laigong, which was initially built during the Tang dynasty, is a seven-story brick pagoda with closely spaced corbel eaves; it is empty inside and topped with a vase-shaped finial. The temple was announced as a provincial cultural heritage site of Henan in 1986.

The Lingquan Temple's grottoes and pagodas, and the Honggu Temple's pagodas, provide rare and precious materials for research on ancient architecture, the evolution of pagodas, sculpture, and the history of Buddhism.

洪谷寺摩崖佛塔：位于河南林州市合涧镇西部山中的洪谷寺，始建于北齐天保初，拓片高160厘米，宽137厘米，于2013年拓印。由塔基、塔身和塔刹组成，单层叠涩和反叠涩檐相轮顶形，造型颇为别致。

Cliff Pagoda at the Honggu Temple: Located at the Honggu Temple in the mountains west of Hejian Town, Linzhou, Henan, first built in the early years of the Tianbao era of the Northern Qi dynasty, it comprises a base, a body, and a finial that tops a single layer of eaves made up of corbels.

洪谷寺大像碑师塔龛 /2013 年 /283 厘米 ×163 厘米

大缘禅师塔铭

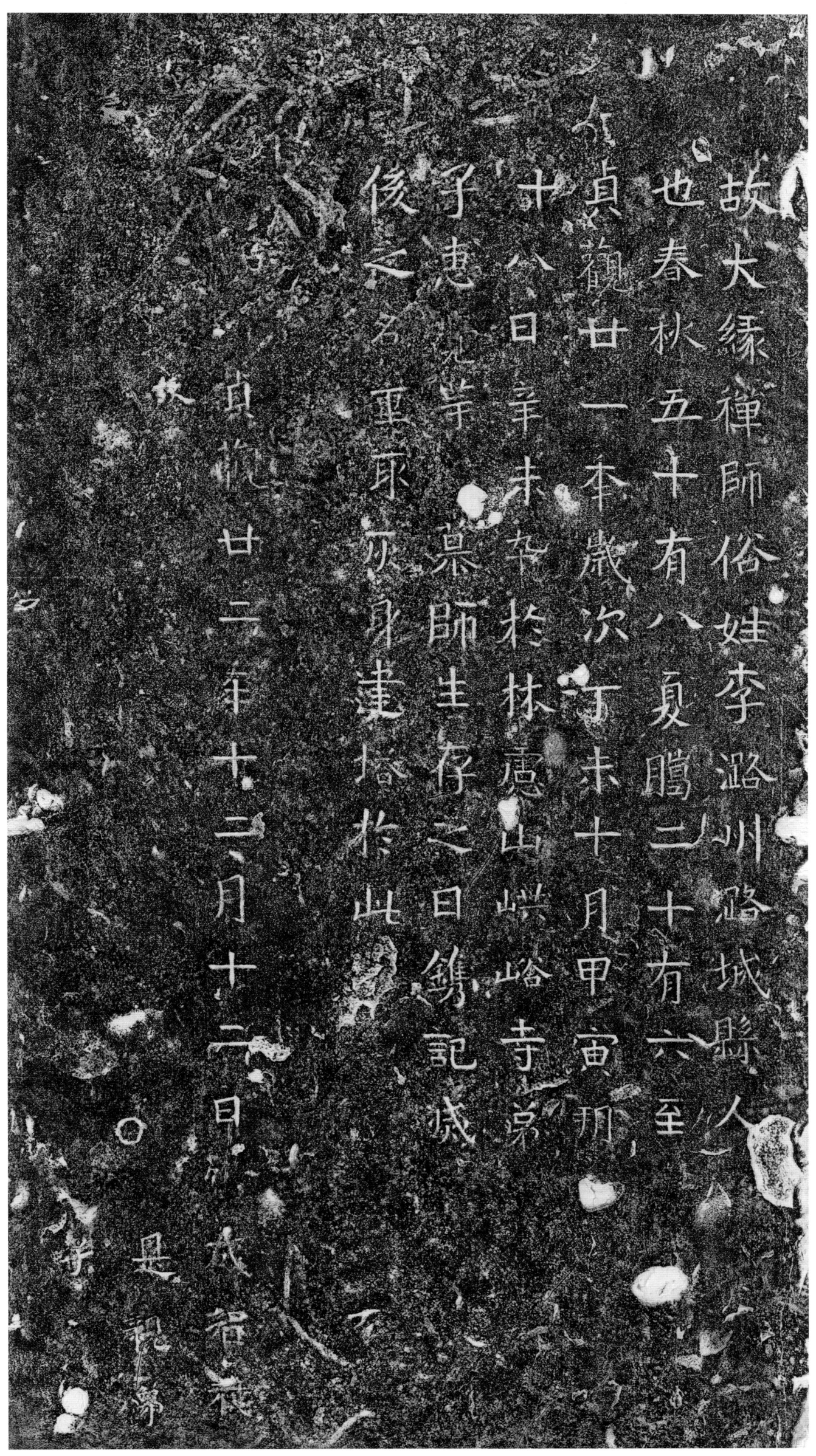

北齐 林州洪谷寺塔龛

北宋巩义宋陵石像

Stone Statues at Northern-Song Imperial Mausoleums in Gongyi

北宋皇陵群位于河南郑州巩义市西村、芝田、市区、回郭镇一带，是全国重点文物保护单位。北宋九个皇帝，除徽、钦二帝被金兵掳去死于漠北五国城外，太祖、太宗、真宗、仁宗、英宗、神宗、哲宗以及宣祖（赵匡胤之父赵弘殷）均葬在巩义，通称"七帝八陵"，依次排列为：永昌陵，位于巩义西村镇龙洼，太祖赵匡胤陵墓，太平兴国二年（977）葬于此地。永熙陵，位于巩义西村镇滹沱村东，太宗赵光义陵墓，至道三年（997）葬于此地。永定陵，位于巩义蔡庄北1公里，真宗赵桓陵墓，乾兴元年（1022）葬于此地。永昭陵，位于市区南郊，仁宗赵祯陵墓，嘉祐八年（1063）葬于此地。永厚陵，位于巩义市区孝义堡，英宗赵曙陵墓，治平四年（1067）葬于此地。永裕陵，位于巩义市八陵村东南1公里，神宗赵顼陵墓，元丰八年（1085）葬于此地。永泰陵，位于巩义市八陵村南，哲宗赵煦陵墓，元符三年（1100）葬于此地。永安陵，位于巩义市西南西村镇常封村西，太祖赵匡胤之父赵弘殷陵墓，北宋乾德二年（964）葬于此地。在每座陵墓都有一对瑞禽高浮雕，每座陵虽大小不同，但石壁上浮雕都刻一只神鸟，马头、龙颈、鹰爪、凤尾、背有翼，后衬山峰，与山穴小兽呼应，怒目圆睁，张嘴露齿，四肢前刻有鱼鳞纹，威猛有力，系象征吉祥之鸟，有"鹏图""祥瑞"之意。另外陵区陪葬皇后22座，皇室宗亲墓144座，名将勋臣8座，形成了一个规模庞大、气势雄伟的皇家陵墓群。地面石刻现存1000余件，堪称北宋历史博物馆，具有重要的文物和艺术价值，是研究宋代典章制度和石刻艺术十分珍贵的实物资料。

The Northern-Song imperial mausoleums are national key cultural heritage sites scattered in the towns of Xicun, Zhitian and Huiguo and in some urban areas of Gongyi. Of the nine emperors of the Northern Song dynasty, except Emperors Huizong and Qinzong of Song who both were taken captive by the Jin forces and died in present-day northeast Chinese province of Heilongjiang, Emperors Taizu, Taizong, Zhenzong, Renzong, Yingzong, Shenzong, Zhezong and Xuanzu (Zhao Hongyin, father of Zhao Kuangyin) were all buried in Gongyi. Their mausoleums are, in the chronological order: The Yongchang Mausoleum, located in Longwa in the town of Xicun, Gongyi, is where Emperor Taizu of Song, Zhao Kuangyin, was buried in 977; the Yongxi Mausoleum, located east of Hutuo Village in Xicun Town, Gongyi, is where Emperor Taizong of Song, Zhao Guangyi, was buried in 997; the Yongding Mausoleum, located one kilometer north of Caizhuang Village, Gongyi, is where Emperor Zhenzong of Song, Zhao Huan, was buried in 1022; the Yongzhao Mausoleum, located on the south outskirts of the city of Gongyi, is where Emperor Renzong of Song, Zhao Zhen, was buried in 1063; the Yonghou Mausoleum, located at Xiaoyipu, downtown Gongyi, is where Emperor Yingzong of Song, Zhao Shu, was buried in 1067; the Yongyu Mausoleum, located one kilometer southeast of Balng Village, Gongyi, is where Emperor Shenzong of Song, Zhao Xu, was buried in 1085; the Yongtai Mausoleum, located south of Baling Village, Gongyi, is where Emperor Zhezong of Song, Zhao Xu, was buried in 1100; and the Yong'an Mausoleum, located west of Changfeng Village in Xicun Town, Gongyi, is where Zhao Hongyin, father of Emperor Taizu of Song, was buried in 964. The mausoleums, though varied in size, each have a pair of auspicious birds in high relief. The birds, with peaks in the background, have a horse head, a dragon neck, eagle claws, and wings in the back, looked up at by small creatures in the carved caves; they have glaring eyes, an open mouth with teeth exposed, and mighty limbs, symbolic of ambitiousness and auspiciousness. Also, there are 22 tombs of empresses, 144 tombs of imperial family members and relatives, and 8 tombs of meritorious ministers, which combine to form a vast, magnificent imperial mausoleum complex. There are more than 1,000 extant stone statues on the ground, which are of vital cultural and artistic importance as precious physical materials used for research on Song-dynasty institutions and stone sculpture.

永熙陵将军像：位于巩义西村镇滹沱村东，至道三年（997）立，拓片高452厘米，宽153厘米，于2011年拓印。永熙陵将军像更加高大，人像面部丰腴，表情威严，给身临其境者以赫赫压人之感。

Statue of the General, the Yongxi Mausoleum: Erected in 997, east of Hutuo Village in Xicun Town, Gongyi. The rubbing, made in 2011, is 452 cm tall and 153 cm wide. Massive in stature, the figure has a puffy face of awe-inspiring countenance.

／北宋／巩义宋陵石像／

服饰局部

李仁清传拓艺术

/北宋/
/巩义宋陵石像/

241

永厚陵瑞禽：位于巩义市区孝义堡，英宗赵曙陵墓，治平四年（1067）封墓。拓片高255厘米，宽166厘米，于2011年拓印。石壁上浮雕刻一只神鸟，马头、龙颈、鹰爪、凤尾、背有翼，后衬山峰，与山穴小兽呼应，怒目圆睁，张嘴露齿，四肢前刻有鱼鳞纹，威猛有力。

Auspicious Bird, the Yonghou Mausoleum: Located at Xiaoyibao, Gongyi, it is where Emperor Yingzong of Song, Zhao Shu, was buried in 1067. The rubbing, made in 2011, is 255 cm tall and 166 cm wide. The sculpture of the bird in high relief, with peaks in the background, has a horse head, a dragon neck, eagle claws, and wings in the back, looked up at by small creatures in the carved caves; it has glaring eyes, an open mouth with teeth exposed, and mighty limbs.

永昭陵西瑞禽：位于市区南郊，仁宗赵祯陵墓，嘉祐八年（1063）封墓。拓片高310厘米，宽195厘米，于2011年拓印。刻一只神鸟，马头、龙颈、鹰爪、凤尾、背有翼，后衬山峰，与山穴小兽呼应，象征吉祥之鸟，有"鹏图""祥瑞"之意。

West Auspicious Bird, the Yongzhao Mausoleum: Located on the south outskirts of the city of Gongyi, the mausoleum is where Emperor Renzong of Song, Zhao Zhen, was buried in 1063. The rubbing, made in 2011, is 310 cm tall and 195 cm wide. The sculpture of the bird in high relief, with peaks in the background, has a horse head, a dragon neck, eagle claws, and wings in the back, looked up at by small creatures in the carved caves; it has glaring eyes, an open mouth with teeth exposed, and mighty limbs, symbolic of ambitiousness and auspiciousness.

艺术展掠影
A scene of the art exhibition

布展场景 | A scene of exhibition preparation

布展中 | Exhibition preparation

布展中 | Exhibition preparation

北京大学常务副校长吴志攀先生致辞
Mr. Wu Zhipan, Executive Vice President at Peking University, gives a speech

北京大学图书馆馆长朱强先生致辞
Mr. Zhu Qiang, Director of Peking University Library, gives a speech

北京大学考古文博学院原院长杭侃先生致辞
Mr. Hang Kan, former Dean of the School of Archaeology and Museology, Peking University, gives a speech.

李仁清先生致辞
Mr. Li Renqing gives a speech.

北大图书朱强馆长、汤燕金石组组长、杨守民中国动漫集团董事长
Zhuqiang Director at Peking University Library, Tang Yan Epigraphy Team Leader, Yangshoumin, Chairman of China Animation Group

专家学者合影
Group photo of experts and scholars

（左一）王红蕾，国家古籍保护中心主任助理
（左二）庄秀芬，国家古籍保护中心研究员
Wang Honglei (first from left), Assistant Director at the National Ancient Books Conservation Center
Zhuang Xiufen (second from left), research fellow at the National Ancient Books Conservation Center

胡海帆先生为本次展览题字
Mr. Hu Haifan writes an inscription for the exhibition

北大中国古代史研究中心副研究馆员史睿
Shi Rui, associate research librarian at the Center for Research on Ancient Chinese History, Peking University

北大常务副校长吴志攀
Wu Zhipan, Executive Vice President at Peking University

故宫博物院研究员郭玉海
Guo Yuhai, research fellow at the Palace Museum

北京大学图书馆金石组原组长（右二）胡海帆先生来郑州挑展品
Mr. Hu Haifan (second from right), former Epigraphy Team Leader at Peking University Library, selects works to be exhibited, in Zhengzhou.

北京石刻博物馆研究员吴梦麟
Wu Menglin, research fellow at the Beijing Stone Carving Art Museum

展览合影 | A photo exhibition

跋

在中国非物质文化遗产项目中，传拓作为一项古老的、重要的技艺越来越受到广泛关注。历代传拓者各擅其能，以宣纸、水墨或颜料为主要材质，施于青铜器、石刻、秦砖汉瓦等器物，乌金蝉翼，留影传形，创造出"下真迹一等"的精美的拓片艺术。

在中国古典文献学研究中，传拓提供了原始、基础的文本资料，一通新发现的碑刻、墓志、画像砖石对历史研究往往起到考遗补缺、勘误正讹的重要作用。从北宋欧阳修、赵明诚直至近现代的金石学，就是建立在传拓技艺及拓片作品广泛流传的基础上的。对于中国书法艺术而言，在现代印刷技术出现之前，传拓是书法作品在墨迹之外流传的重要载体。汉唐名碑拓片被视为书法研习的童蒙读本、登堂入室的必由津梁。许多书家学习魏晋、宗法二王，大多从临习《淳化阁帖》入手，这部丛帖就是北宋辑录前代优秀书法作品并广为传播的一部拓片总集。

在传拓技艺传承发展过程中，良工善拓虽然为人所重，但囿于轻工匠、轻技艺的传统，今时传拓往往被视为一般性资料建档留存，艺术的独立性、本体性被忽视、弱化了。

李仁清在现代传拓技艺传承创新上，是有许多难能可贵的"过人"之处的。他对前人传拓技艺做到了全面、深入地研习，博学笃行，融众为我。他对淡墨蝉翼的拓法颇有心得，多以简淡的墨色凸显石刻的刀法、肌理变化，随物赋形，雅致自然，形成了极具个性的表现风格。在传拓上纸、施墨揭拓等环节，他都有许多长期精研、熟能生巧的感悟和总结。

李仁清对传拓技艺的创新，主要体现在他创造性地解决了对古代高浮雕、圆雕石刻进行立体传拓的难题，通过水墨传拓使雕塑作品回归到平面的构图"粉本"，解析、还原了一大批珍贵的汉魏唐宋艺术珍品。这一创新极大拓展了传拓这一古老技艺的创作领域及表现方式。近年来，李仁清配合文物部门开展了大运河申遗、天地之中申遗、中小型石窟调查、北宋皇陵等一批重要传拓项目。他从文物测绘中学习借鉴了对雕塑的空间透视方法，从绘画、书法艺术中参悟了墨分五彩、干湿润燥的水墨变化，通过艰苦、不间断、大型的传拓实践，较好地推动了传拓技艺的现代创新与发展。根据传拓工作的需要，李仁清尝试了巨幅整张的传拓表现形式，先后对登封汉三阙汉阙形制、石刻图像与铭文，对巩义石窟寺中心柱佛龛、窟顶藻井等进行了整体性拓印。巨幅拓片的成功制作，更加准确、如实地展示了被传拓器物的原始形态，丰富了拓片艺术的空间表现力，给人以前所未有的强烈视觉冲击。

值得特别提出的是，近年来传拓技艺的传承创新得到了政府和社会的关注和支持。国家古籍保护中心专门批准设立了国家级古籍修复技艺传习中心李仁清传习所。出版这部作品集，是中共郑州市委宣传部推进郑州国家中心城市建设、宣传推介优秀文化领军人物的一项重要举措，集中展示了2017年李仁清在北京大学图书馆举办传拓艺术展的一些代表作品。

作为传拓技艺的当代发展，其社会价值的重要性不仅仅体现在历史学、文献学、考古学、艺术学等学术范畴，也是弘扬优秀传统文化中国气派、中国元素、中国故事的重要内容。

与李仁清相识多年，约赘言为记。

石　桥

2019年端午

Epilogue

Among intangible cultural heritage programs in China, rubbing as an important ancient technique has drawn widespread attention. Throughout the ages, rubbing artisans created exquisite rubbings that are "second only to the originals", by applying rice paper and ink or pigment on such objects as bronzes, steles, Qin bricks and Han tiles.

In classical Chinese philology, rubbings provide original and basic textual materials, and a new discovery of a stele, an epitaph, or a portrayal brick or stone may often prove crucial in filling gaps or correcting errors. Chinese epigraphy since Ouyang Xiu and Zhao Mingcheng of the Northern Song dynasty has been grounded in the wide currency of rubbing techniques and rubbings. To Chinese calligraphy, rubbings had been the most important carrier of calligraphic works other than originals before the advent of modern printing technology. Learning from the rubbings of well-known steles from the Han and Tang dynasties have long been seen as a road that one must take to become a calligrapher. Many calligraphers studied calligraphy of Wei- and Jin-dynasty styles, most notably that of Wang Xizhi and Wang Xianzhi, largely by copying the *Chunhua Getie* (Copybook from the Imperial Library of the Chunhua Era) - a widely circulated collection of rubbings made up of best calligraphic works from the dynasties preceding the Northern Song.

In the preservation and development of rubbing techniques, though techniques and skills are something important, the tradition that artisans are not thought highly of persists so that today rubbing is often seen simply as a job done for archival purposes, and its independent and ontological nature as an art is overlooked or weakened.

Li Renqing has a lot of estimable and "extraordinary" qualities with respect to the preservation of and the innovation in rubbing techniques. He studied rubbing techniques of the masters before him extensively to inform himself thoroughly of the craft. He excels at using light ink in making rubbings to underscore the artistry of carving and the change in texture as naturally as possible, in a style that distinguishes his work from that of others. He is particularly skilled, as a result of his careful study and practice over the years, at placing paper over the object, applying ink, and peeling off paper among other aspects of the process.

Li's innovation in the technique of rubbing, prominently manifested by his creatively solving the puzzle of making rubbings of ancient sculptures in high relief and in the round to turn them back into "powdered sketches" on the plane, has helped unravel and restore a multitude of works of art from the Han, Wei, Tang and Song dynasties. This innovation drastically broadens the field of creation and the form of expression for rubbing as an ancient craft. In recent years, Li worked with cultural heritage departments on such important rubbing projects as the application for the World Heritage Site inscription of the Grand Canal and the Center of Heaven and Earth, the surveys of small and medium-sized grottoes, and the Northern-Song imperial mausoleums. He studied and borrowed the idea of perspective with respect to sculptures from cultural heritage surveying and mapping, acquired insight into the shading and change of ink under different conditions from the arts of painting and calligraphy, and through persistent and extensive practice, furthered modern innovation in and development of the rubbing craft. As needed by his work, Li experimented and made holistic rubbings of the three ceremonial gate towers, and engravings and inscriptions thereon, in Dengfeng, and the Buddhist statues on central pillars and the caissons at the Shigu Temple in Gongyi. His success in colossal rubbings made it possible to present the original shapes of objects more accurately and authentically and enhanced the expressiveness in space of the art so greatly as to give an unprecedented sense of visual impact.

It is worth special mention that the craft of rubbing has in recent years drawn attention and support from the government and the public as well. The "Li Renqing Apprenticeship Institute, National-level Ancient Texts Restoration Training Center" was founded under the auspices of the National Ancient Books Conservation Center. This book is published as a major action that the Publicity Department of the CPC Zhengzhou Municipal Committee has taken in furthering its effort to build Zhengzhou into a national central city and give publicity to culturally leading figures. The book contains some representative works that Li exhibited at the Library of Peking University in 2017.

Embodying contemporary development of the rubbing craft, Li's works hold great importance which lies not simply in reflecting the academic disciplines of history, philology, archeology, the science of art and so on, but in promoting the manners, elements and stories in traditional Chinese culture.

The above is my word about Li Renqing whom I have known for years.

Shi Qiao

June 2019